12.00

Victoria, Albert, and Mrs. Stevenson

Books by Edward Boykin

GHOST SHIP OF THE CONFEDERACY

CONGRESS AND THE CIVIL WAR

THE WISDOM OF THOMAS JEFFERSON

LIVING LETTERS FROM AMERICAN HISTORY

THE AUTOBIOGRAPHY OF GEORGE WASHINGTON

FIRST AMERICAN HISTORY QUIZ BOOK

SECOND AMERICAN HISTORY QUIZ BOOK

SHRINES OF THE REPUBLIC

VICTORIA, ALBERT, AND MRS. STEVENSON

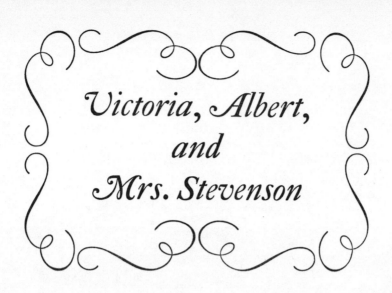

Victoria, Albert, and Mrs. Stevenson

Edited by

EDWARD BOYKIN

RINEHART & COMPANY, INC.

New York   Toronto

PUBLISHED SIMULTANEOUSLY IN CANADA
BY CLARKE, IRWIN & COMPANY, LTD., TORONTO

© 1957 BY EDWARD BOYKIN
PRINTED IN THE UNITED STATES OF AMERICA
LIBRARY OF CONGRESS CATALOG CARD NUMBER: 57-5218

For
Virginia

Foreword and Appreciation

To AN EDITORIAL eulogizing Sallie Coles Stevenson the day after her death, in 1848, Thomas Ritchie, editor of the *Richmond Enquirer* and close friend of this extraordinary woman, appended this personal note:

> We knew her long and intimately, yet we shall not attempt to sketch her many virtues and noble qualities—her brilliant intellect—her fascinating manners, which, whether in the glitter of a court or the quiet of the domestic circle, won the love and admiration of all who came within the magic circle of her conversation—her self-sacrificing devotion to her affectionate and watchful husband—her unostentatious charity and deep and sincere piety. We trust that the pen of some one of her numerous and devoted admirers will pay a proper tribute to her noble character and virtues.

The "pen of someone," indeed, the pens of many, were quick to respond. Here is one of innumerable tributes:

> We venture to say that her private correspondence with her friends, when she was residing in England as the lady of the American Minister, the portraits she drew, the scenes she described, are not surpassed by the letters of any other person who has ever visited England.

Today, in Albemarle County, Virginia, where "charming Sallie" was born, raised and buried, her name is virtually un-known. Although she is easily the first lady of this ancient county that boasts Thomas Jefferson, George Rogers Clark and Meriwether Lewis among its sons, Sallie Stevenson is buried and forgotten, her grave marked by a weather-beaten slab in a remote graveyard deep in the Virginia forest.

One wonders why the letters of Sallie Coles Stevenson, written between 1836 and 1841 when her husband was Minister at the Court of St. James's, have so long escaped publication. This book does not attempt to include the entire correspondence, which is collected in Duke University Library, at Durham, North Carolina. The collection is too vast. Many of her letters were undoubtedly lost or discarded. It is highly possible others may someday be discovered. Perhaps publication of this book may bring them to light.

After Mrs. Stevenson's death one member of her family, at least, thought her letters were interesting and valuable enough to collect and save for posterity. This was her sister Emily, Mrs. John Rutherford, the "Beloved Emm" of these letters.

For the most part Mrs. Stevenson's letters are printed here just as she wrote them: punctuation, spelling and grammar. Very occasionally the letters have been cut to spare the reader repetition. Mrs. Stevenson's chirography is not always the easiest to read. Her *o*'s, *i*'s and *e*'s frequently look alike; so with her *k*'s, *h*'s and *b*'s.

The editor has hesitated to clutter up his pages with footnotes and reference numbers. Mrs. Stevenson herself identified, in one way or another, many of the personages she alluded to. Others needed no identification. For closer identification of England's lords and ladies, dukes and duchesses and other socially distinguished persons mentioned by Mrs. Stevenson, the best sources are Britain's DICTIONARY OF NATIONAL BIOGRAPHY; Charles Greville's JOURNAL OF THE REIGN OF QUEEN VICTORIA, and John Gore's CREEVEY'S LIFE AND TIMES. Dormer Creston's THE YOUTHFUL QUEEN VICTORIA has been helpful as has Harriet Martineau's AUTOBIOGRAPHY.

Without THE COLES FAMILY OF VIRGINIA by William B. Coles this editor could scarcely have compiled this book. Francis Fry Wayland's scholarly ANDREW STEVENSON—DEMOCRAT AND DIPLOMAT has been of considerable help. Marie De Mare's G.P.A. HEALY, AMERICAN ARTIST supplied the editor with details of Healy's social and artistic connections with the Stevensons in London. THE LIFE AND WORKS OF THOMAS SULLY by Edward Biddle and Mantle Fielding was revealing as to Sully's experience in painting his celebrated coronation portrait of Queen Victoria.

Rendering thanks is always a difficult task because one hardly knows where to begin, yet of the many obligations the editor has incurred in preparing this book the greatest is that owed to the Manuscript Department of Duke University Library. This splendid library gave unfailing co-operation as well as generous permission to publish these selections from its "Sarah Coles Stevenson Letters Collection." The editor wishes to acknowledge a debt to Mrs. Pauline C. Beers, former Assistant in the Manuscript Department, for her help and for annotations in respect to the letter describing Queen Victoria's Coronation. Nor should he forget the present Assistant in the Manuscript Department, Mrs. Elizabeth C. Harrison, to whom he is grateful for many favors.

Mrs. Clarence S. A. Williams of South Orange, New Jersey, great-great-niece of Mrs. Stevenson, was most helpful in supplying information about her accomplished forebear and the whereabouts of letters written over a century ago.

At the Library of Congress, the Stevenson Letter Books, containing the Legation records between 1836 and 1841, were placed at this editor's disposal, one of the many courtesies received there. The State Department supplied, through G. Bernard Nobel, Chief, Historical Division, essential data relating to the American Legation in London at the time the Stevensons occupied it.

As always, the Alderman Library of the University of Virginia placed its facilities and collection at the editor's disposal. He is specially indebted to Mrs. Virginia Corey and to Mrs. Robert Hoskins of the Library's Photostat Department for courteous co-operation.

The editor extends thanks also to Mrs. Bradley T. Johnson of Charlottesville, Virginia, whose home is graced by the surviving portrait of Mrs. Stevenson—there were two of them—painted by G.P.A. Healy in London in 1839. This painting is as lovely today as when it came from Healy's gifted brush. Mrs. Johnson graciously permitted reproduction of the portrait in this book.

To the Speaker of the House of Representatives, Honorable Sam Rayburn, thanks are in order for permission to reproduce the portrait of Andrew Stevenson that hangs in the Speaker's Gallery of the Capitol at Washington.

I wish to express my thanks to George Coles of Charlottesville, Virginia, for assistance rendered and for obtaining access to Coles family history.

Appreciation goes also to Mr. and Mrs. Edward Michael Keating, who reside at Enniscorthy, near Charlottesville, Virginia, where Mrs. Stevenson was born. The picture of Enniscorthy as it looks today—restored and little changed from the original—was contributed by these two hospitable people.

The editor is also indebted to Lois DeBell of Charlottesville, Virginia, for her help in unraveling these letters and for typing the entire script, no small task.

EDWARD BOYKIN

Charlottesville,
Virginia.
June 1, 1956

Victoria, Albert, and Mrs. Stevenson

Prelude

JUST SIX DAYS after George Washington took the oath as First President of the Republic a baby girl was born at Enniscorthy, home of Revolutionary veteran, John Coles, in the Green Mountain section of Albemarle County, Virginia.

After the doctor had mounted his horse and ridden away, John Coles went to the family Bible and made a tenth entry, "Born, Sarah Coles, May 5, 1789." This done, he made sure his decanters were filled. Neighbors would soon be dropping by to offer felicitations and drink to the newcomer and her mother, Rebecca.

Enniscorthy was a hospitable place. It boasted none of the splendor of the baronial homes along the James River, yet two generations of Coleses had found it solidly comfortable.

The Coles home was in a neighborhood where clay roads wound through the foothills and valleys like broad red ribbons. To the west, the ranges of the Blue Ridge Mountains bordered the landscape like a purple wall. Northward, two hours by horseback, lay the county seat, Charlottesville, named for Queen Charlotte, wife of King George III.

Enniscorthy had twenty-four rooms. The nursery was huge and well filled. There were eight living children; two had died in infancy, and three more would arrive before the nursery was quiet.

The house was well furnished—highpost beds, pier glasses, presses gleaming with glass and china, glass chandeliers that

(3)

tinkled in the summer breeze descending from the Blue Ridge at dusk, family portraits by itinerant painters, and an amply stocked wine cellar.

Enniscorthy faced a broad lawn, bordered by oaks and spotted with patches of lilac. There was no coach-and-four at Enniscorthy. John Coles, a practical man, used a huge carryall of a carriage that lurched and creaked over the rutted roads, but always managed to get him and his large brood where they were going.

Not far from the house, a low wall surrounded the cemetery where the Coleses were buried. One can still read their dates, chiseled on weatherworn stone.

The region teemed with history. Under the oaks in front of the house youthful Revolutionists—Jefferson, Henry, Pendleton and others—had assembled to demonstrate their indignation at British infringement of their liberties. In June, 1781, when Banastre Tarleton and his dragoons went to Monticello by night to seize the author of the Declaration of Independence, they arrived too late, for Jefferson with his wife and daughters had already sought refuge at Enniscorthy.

Slicing his way through the forest near Enniscorthy, Lafayette had outflanked Cornwallis and turned him toward Yorktown and surrender. Colonel John Coles himself had commanded the prison compound near Charlottesville where British and Hessian prisoners captured at Saratoga were stockaded for the duration of the Revolution.

Monticello was the show place of the area. When Sarah Coles was in her teens, she would frequently accompany her father to pay respects to President Jefferson on his Little Mountain. While the President and her father, over sips of wine, discussed politics or agriculture, she would roam the mansion fascinated by the ingenuity of its designer or read a volume from Mr. Jefferson's collection of poetry.

From the first, Sarah was called Sallie, and like her three sisters, grew into a beautiful young lady. Suitors besieged Enniscorthy. In summer there were dances, picnics on the top of the Blue Ridge, and trips to the Springs—the White and the Sweet.

Most exciting of all were visits to "Cousin Dolly" Madison at the President's mansion in Washington. Dolly Madison called Sarah "my beloved Sallie." Sallie Coles flitted back and forth, now to Richmond, now to Washington, now to Enniscorthy. On February 14, 1815, she was "Cousin Dolly's" guest at the Octagon House in Washington when a coach-and-four came thundering up to the door. Out leaped a messenger bound for the President's study with news of the peace with England. It was Sallie Coles who stood at the head of the stairs and echoed the joyous news, "Peace! Peace!" to the excited throng below.

Through such scenes she moved like a young queen, meeting politicians, statesmen, soldiers, adventurers. Once the matchless Stephen Decatur bent over, kissed her tapering fingers and paid tribute to her charms. At twenty she was an experienced belle, "reigning over a multitude of willing subjects." Matchmaker Dolly tried often to pair off her fascinating protégée with one of the young men who graced her soirées, but Sallie Coles demurred until, at last, in 1816, she met and married "the man of my choice," Andrew Stevenson, a Richmond lawyer, widower, and son of an Episcopal cleric in Culpeper, Virginia. Sallie Coles and Andrew Stevenson had one child, a daughter who, at five, lost her life in an "agonizing casualty." She fell into the fireplace. Her death brought grief that was never assuaged.

Stevenson's political ambitions were already flowering. Soon he would enter the Virginia Legislature, only to step from there onto the broader stage of the House of Representatives in Washington. He took his seat in the House in 1821. Six years later, in 1827, he was elevated to the speakership, succeeding Henry Clay. A turbulent period it was. Andrew Jackson's battles with Congress began in 1828, and the floor of the House became a fierce political arena. Stevenson was a staunch Jacksonian. As Speaker of the House he wielded the gavel with rare discernment, tempering his rulings with dignity, courtesy and authority.

Handsome, suave, politically astute, ready with wit and anecdote, Stevenson was a presiding officer of great distinction. He seemed to have inherited much of the charm of Henry Clay whom he had succeeded to the chair.

As wife of the powerful Speaker of the House, in Washington Sallie Coles Stevenson mingled with the leading personalities of the day. It was the age of oratory. Webster, Clay, Benton and Calhoun were at the peak of their powers. Sallie frequently matched wits with these powerful men. Implementing her husband's political talents were her own many social graces. Nor should the deeply pious side of her character be overlooked. She had great faith in divine destiny.

The year 1836 was an eventful one in America. Andrew Jackson's eight-year reign in the White House was closing. Three giants, Daniel Webster, Henry Clay and John C. Calhoun, ruled the Senate. A new party, the coalition Whigs, entered the political scene with a surge that would capture the presidency four years hence.

Things were happening around the nation. Texas broke her Mexican shackles and proclaimed her independence. At his home in Virginia, James Madison, Father of the Constitution, died. In July, a red-haired Ohio youth of seventeen, William Tecumseh Sherman, entered West Point to learn how to lead an army. At St. Louis, young Robert E. Lee, lieutenant of engineers, was pioneering flood control, trying to make the Mississippi behave. The West was beckoning. Steamboats were opening a new era in Atlantic navigation.

The arbiter of fashion and etiquette in America was *Godey's Lady's Book*. American literature was in its first fine bloom. What Dickens called American "go-ahead-itive-ness" promised an era of unparalleled expansion and invention.

On the darker side the cold war between North and South was gathering intensity. Jacksonian prosperity was still rolling in high gear, but shadows of the nation's first major economic depression showed faintly on the horizon.

Overseas affairs were reasonably under control. Jackson had settled the long-standing spoliation claims against France. But there were still problems to be solved in the northeastern boundary disputes unsettled since the close of the American Revolution.

On March 16, 1836, the United States Senate confirmed the appointment of Andrew Stevenson of Virginia as "Envoy Extraordinary and Minister Plenipotentiary to Great Britain." It was the second time Old Hickory had nominated the distinguished Virginian for the coveted post at the Court of St. James's.

This pre-eminent diplomatic station had been vacant since 1832. Politics had kept it so. Jackson's war with the Great Triumvirate and their allies in the Senate still raged. The fight over the Bank of the United States had left the upper chamber a political shambles. Whatever Jackson did, every word he uttered, was anathema to Clay, Calhoun and Webster. They heaped scorn on his policies, blocked every move, and labeled him King Andrew the First.

In 1832, when Jackson sent to the Senate the name of his favorite "courtier," Martin Van Buren, recently resigned Secretary of State, for confirmation as Minister to Great Britain, the Webster-Clay-Calhoun combine closed in. The vote against confirming Van Buren was close, so close, indeed, that Calhoun, then Vice President, had to use his casting vote to reject the appointment.

Indignant at this rebuff, Jackson took his time seeking an alternate. His choice fell on Andrew Stevenson whose health had crumbled under the nerve-wracking task of presiding over the highly charged House for seven controversial years. In 1834, Stevenson resigned. He needed to recuperate, but Jackson promptly nominated him to the London post. The Senate rejected Stevenson with equal alacrity. With characteristic stubbornness Jackson waited two years before renaming him. This time the appointment squeaked past the opposition watchdogs.

On June 8, 1836, Andrew and Sallie Coles Stevenson embarked at New York for London aboard the packet ship, *Montreal*. Three weeks later they docked at Portsmouth, England, pausing there to recuperate from the debilitation of their first transatlantic passage. Reaching London on June thirtieth, the Stevensons were greeted by the American *Chargé d'Affaires*, Aaron Vail, who had directed the American Legation at London during the four-year lapse between Van Buren's rejection in 1832 and Stevenson's assumption of the ministerial duties in 1836.

The Stevensons reached England at a memorable moment in its history. William IV, third son of George III, sat on the British throne, but he was slowly dying. Heir presumptive to the crown was a slender, rosy-cheeked girl of seventeen, Alexandrina Victoria. On her the hopes of Britain were fastened. To this fresh, young creature the scepter was soon to pass, and the Stevensons had arrived just in time to watch the curtain rise on the fabulous Victorian Era.

At the top of Britain's political hierarchy sat Whig Prime Minister Lord Melbourne, who bore also the milder appellation, William Lamb. Melbourne was one of the most paradoxical figures in Britain's history and a master politicial craftsman. A man who had a way with women and a habit of spicing his conversation with "damns" and "dammits."

Foreign Minister in Melbourne's Cabinet was Viscount Palmerston, brusque, blustery, unyielding, but fair in diplomatic dealings. With Palmerston the new American Minister was to resolve many questions causing friction between the two countries.

Chief luminary and grand old man of England in 1836 was the Duke of Wellington, conqueror of Napoleon. His blue coat and white trousers were symbols of a moral power no less great than his military strength on the historic day at Waterloo. Trouble shooter for the Royal family, he was likewise their chief conciliator and consoler. The Iron Duke was respected, looked up to and consulted by all parties. And the Stevensons were to find him a friend of America.

Pomp, splendor and worldliness had been the legacy of the Georges, and it is little wonder that Sallie Coles Stevenson, with her "republican" tastes and background, found England a procession of social and regal magnificence "so splendid it dazzled one's eyes to look upon it."

Rare, indeed, were the endowments she brought to the task of consort to the American Minister at the Court of St. James's. Witty and imaginative, her conversation was brilliant. All her life she had had literary leanings. Her pen was facile. Kindly, charitable, she had hosts of friends. In Britain she was to make many more. Striking to look at though not beautiful, there was a glamour about her. Healy's portrait of her bears this out. One who knew her said, "She was tall and almost gypsylike in her style." As wife of the "Envoy Extraordinary and Minister Plenipotentiary," she achieved an unrivaled social success.

Stevenson himself was superbly equipped by nature and experience for the diplomatic duties at the British Court. The former Speaker of the House of Representatives was a political figure of no meager stature. He possessed most of the attributes that bring social and political success. Dear to British hearts was his eloquence. His engaging personality won immediate popularity with all parties and classes in Britain. The Legation was flooded with invitations to great homes, castles in the country, princely mansions, to Windsor itself and to Buckingham Palace.

The Stevenson letter books are dotted with these cordial, precise invitations.

Naïvely, Stevenson wrote a friend from London, "We have indeed made friends, instead of acquaintances, and have been welcomed by all parties, Tories as well as Whigs. Probably no Minister from America has ever been more welcomed or so well received by the English. We have been ushered at once into the higher circles and have seen all the elite."

Sallie Coles Stevenson began the voluminous private correspondence—from which the letters in this book were selected—the day she landed in England, June 29, 1836. Seldom, if ever, was her pen dry from that moment until she boarded the *Great Western* in October, 1841, for New York and home.

For her American relatives and friends she drew fascinating portraits of British society and court life. Her brilliant descriptions of young Queen Victoria rival the best—and it should be added that the girlish sovereign found the Stevensons a charming couple. Mrs. Stevenson's close-ups of dukes, duchesses, lords and ladies, of the literati and ranking personalities of the day are delightful. For almost five years she was in the front rank of British society, but she retained her objectivity and she knew how to describe what she saw. Flashes of humor, bright comments, and an occasional bit of gossip, enliven her correspondence.

Her letters, those now extant at least, were addressed mostly to her family in Virginia. Headed "My Beloved Sisters," or "My Namesake" or "My Dear Sisters and Brothers—All," they were routed through the home circle, as she intended, yet read by friends and neighbors as well.

It is pertinent to know that in 1836 when Sallie Coles Stevenson went to England she left behind nine brothers and sisters. Oldest was Walter Coles whose home was Woodville, Virginia. Youngest was Emily Coles, or "Emm," wife of John Rutherford of Richmond, one-time acting Governor of Virginia.

The others were: John Coles III who lived at exquisite Estouteville, Virginia, named for Count d'Estouteville who served with William the Conqueror; Mary Eliza Coles who married Robert Carter and lived at Redlands; Isaac Coles to whom Colonel John Coles II left Enniscorthy and who for a time was President Jefferson's private secretary; Tucker Coles of Tallwood, Virginia; Rebecca Coles, wife of Richard Singleton of South Carolina; Elizabeth Coles, or "Bett," who was unmarried; Edward Coles, who served President Madison as private secretary for six years and later became second Governor of Illinois where he had emigrated. A strong antislavery man, Edward Coles emancipated the slaves he had carried with him to Illinois and his campaign for governor virtually assured free status for Illinois.

Mrs. Stevenson's letters are long ones, ranging from several hundred to several thousand words each. One or two run almost five thousand words. She wrote fast, punctuated little, made mistakes in spelling (which she freely admitted) and grammar, and, like Thomas Jefferson, used few capitals. She had a newspaperman's knack of describing what she saw in few words, seldom missing a feature. Her "Coronation Letter" portraying the elaborate and colorful pageantry of Victoria's crowning is a good example of modern newspaper technique. It might have been written about a more recent coronation in Westminster Abbey.

Mrs. Stevenson complained often of the drudgery of writing yet she continued to write dutifully, regularly, lengthily. She closed her letters apparently always one jump ahead of the sealing of the State Department packet, which traveled by steamer, often by the same *Great Western* that in 1838 began regular transatlantic service between New York and Liverpool. On reaching Washington her letters were committed to normal postal channels.

Letters of even the greatest figures in our history have hard sledding. Wear and tear, careless handling and time take their toll of everything written with pen and ink. Sallie Stevenson's letters were no exception. How many she wrote can only be guessed at. She gave a clue now and then by numbering her letters though she apparently abandoned the idea. Those that have survived were handed down through her family until they reached her great-great-niece, Mrs. C. S. A. Williams of South Orange, New Jersey, from whom they were acquired in 1942 by the Library of Duke University, Durham, North Carolina. The Sallie Coles Stevenson Collection comprises one hundred and ninety-one letters, on approximately eleven hundred closely written sheets. She probably wrote two hundred and fifty letters while in England.

Not only did this talented lady write voluminously to her family, but often she pitched in to transcribe for hours on end her husband's diplomatic papers and letters. The American Legation was notoriously shorthanded. Etiquette was strict in demanding acknowledgment of the least social attention. This task fell to her also.

As lady of the Minister from the great Republic in the West she wrote more constantly and entertainingly than any other who had occupied her position, save perhaps Abigail Adams, wife of the nation's first Minister to the Court of St. James's.

She occasionally chided her family for not writing more often to the "exile," as she called herself. Probably she never realized that only one with a passion for writing to match hers could have done so. In her third letter home she says that Mr. Vail, the *Chargé d'Affaires,* was much amused to see her plop down "anywhere with my portfolio on my knee & inkstand in one hand whilst my other scribbles away so fast that he does not know how I can arrange my ideas so rapidly."

Her letters dealt sparingly with politics, for the Stevensons found it refreshing to get away from the intrigue of Washington. However, she thought President Van Buren an ingrate, lacking in appreciation of past political favors performed by her husband, and she said so quite frankly. She knew the Little Magician too well not to know his traits. She flew to her husband's support when politicians back home began sharpshooting at him and bitterly remarked that he was more appreciated in England than in his own country—or so she felt.

Homesickness weighed heavily on her at times. Frail all her life, she feared she might never live to see again her people and native land. In 1840, her delicate constitution began to break under the rigors of British climate and the heavy social requirements of her station. English spas and the seashore brought only temporary relief. The disease that finally won out was making serious inroads and she was forced to withdraw considerably from the social whirl. No longer could she stand hours on end at a "Drawing Room" or permit herself to be "royally squeezed" at Lady So-and-So's Grand Ball.

In 1840, on learning of the Democratic debacle at the hands of the whooping Whigs, Andrew Stevenson offered his resignation to defeated President Van Buren. Vexed by the long-delayed arrival of his successor, Edward Everett of Massachusetts, Andrew Stevenson said good-bye to Queen Victoria at a farewell audience at Buckingham Palace on October 21, 1841. Two days later he and his wife embarked at Bristol on the *Great Western* for New York.

Having seen and enjoyed to their heart's content (as well as discontent at times) all that "Royalty, wealth and luxury can do in this world," the Stevensons resumed their quieter way of life near Richmond, Virginia. Here Sallie Coles Stevenson was to spend the rest of her days in a wheel chair. Never again was she to enjoy even a small measure of health. Summers her husband took her to visit relatives in Albemarle County and sometimes, if her strength permitted, to the Springs farther west.

In 1846, Andrew Stevenson purchased the ancient estate of Blenheim, near Charlottesville, and here erected a cluster of buildings that still charm the visitor with their beauty and setting. The main house followed English Gothic cottage lines so much admired by the Stevensons in rural England, but Sallie was never to live in their new home. She died at the "Retreat," near Richmond, January 2, 1848. She was buried in the old Coles burying ground near Enniscorthy. On the marble table above her Andrew Stevenson inscribed his tribute to this remarkable woman. It read in part:

> Few women possessed in a more eminent degree all the admirable and Christian virtues. As a daughter, she was unremitting in her duties; as a wife and mother, tender and devoted; as a sister, most affectionate; as a mistress, just and kind.
> Blessed with rare intellectual endowments, she possessed nearly all the elements of moral grace and dignity. Peculiarly captivating in her manners, she imparted pleasure and instruction to all around her. Inspired by the truths of Christianity, and the hope of immortality, her life was beautifully illustrated by devoted piety and expanding benevolence. Meek, gentle, frank, artless, and confiding, she seemed to have been created to be loyed.

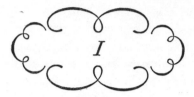

_I_

FROM THE _Montreal_—at sea—Mrs. Stevenson wrote her first letter home. Later, she was to tear it open and record for "My Beloved Friends" her first thrilling impressions of England as her ship slowly ran past the Isle of Wight and into the harbor of Portsmouth.

The "Fs" she mentions were the Fays—Theodore Fay and his wife—who had accompanied them. Fay was slated to take over the duties of Secretary of the Legation.

Portsmouth Wednesday [June] 29th 1836

My beloved friends

I have opened my letter written at sea to inform you of our safe arrival on British ground. I can scarcely realize it to myself that I am indeed in England! Yesterday was one of the most exciting days I have ever passed. Soon after I closed my letter the scenery which opened upon us on both sides of the Channel became so beautiful & interesting that we could not leave the side of the vessel except to pass from one side to the other. The beautiful village of Symington, the castles, country seats—villages—every thing looked so new & strange. Even the stile of buildings; the very tree's & verdure looked different from what it does in dear America. About 2 oclock we passed the

(_13_)

Needles, & at six bid adieu to the ship two miles distant from Portsmouth, & in sight of the sweet & beautiful village of Ride. It was quite an animating scene when the passengers had been all lowered in a large arm chair into the boat. Loud cheers burst from all the ships crew which to my ears were most pleasant sounds tho' some of the passengers were sentimental enough to talk of regrets &c &c. The day was bright & beautiful, & every thing seemed to inspire us with feelings of joy & happiness & with thankfulness too to that Almighty Being when Providence had watched over us, & brought us safely over stormy & pathless ocean in so frail a thing—such a nut shell as is the largest vessel when compared to the immense & boundless waters through which we had passed. Oh, it is worth going to sea & suffering all the miseries of seasickness for the happiness of reaching land again. For the first time since we parted, my beloved sister, I wished for you as I shall ever do when any enjoyment presents itself. Soon after we left the ship a boat joined us from Portsmouth with a messenger bearing a letter to Mr. S. from Mr. Vail with an order to exempt our luggage from search. Mr. Vail's letter was more than friendly. He says, he "has just seen a New York paper announcing our departure in the Montreal, and he had sent to anticipate our arrival, that every hole & corner of London is filled at this time; (Parliament will sit untill August)," & adds, "There is hardly left any prospect of your being better accommodated than in my own house, part of which will be prepared for your reception, & which Mrs. Vail joins me in offering you & Mrs. Stevenson, untill you can make more permanent arrangements" &c. He requests Mr. S. to drive immediately to his house, giving him the number, &c, if he should post up to London; but if he decides to take the stage coach entirely to ourselves, which he recommends, his carriage shall meet us. Mrs. Vail greets [*a few words were torn off here*] There is in the whole stile of the letter a tone of cordiality & kindness which went straight to my heart in this land of strangers, & takes from me in my approach to the great city something of that feeling of loneliness & desolation which every stranger in a foreign land necessarily feels. It at least assures

(*14*)

me of her friendly feeling towards us. Just before a brilliant
sun set we landed at the custom house where notwithstanding
the order from Mr. Vail our luggage with difficulty escaped a
search. Scott, our servant, amused me by declaring as he brought
a trunk into my chamber, that he believed they would pull his
eyes out, if they could. Mr. S. invited the M's to share our
parlour with us. With good appetites we sat down at 10 oclock
to a sumptous supper. Two kinds of fish, the most delicious
bread & butter & mutton chops such as I never tasted before,
green peas & lastly two dishes of strawberries—very fine—altho'
I do not think they have as much flavour as ours or are so deep
a colour—but perhaps this is partiality. I must admit however
they were excellent. Again, this morning, a most abundant
breakfast wound up with a dish of strawberries & cherries, the
latter very inferior to ours. Altho' this place is not remarkable
for good hotels, this, "The George," leaves the City Hotel at a
sightless distance behind—& I only wish our host of the said
Hotel could be sent over with his cook & chamber maid for a
little drilling. To morrow we shall take a coach and proceed to
the great metropolis of the world. The F's, who are chattering
around me, are going to day to visit an old abbey about 18 miles
off and to morrow, to the Ile of Wight, & from thence to Haver
on their way to Paris. The rest of our party have scattered some
to London some to Paris & others to travel about the country.
The sun is shining brightly even as much so as in my own native
land—and Mrs. F. has come to invite me to walk & see the town.
The ramparts—fortifications &c. You must give me credit for
this scrawl for my head is still turning around as if I was on
ship board. My love to all the dear ones we have left behind
us. Your sister—SCS

II

As Sallie Coles Stevenson promptly was to discover, being the American Minister's lady in the gayest capital in the world was a full-time task. London was unbelievably festive. Well-dressed people crowded the streets and parks. Elegant carriages streamed by, decorated in scarlet, blue and gold, with footmen and coachmen in sumptuous liveries.

It was not long before the American Minister and his wife fell under the spell of English life at its best and brightest. Castles, palaces and great houses opened to them as if by magic. Hospitality and kindness greeted them wherever they went. They were accepted in record time.

The names of the personnel of the Legation appear frequently in Mrs. Stevenson's letters. After Aaron Vail's departure, Stevenson appointed as Secretary *ad interim* Theodore S. Fay, who had accompanied the new Minister to England on the *Montreal*. It was an unhappy choice, both for the Stevensons and for Fay, who was replaced in July, 1837, by Attaché Richard Vaux, a young gentleman of much charm. Vaux served as Secretary *pro tempore* until the arrival of Benjamin Rush of Philadelphia in September 1837. Rush—"one of the most sensible and correct young men I have ever known" wrote Mrs. Stevenson —held his post until a few months before the close of Stevenson's ministry. Like Vaux, he was warmly attached to the Stevensons—and they to him.

On July 13, 1836—the day Mrs. Stevenson wrote the following letter to her sister, Mrs. John Rutherford (Emily) at Richmond, Virginia—Andrew Stevenson sallied forth for his first audience with his Britannic Majesty, William IV. Sir Robert Chester conducted him into the royal presence; Lord Palmerston, Foreign Minister, presented him.

Mrs. Stevenson was busily writing her letter, giving the details of the domestic ménage of the Legation over which she was to preside, when her husband returned from this, the first of many ceremonials to come.

The Mrs. Morrison to whom Mrs. Stevenson refers here was the wife of James Morrison, member of Parliament for Wiltshire. One of England's first self-made men, Morrison began his business career as a lowly workboy in a London warehouse. His estate, Fonthill, in Wiltshire, was fabulous.

London July 13 1836

My dear Emm,

I wrote a volume from Portsmouth & addressed to my dear friends generally & again from this place to my precious Betsy, the longest dispatch, Mr. Vail said, that had ever been sent to the office of the present secretary who is not remarkably fond of reading long dispatches. Since my last to Betsy nothing here that is interesting has occurred. You will scarcely believe it possible.

I have been in London nearly a fortnight & have seen none of the Lions. I have not yet been to visit Westminster Abbey, St. Paul's, the opera or indeed any thing that is to be seen in this wondrous Queen of Cities. Having so much time before us we thought it best to wait until the Vails left us when we shall have more leisure & a carriage at our command. Today we take the house, servants &c &c & they become our guests whilst they remain in town. Mr. & Mrs. Vail were both very unwilling to make the transfer untill a few days before they were ready to depart but we insisted on its taking place today as Mr. Stevenson is presented & Mr. Vail's function as Chargé ceases on the day of the Minister's presentation.

(*17*)

Mr. & Mrs. Vail have been very kind to us. I shall never cease to think of their kindness with the deepest gratitude. They have been of infinite use to us. We take their house, servants & equipage untill we can find a house & carriage we like better. The butler has been in the Legation for five years & is one of the most valuable servants in London. Many attempts have been made to get him from Mrs. Vail but without success. He seems to think he belongs to the American Legation. He is a man of about 50, has most respectable manners, perfectly accomplished in his department, & the most kind & faithful of servants. Such is the character given of him by Mr. Van Buren & Mr. Vail. He has the charge and superintendence of everything, delivers in his accounts once a week, or fortnight, & takes the orders of the lady every morning as to what she will have for dinner &c. He stands between her & the other servants, dismisses them if they do not please, pays their wages, accounts, &c & receives 50 guineas a year, about 250$.

Mr. Vail tells me Cates has generally been considered as belonging to the Legation. The coachman, a most admirable driver, who could drive to Petersburg whilst Peyton was wending his weary way to the turnpike gate, receives something like the same amount of wages, & finds his place no sinecure at that, for people in London do not permit their coachman to have much idle time. A cook at 18 guineas, footman at 15, a chambermaid at 12 (lower wages than I give Rhoda) and she waits on Mrs. Vail, cleans the chambers, parlours dining room and office, that is to say she does all the cleaning, makes all the fires, sometimes shops for her mistress as she calls Mrs. Vail, & even finds time to sew for her & renders these services with a cheerfulness and alacrity that is delightful & withall is so affec and attached that last winter when Mrs. Vail was sick she sat at her door all night. Rhoda is astonished & frightened at all this and reminds me every day that she engaged to wait on me and do any little sewing. She is a good creature but excessively indolent & laces so tight that it renders her incapable of any exertion.

I am sensible of the folly of bringing American servants

to this country. They are in every way inferior and an incumbrance rather than "helps". They tell me here I shall be obliged to get a ladies maid. If so Rhoda, the maid I brought with me, will be a supernumerary and as yet Scott has been of no use. When we get a larger house we may find employment for them. Mr. S. has been looking at a great many furnished houses, & thinks he has found one in Manchester Square, which will suit him. It is a very central & fashionable part of London about half way between Regent & Hyde Park but we have not yet decided upon taking it. It rents very low, they say for its appearance & comforts only 400 a year. All the knowing ones advise Mr. S. not to be in a hurry, but take time to look about him, as we are very agreeably fixed here, & can keep this house for a week or a month, or as long as we please & it is more like the country than the town.

Since I wrote you last I have only been out to return calls, & visit some of the shops. Mrs. Vail took me one day to a Bizaire, where every thing is to be seen & bought. I could have formed no idea of any thing like it. Brother J or E will describe it to you. I thought of Helen & wondered what she would do in the multiplicity of beautiful things which claim ones attention. I thought too if brother had been there with his $55 he might have got more for them & turned them to much better account than he did in New York. On Sunday Mrs. Morrison called & took me to Trinity Church where I had the pleasure to hear a most excellent sermon, & returned home refreshed in spirit, for to confess the truth I have been sadder than I am wont to be, but I dare say it will wear off after a while. The sun has come forth to welcome us every day since our arrival in England and I have found friends & kind ones too, yet still they are not brothers & sister's & such dear ones as I have left in the land of my birth, & the home of my Fathers—but you know how elastic my spirit is & I hope it will revive some of these days. On Sunday about 3 oclock we set off in an open barouche to dine nine miles out of town at an English cottage with Mr & Mrs B——, Americans long residents in this country, & very amiable people. They are wealthy—with only one daughter about 16. They lost an only son about 18 months ago, by an accidental shot from the hand of a young man, his friend & school companion. They have not recovered & probably never will from the shock. Mrs. B—— is very amiable, frank, & unpretending; if I had the pen of our Miss Sedgewick I would attempt to describe this beautiful & secluded spot, where every elegance was united to every comfort, where we sat under the trees, & inhaled the fragrance of flowers, or walked through shaded & secluded paths, every ray of sunshine excluded, catching through the openings in the trees glimpses of the lawn, ornamented with clumps of shrubbery or white vases filled with beautiful flowers. Poor Lady! in the midst of all this rural beauty, & surrounded by all these enjoyments her heart was in the grave of her departed child, her conversation with me was constantly of her son, for in me she found a sympathetic listener. My tears flowed with hers. We wept as bereaved mothers only can weep. Dined at 8 & got home a little before 12. The drive was delightful, I cannot tell you how much I enjoyed it, & as I looked upon the calm & beautiful heavens, & then upon the scenery through which we were passing, illuminated by the brilliant gas lights which shone upon us either from houses or villages the whole 9 miles, I slept soundly, & awoke well. Is it not strange, that one so delicate as I have been should be able to change old habits so entirely and with impunity? Both Mr & Mrs B—— urged us to go out & spend a week or as long as we found it agreeable. We have also a kind & pressing invitation to visit the Morrison's at Fonthill Abbey. She has just called to bid me good bye, show her little son, & repeat her invitation. She does not reside in the abbey as it has become a ruin. They lived, she said, in a small house very near, quite in cottage style. "The house did not contain more than forty rooms".

After seeing my husband off to the palace at one, I sat down to scribble to you, & my dear Sister, during the interval of his absence, and had just finished the account of our domestic arrangements when Mrs Morrison called, and now as Mr. Stevenson has not returned, I will give you some account of his general appearance. I will not describe his dress, as I hope some day, not very distant, you will see him in it for your especial gratification. It is very becoming to him, and I thought he looked very well. After contemplating himself in a full length mirror, he said, "How I wish Betsy could see me". You may guess, as the Yankee's say, what he thought of his appearance from the involuntary expression of this wish. He looked at least two inches taller buttoned up to the throat, & his clothes fitted him to a charm—cocked hat—very rich & handsome sword by his side, of exquisite workmanship—gold lace enough about him to adorn at least a dozen well dressed footmen— American boots (the best looking article of his dress) & French gloves. In this costume, he departed about two hours ago for the Palace of St. James, attended by the Chargé, Mr Vail, & the Secretary pro-tem Mr. Fay—& now, I hear the knock & ring of the footman—Mr. Stevenson has just given me an account of his presentation. His Majesty received him very graciously, addressed some commonplace questions to him, such as related to his arrival—voyage, &c, &c—having answered these enquiries, Mr. S. made a short speech to him, somewhat in the tone of conversation, only more dignified & emphatic. Mr. Vail tells me, it was very admirably done, and made a most favourable impression upon the King. Lord Palmerston it seems paid him a high compliment, a good beginning. Tomorrow he will have to call upon the Royal family, the Cabinet Ministers —foreign ministers, & some of the most distinguished of the nobility. As to myself I shall not have much of this until I have been presented which will now probably take place at Windsor, in a more private manner, as the drawing rooms are over. We received to-day an invitation from the Duchess of Kent, the Mother of the future Queen, who will be Regent in case of the death of the present King before the princess Victoria comes of age. We have both declined not being yet ready for so grand a debut. Mr. Stevenson went at a grand dinner given by Lord Palmerston and was treated with distinguished attention. As yet I have not been thrown in direct contact with any of the nobility, a titled Lady called yesterday, but I had the good fortune to escape an interview. It is astonishing to an American

(*21*)

how distinctly marked the different classes of society are here. Wealth is nothing, as to the rank it gives, tho' all important as to the comforts. In vain the rich Bankers & merchants give feasts of which Lucullus might have been happy to have par- taken, they are forced to keep within their own magic circle and thus it is they are so delighted to get hold of a foreign minister, who may if he chooses feast every day in the week. We have already declined several invitations, & dined only with those whom we knew, the M———'s and W———'s. Mrs. W——— is an English lady but neither so graceful nor as pretty as our Mrs. W———, tho' a lady of very high pretensions, & the most extravagant dresser, in her way in London. Mr. V. tells me the nobility may always be distinguished by the extreme simplicity of their dress, unless when they go to Court, or upon some grand occasion. The W's have been very civil to us, & invited us to make them a visit at their country seat a few miles distant from town. They live in great stile & fashion. Say to the Mann's when you see them that I delivered their beautiful present, and had the pleasure to witness the delight of the young people. The girls are very sweet & interesting, especially, E———, who is very like her cousin's in Richmond. Mary plays delightfully on the harp & they both promise to make lovely young women. Mrs. Mann seems to be a most excellent & exemplary mother & the children are devoted to her. They leave town on Saturday for a tour in Wales. Many of the fashionables are leaving London, & the town they say will soon be empty. The season is thought pretty well over when the drawing-rooms cease. All this is fortunate for us, as it gives us breathing time, & enables us to get acquainted with the ways of this new people. Every thing here is so different from what it is with us, even the manner of knocking & ringing at the door—a visitor, knocks & rings, a servant rings—the postman knocks twice & the master of the house has a knock, & ring peculiar to himself—all this I like, because it prevents disturbance—but the manner of serving tea is very disagreeable to us, the servants, generally the butler, & James the footman bring in the waiter with the tea things on it, & the urn hissing is sat before the lady of the house. She draws towards her a little table, or stand, containing tea, sugar,

&c, unlocks it, & makes the tea, when the gentleman of the house, or any familiar friend present, hands to each person a cup, sugared & creamed, or each individual may approach the table & help himself, & it is the same thing with coffee after dinner—and at breakfast the servants also retire, but at dinner you must be looked at by a dozen if there is as many in the house each one with napkins over their right thumb—poor Scott makes a sad figure among them as yet—but I hope he will improve. And now dear & precious friends am I not a peerless correspondent. Mr Vail amuses himself very much with me, he says I sat down any where with my portfolio on my knee, & ink stand in one hand, whilst my other scribbles away so fast that he does not know how I can arrange my idea's so rapidly. I tell him if he could take a peep into my scrawls the wonder would cease, for he would find there as little arrangement as in a ladies work box—or dressing room—and now my dear friends this is my third long dispatch & not one word from any of you. My dear sisters I know have neither neglected, or forgotten me, but why I do not hear, I cannot tell. Sally must write long & often and I will reply—my best love to her, & dear Mr Rutherford—John—Emm—& dear little Helen with her bright eyes. Heavens blessings rest upon you all here & hereafter & all the dear ones on our happy mountain. Do present me kindly to all enquiring friends. I had intended folding this for Mr. S. to put under cover, but find I have not space enough to do so. I shall therefore fill up this with some of the little nothings I have to say. Mrs. Vail told me last night her Court feathers only five in number cost her 65 dollars. I very much regret not bringing mine. They would have been worth a great deal to me, & nothing to you. I understand also it is the fashion here to rouge when you attend the drawing rooms. Ah, for a little poke juice—to bring the blood into my poor faded cheek. This is the only rouge I could ever bring myself to wear even at the risk of exclusion from the royal presence. I dare say I shall pass unnoticed. I must hope to be rouged by the climate. A pity I did not think of bringing some of our native rouge the mullen leaf of famous memory, or the still more venerable poke. Adieu! Adieu!

III

IN SEPTEMBER 1836, the Stevensons accepted a "pressing invitation" from the James Morrisons to visit them at their home, Fonthill, in Wiltshire. This letter was one of the first of Mrs. Stevenson's excellent descriptions of places and things she saw in England.

On this trip she also visited celebrated Longleat, home of Lord Bath—and, today, of the fifth Lord Bath. Longleat was a "feast of beauty" for the romantic lady from Virginia. One of the great places of England it is open today to visitors—at thirty-five cents per head. Queen Elizabeth and George III were both guests at Longleat—two centuries apart, of course.

It is worth noting that the fame of Mrs. Stevenson's brother, Edward Coles, former governor of Illinois, who had emancipated his slaves, had preceded her to England.

Wiltshire Fonthill
Sepr 1836

My beloved sister's & friends
We left London on the 19th in the stage coach for Salisbury and had a most agreeable journey. The day was fine, the country beautiful, and the roads as smooth & as hard as marble. What added greatly to our pleasure was the company of a most in-

teresting fellow-passenger whose conversation we found both amusing and instructive. We passed over the plains of Salisbury which Miss More has made classic ground, our coach acquaintance told me he had seen her "Shepherd" such as she had described him in her beautiful book. We spent the night at Salisbury, where we found most comfortable accommodation, but an extravagant bill. We suspect Louisa must have told who we were. The next morning I persuaded my husband to go with me to the celebrated Cathedral, & we were well repaid for the walk. It ranks next to St. Pauls, not only in antiquity but for its grand and noble proportions, its stile of architecture is, I believe, purely Gothic. The spire is said to be the highest & the most graceful in the world. I never saw my husband more deeply impressed than when he approached this noble structure. He paused, & gazed upon it with deep emotion, & what do you think he said? Why only—"I wish B was here"!—Need I say, dear sister, how warmly my heart responded to this wish. We remained to witness the morning service from an elevated pew belonging to one of the nobility, afterwards, went over the vast building—paid two shillings—& departed for Fonthill. The country as we approached this far-famed spot became even more beautiful & peculiar. The downs spreading on one side like a sea of green turf dotted here & there with flocks of white sheep attended by the shepherd & his dog, on the other the high state of cultivation with the woods and towers of the abbey in the distance, presented a prospect on which the eye of an American would gaze with unwearied pleasure. The Pavilion the residence of Mr. Morrison is about a mile from the Abbey, & is connected by a Terrace drive which is said to be the most beautiful in England. The approach to the Pavilion is through the village of Fonthill Bishop, & some fine woodland brings you to the entrance lodge a building of considerable elegance. Tradition ascribes its design to Inigo Jones, that great master of English architecture, it was built in the time of Charles the 2d. On passing the Lodge a wide & extensive lawn opens upon you adorned with plots of flowers & rare shrubs. Trees of every graceful form which lead the eye by fine gradations to those distant clumps of massy foliage which surround the lawn on two sides, on one of which is the church of Gothic architecture just showing itself through the trees, on the other is a gentle undulation rising from the back of the house, and cut into walks which wind up amidst flowers & shrubs to a very pretty summer house from whence you command a most beautiful & extensive view—but the most striking object is the Lake winding in front of the house looking like a broad deep river & covered with swan's who proudly floating on their glassy Empire give life and animation to the scene. There are also pleasure boats and a beautiful Yatch with its gay colours flying. The House is indeed a cottage as Mr. Morrison called it, when compared with the magnificent Palace of Fonthill, altho' it contains twenty six rooms some of them rich, tastely and beautiful beyond any thing I have seen except in the Palaces of the Nobility but I shall not attempt to give you any discription of the style & fashion, it is so very different from ours. The ceiling of a room here will cost as much as a comfortable house with us. Mrs. Morrison told me that the ceilings of my chamber, dressing room, & the one adjoining, had cost 800 pounds. But I dare say you would rather hear of the charming inmates than of the house, and of the very kind & cordial manner which marked their reception of us. We found company staying with them, or as they say here, stoping. They had also invited some friends to meet us, a Mr. & Miss Bennet, he is a member of Parliament & his canvass cost him only the trifling sum of 60,000 pounds. He is much respected & thought to be a high minded chivalric person. His family is one of the oldest in Wiltshire, & he possesses a splendid establishment in the modern stile. Miss Bennet is what they call here, "a nice person" sensible, accomplished, & full of feeling & sensibility, with a good deal of excentricity. We soon became friends, & my partiality has strengthened on every interview I have had with her since. The day after our arrival Mr. & Mrs. Morrison took us to see Stocken House, owned by a Mr. Biggs, it is only remarkable for its antiquity, & giving a correct idea of the Elizabethan stile of architecture. The roof is formed of many pointed gables, and in the interior is a porch of oak projecting into the apartment & seems to have been so placed to break the force of cold air issuing from the door. In the same apartment is the Orice window of which we have so often read, another peculiarity is a rich & heavy ceiling divided into compartments and ornamented with various devices. It was all very curious to American eyes. We also visited the horses—dog—& dalia's which formed a very pretty garden. We went in the evening four miles to dine with a parson, where we found some very agreeable persons & a good dinner. The next day was one of the most pleasant I ever passed in making a visit to the celebrated seat of Lord Bath, called Longleat, which is considered as among the most splendid establishments in England both on account of its majestic pile of buildings & the variety of its surrounding territory, the approaches to it from three different points vary in character & each possess much natural beauty. The one selected for our approach is considered the most picturesque for displaying the stately mansion & its fine surrounding woods to the greatest advantage. No verbal description can do justice to this enchanting place. The park with its magnificent trees, its pure emerald green turf, and seven hundred deer sporting over it, may be imagined, but the thousand beauties of nature & art which present themselves here can neither be copied or described in appropriate colours or terms, a faint out line is all I can attempt. It was originally a priory before the time of Henry the 8th when the present noble mansion was erected, & in all the changes which have taken place the utmost care has been used to adhere in all the various decorations of ceilings, cornices, &c to those of that period when this noble structure was first erected—even the stables & out houses present a magnificent pile of building of an architecture corresponding with that of the mansion. The grounds & gardens with their parterres, fountains, &c, are in the most exquisite taste and beautiful as the fabled gardens of Armida. The house, or Palace is of vast extent but the grandest features in the building is the Baronial Hall & the principal stair case. The former is in its pristine state, most appropriately decorated with armorial escutcheons, head pieces, & stag horns and though

of spacious dimensions has been rendered completely warm &
comfortable by flues & stoves—such were the Halls in which
the ancient Barons received and welcomed their vassals and
which Scott has so well described. The stair case leads to the
gallery & upper range of apartments & is a modern appendage,
it reminded me a good deal of the stair case in the former Presi-
dents House, which was considered so remarkable. The house
keeper carried us to a suite of bed rooms kept exclusively, she
said, for guest, twelve in number with their dressing rooms
attached. This was only one range, there were others she said
appropriated to the same purpose. The decided character of
these rooms is that of simple elegance & solid comfort, uniting
the utmost delicacy & neatness with that air of hospitableness,
(if I may use such a word,) which can alone render any mansion
a desirable residence. These rooms are furnished alike with fine
coloured chintz lined with green or yellow to correspond with
the paper. They are also ornamented with china & pictures, &
the dressing rooms have the most inviting looking easy chairs,
lounges & sofa's, I longed to rest my weary limbs upon their
down cushions for after all, this sightseeing is a very wearisome
business. The library is a very fine apartment, & is adorned with
some original paintings by the best masters, a Madonna by
Carlo Dolce, so exquisitely beautiful, & the expression of
modesty is so fine that it looks almost divine. The suffering
Christ, by Guido, is too affecting to be gazed upon without deep
emotion. Now I dare say, dear sisters, you are heartily tired
of discription & will be glad to return with me to the Pavilion,
after taking a lunch on the side of the road on our way back,
dress, & go four or five miles to dine with a Mr. & Mrs. Seymour one of the elite of the neighbourhood, a travelled gentleman possessed of great wealth, living in fine stile, & a very
agreeable person, who reminded me very often of Mr. Ritchie
both in person & manners. We did not get back until nearly
twelve oclock, I passed the evening very agreeably in playing
chess with Miss Bennet, the company was large, & some very
pleasant & high tone persons. When we got home dear Mrs.
Morrison made with her own hand a glass of hot gin toddy &

insisted on my taking it to prevent cold. I cannot express to you how very kind & affc she is to me, & it has gratified me to see how her manner has changed from hospitable to cordial kindness, & then to affectionate confidence. It seems to me as if Heaven had inspired the hearts of these strangers in a strange land with such very kindly feelings towards us, possessed as they are of all that this world can give, their friendship for us, is purely disinterested. Mr. Morrison is a member of Parliment, immensely wealthy, which of course gives him what all men covet, power, & influence, & when to this you add health, a well regulated mind & temper, with the most perfect domestic happiness & prosperity, I think you will admit he has nothing more to desire in this world. His manners are very pleasant & amiable, his conversation sensible & entertaining, & he has strong prejudices in favour of us Americans. His wife has presented him with nine lively children & looks the elder sister of the family, still blooming & handsome & what is even better than beauty, is a pious, sensible, useful woman to whom the poor around look up as a benefactress & friend to whose kind & benevolent feelings they never appeal in vain. She is not only the lady Bountiful of the village but a most admirable wife & mother, & indeed, exemplary in all the relations of life. She pays from her own private purse 20 guineas a year to a school mistress to teach the poor children of the Parish besides hiring a room, paying for fire, books, working materials, &c, and clothing all who are not able to get decent garments to attend the school in. She took me to her school & to visit with her the cottages of the poor, one poor woman said they allowed her one shilling a week & a quartern loaf to subsist upon, that she was very well content upon that, but when she got only sixpence it was hard getting through the week. Another we found patching a shirt which had nothing of the original garment left, she said her husband was out of employment & could get nothing to do, & a shilling for herself, husband, & three little children was starvation. They pity our slaves, but how much more miserable & wretched is the condition of the poor in this country, who have not the means of existence here, nor the power of going where they might earn a subsistence. Notwithstanding the extreme poverty I found among these people, their cottages bore the air of neatness & attention to cleanliness & order in every thing, & every cottager, however poor he might be, yet found time, & space to cultivate a few flowers. We called to see a Mrs. Humphreys, the Miss Merillies of the village, and her tall figure, stately step, & piercing black eyes, which peered at me from under her gipsy bonnet, reminded me very forcebly of Scotts discription. Mrs. Morrison says she hopes in a few years to be able to ameliorate the condition of her parish but Mr. Beckford has left her much to do. Mr. Morrison contemplates purchasing the whole property & bestowing it upon his son Charles who is a fine young man of nineteen, handsome in person & possessed of uncommon talents. Unfortunately he has the English reserve of manner which makes it difficult to know him but once known he can never be forgotten. Alfred, the second son, about fifteen, is what the English would call a "nice young man" devoted to field sports, as all young men of his age are, when freed from the trammels of school discipline. I have promised if he is a hard student, & will become an American, to use my interest with my little niece S— & get her to bestow upon him her brightest smiles. Three of the daughters are at school Lucy—Emily—& Mary, the latter is said to be a perfect beauty, and even the modest Mother speaks of her as the gem of her casket. If she surpasses in loveliness a little fellow they have here in the nursery, she must be exquisitely lovely. This fair boy is only four & a half years old, & rides his shetland poney with the confidence of a man. Twice since I have been here he has been permitted (with a servant to attend him) to follow a fox chase in the rain until 5 in the evening, and then make his appearance with the fruit after dinner, looking as blooming & beautiful as a poets dream, partaking of whatever he liked in the way of fruit nuts, &c and his Mother says sleeping without moving until the morning. The children, & indeed, no one here keep in the house for a little rain as with us. The climate is so variable, if they were not brought up to take an occasional wetting they would be good for nothing. I can not tell you how I covet one of these little shetlands for my little nephews. Stricker would look as bright as an American sun upon the back of one of these delightful little animals, and my own Isaetta would soon learn to course it over her native hills, dear little Emma would like something more quiet at home. As to Helen you must tell me what she promises to be, I hope like her namesake. I often think of brother Walter when I see the fox hunters with their red coats mounted on their beautiful hunters & surrounded by their dogs. Mrs. Morrison and myself have once joined the chase in the Poney Phaeton but I cannot say I liked it much. Since our arrival here we have been constantly engaged in a succession of agreeable engagements. We dined out three times last week after spending all the mornings in visiting the beautiful seats & objects of curiosity & interest in the neighbourhood—both Mr. & Mrs. Morrison seem never so happy as when carrying some scheme into execution which they think will give us pleasure. Their neighbours have also payed us very great attention, they are very numerous, & consist of the elite of fashion—wealth, & elegance & most of them have a long list of noble ancestors to boast of. We have become acquainted with some of the most agreeable & intelligent persons I have ever known since our arrival here & spent my time delightfully. I have felt like one suddenly transported to Fairyland ever since I have been here. I have wished for you dear sister & in the fullness of my heart have talked of you all. I was highly gratified the other day dining at Mr. Bennet's when he spoke to me of my dear Edward as one whom every Englishman knew, and would delight to honour as the liberator of his slaves —my heart was full—even to overflowing—for I felt he deserves the love of all good men.

Our kind friends here insist so earnestly on my husbands leaving me here and going to London on the business of the Legation that he has consented to do so and Mr. Morrison will take him up in his Brisker to morrow. You who know how sensitive both Mr. Stevenson and myself are about outstaying our welcome may imagine from this how very kind we have found our English friends, indeed it is impossible to be more so,

& there is a frankness about the English which shows at once when they are in earnest. They understand in this respect better than we do the duties of hospitality, and it is understood no one is asked to come or stay from mere politeness. They have also the art of making you feel "at home" and do not remind you every moment by the excess of their attentions that you are a visitor whilst they contrive to give you the gratifying feeling that you are bestowing as well as receiving pleasure, and provide for you a succession of pleasures and amusements without seeming to be occupied with you. As you may like to know the habits of an English family, such as I have found them, I will give you a day spent en-famille. The usual breakfast hour is about half past nine, when everybody drops in, as they are ready. The breakfast consist of a variety of cold bread—dry toast—& excellent butter, with eggs on the breakfast table— on the side table, is every variety of cold meats, to which the gentlemen help themselves, & the ladies, who wish for any. The servants disappear after bringing in the urn & coffee, & every body helps themselves. When the meal is over, every one moves off to the library, drawing room, or their own apartments, as fancy or inclination dictates. Those who choose to walk in the grounds, or row on the lake do so. Mrs. Morrison & myself generally rode the poney phaeton until after lunch, when the real business of the day commences. About two o'clock the horses & carriages are at the door for some previously arranged plan of amusements & about six the family assemble in the drawing rooms, dressed for dinner, &c. Coffee is handed after dinner, & is followed almost immediately after by tea, the usual hour for retiring is between eleven & twelve. I have become accustomed to these hours altho' I cannot say I like them. October the 1st. Your letter my dear sister has just been forwarded to me from London & I return you many thanks for it, altho' I feel a little mortified that they should have occasioned you so many tears but I know dear Bett you weep not so much at what I write but because I am so far away from you. You have misunderstood also that part of it which related to dress. It was intended merely to show you the difference of fashions & customs in the two countries, what with us would have been an elegant & appropriate dress was so entirely unsuitable here. It was my leghorn & India fan which attracted so much attention, articles so costly here that only the nobility can afford to use them. Mrs. Vail was so delighted with my fan, that her husband after searching London procured one at an extravagant price. I will not complain but I certainly feel mortified that not one of my brothers have written me but dear Ned. Surely their memories & their affection might reach 3000 miles off as my family is so numerous I shall not attempt to write separate letters to them. Those who wish to have a letter from me must write me I have answered every one I have received immediately & written so many I cannot number them. I wrote first a general letter to the family.

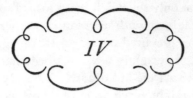

IV

LADY WELLESLEY whom Mrs. Stevenson mentions in this short letter to her sister, Mrs. Richard Singleton of South Carolina, was an American, formerly Miss Patterson of Baltimore. Lady Wellesley's sister was the first wife of Jerome Bonaparte, brother of the Emperor Napoleon.

The Queen, of course, is Adelaide, spouse of King William IV. The "celebrated Mrs. Somerville" is the renowned mathematician and astronomer, who was regarded with considerable awe in England, even by the acid-tongued political diarist, Charles Greville.

The "fair lady" is Angelica Singleton, Mrs. Stevenson's niece, who had blossomed into a girl of rare beauty and attainments.

It was most likely Henry Peter Brougham, Baron Brougham and Vaux, to whom Mrs. Stevenson refers as "Lord Chancellor." He had only recently retired from the second Melbourne Cabinet. One of the great men of British politics, his name is famous in another way: he gave it to a little specially built carriage, the brougham, that Thomas Moore, the poet, called "an odd little sort of garden chair."

Decr 12th 1836

My beloved sister

This letter ought to have gone by the last packet, but Mr. Fay disappointed me by closing it without informing me it was dispatch day. I have just received a very long & affec letter from my dear Edward & another from my ever attentive Bett who never forgets me. No one who has not been separated from country—home—& friends can form any idea of the pleasure of a long letter—next to seeing those we love it is the greatest happiness. For six months my eyes have rested on no human face it has ever known before save my husbands. We both sometimes pine for dear familiar faces, but try to bear the privation —especially, since it has pleased Providence to raise us up so many kind friends in this land of strangers. We have quite an agreeable circle of English, besides a number of American's who are always here. Lady Wellesley has been very polite & kind. She is an elegant creature—& the Queen is devoted to her. She told us the other day that she understood no American Minister & lady had been received with as much cordiality & kindness by the English. We are invited to morrow to dine with Lady Alderson, the next day to Lady Parker to meet the Lord Chancellor. The next evening to a Mrs. Mathison's to meet the celebrated Mrs. Somerville &c &c so you see we are likely to have our hands full. Notwithstanding, as Christmas approaches I think of you all & wish I had Fortunatus' 'cap'. I would take a trip across the big waters, call at the Green Mountain—stop a while in Richmond & then to Carolina & peep at you all & may be I might see a fair lady stand before the holy man & offer up her lips to one worthy of them. I would stay long enough to kiss her lips, & say God bless you my child!!! and may He bless you all dear friends is the earnest fervent prayer of your attached & devoted

Sarah C. Stevenson

Mr. S. sends much love—kind wishes &c &c & sometimes wishes for your nice sausages &c &c and I for the hominy.

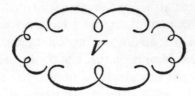

THE MOST PRESSING diplomatic problem confronting Andrew
Stevenson at London was the long-standing controversy with
Britain over the Northeastern Boundary between Maine and
Canada. Secretary of State John Forsyth had briefed Stevenson
carefully on this phase of his diplomatic mission. The situation
was fast becoming inflammatory: sabres were rattling in Washington and President Van Buren had asked Congress for fifty
thousand men to enforce the American border claims.

Andrew Stevenson began sounding out Lord Palmerston,
Foreign Minister, the moment he reached Britain. Palmerston
was not yet lovable "Old Pam." But he was amenable to discus-
sion. Stevenson and his Lordship were to have many a heated
engagement, but out of it would emerge a cordial *entente* that
augured well for amicable relations between England and the
United States.

Stevenson has never been given due credit for his zeal and
adroitness in handling the boundary dispute, although his wife
fully appreciated his amazing ability for diplomatic tightrope
walking. The issue was finally settled in 1842 by the Webster-
Ashburton Treaty. But Andrew Stevenson's work had an important bearing on the final settlement.

In December, 1836, Lord Palmerston invited the American
Minister to visit him at his estate, Broadlands, in Hampshire.
An invitation to the Minister meant, unless stated otherwise, an
invitation to the Minister's wife as well.

So, on New Year's Day, 1837, the Stevensons climbed into their carriage and went rolling through the countryside to Broadlands where Lord Palmerston himself greeted them with gracious courtesy.

London Decr 27th 1836

My dear Sisters,

I feel particularly inclined to be with you in spirit at this season of the year to commune with you as I do with my own heart. I went to Church on Christmas day with my sweet friend Sarah Moore, her brother, Dr. Moore, & a Miss Cochrane, three of the most amiable and intelligent Americans we have had in London—all communicants of our Church. My heart was full —first of thoughts of my own sinfulness, and unworthyness of the great mercies I have received in the last year, in a foreign land, far away from friends & kindred—and especially I thought of you my dear sisters, with whom I have so often knelt to commemorate this solemn rite, & to supplicate for pardon & peace, and almost I dared to hope our prayers might meet at His footstool, and find acceptance through Him, who lived & died for us. The life I lead here, I am sorry to say, is not favourable to the growth of piety in the soul. The mind and attention is so distracted by a thousand things, that the life of a Christian, or one who would be a Christian, in spirit & in truth is a communal warfare—it is in vain to bid the world go by with all its deceiving vanities, there is so much to lure one to folly, or to ensnare one in sin, so many calls upon ones time, no matter how frivolous, or how tiresome, which must be attended to, that we feel on each Sabbath day, when we come to settle the account with Conscience this is not the life which an immortal being should lead. This is not a preparation for Eternity—not the one thing needful—and yet, I feel it is my duty to be where my husband is. I am bound to follow his fortunes whether for weal or woe, to be a helpmeet, if I can— and in a foreign country, we feel even more than in our own, the want of this domestic friends. You know my dear sisters I have always said, I did not consider giving up the world, consisted in renouncing its amusements—its company—its pursuits—so much as in pulling off its temper & spirit—but alas! that is the difficulty—in such a vortex as this, we feel, we must be swallowed up—unless our Heavenly Father will throw His shield around us. It is the remark of an old Divine "That we may not complain of the present, let us view God's hand in all events—and that we may not be afraid of the future, let us view all events in God's hands". You will think me sadly out of spirits dear sisters, nor would you wonder, if you could breathe this London atmosphere for a little while. For two months the sun has scarcely been seen here, constantly a heavy mist, or drizling rain—or snow—or worse than all this, a darkness so complete that at my window I could not see any thing passing in the street—indeed, it was awful—besides the inconvenience & disagreeable necessity of lighting candles at one oclock in the day. I see from the papers many accidents happened during the darkness & one or two lives lost. Oh! for the bright sun of my native land, the pure dry air—here the dampness is so excessive that the external air feels like a wet blanket—and the effect upon my health & spirits has been very trying. I have had a cough ever since I came to England with the exception of the few weeks I was in the country.

I wrote you that Lord Palmerston had invited us to Hampshire, where he has a fine old country seat, called Broadlands. I feel desirous to go in hopes change of air may do me good, & raise my spirits. Adieu, till then!

Broadlands Jany 7th 1837

Permit me dear sisters to wish you a happy new year from this scene of gay & festive enjoyment. We left London on the first day of the new year about nine in the morning, in our own carriage with post horses, & reached this place a distance of 73 miles by seven in the evening. The noble host received us with smiling courtesy, and introduced us to his two sisters, the honourable Mrs. Bowles, & Sullivan, & as the dinner hour was very near showed us himself to our rooms, and said, dinner should wait half an hour. This I resisted so earnestly that he proposed my coming down in my travelling dress, and as my maid Plumb encountered some difficulty with the lock of the imperial I changed by bonnet for a cap, and accompanied Mr. S. down to the banquet room. Now I know you so well dear sister you will not be content unless I tell you what this travelling dress was made of, &c—a French silk of maraxine blue with bonnet to suit—the cap was of blond with French flowers &c. We found a large party assembled at dinner. Ld Palmerston rose welcomed me again to Broadlands, and placed me next to him. The dinner and evening passed very pleasantly, & I found Lady Anna Marie, a "very nice person". She is sister to the Earl of Minto, & is remarkable for her fine sense, & good heart. She married about three years ago, Sir Rufane Dunken, who is verging upon 70, tho' he looks not more than 50. She is fifty four or five, and looks about thirty five, bare arms, & neck, gold chains & bracelets, one single bracelet her brother had given her cost 50 pounds. It is delightful to see the sincere & honest attachment which seems to exist between her & her dear Sir Rufane. Every night when the tray is brought in just before we retire to bed, he mixes and carries to "my Lady", her hot Negus. We have also had with us for two days Lady Gertrude Stanley, of the noble family of the Howards. She is also aunt to the Duchess of Sutherland, & sister to the Duke of Devonshire, & related or connected with some of the first families in the United Kingdom. Notwithstanding so much "good blood" I liked my simple Mrs. Nightengale better. She has also spent her days with us, & is what we Virginians call a "charming woman", full of intelligence & feeling, and converses in a natural tone of voice which may be heard, not in the subdued tones of the high bred aristocracy. However, I must say, the more I saw of this Lady Gertrude, the better I liked her, especially, after giving her a good beating—at chess— We have also had all the Diplomatique Corps here. Lord

Palmerston came to me last night from a full band of music he had playing in the Hall, to say I must listen, for they were about to do their best, as he had just informed them they had four foreign ministers to listen to them. I gave you so much description in my visit to Wiltshire, that I am afraid I tired you heartily. I will therefore content myself with saying very little now. The house is large, elegant, & convenient, without being fine or gorgeous. There are two halls of entrance, the inner one filled with statuary, &c—& opening into the entertaining rooms six in number, & all en-suite. These apartments are large, high pitched, & filled with furniture of every description, easy chairs, sofas, lounges—tables of every size & shape, musical instruments &c. The walls are covered with paintings by the first artists, and some rare, & beautiful antique statues, & vases. The chambers with their dressing rooms contain every thing which can contribute to ease or luxury. The grounds are extensive, in good taste, & highly improved, with a deep & rapid river called, the Test, running through them which gives even at this season a very bright & cheerful aspect to the landscape. In short nothing can be better arranged, better ordered—or better conducted, than the whole menage of Lord Palmerston, who appears as little like the master of the revels as any of his guests, unless, indeed, any thing is required for the comfort or enjoyment of any individual of this numerous party, then indeed, he never fails to come forward with his bland & gracious smile. He is the beau-ideal of elegant high bred, courtesy, & his sisters are very like him. The wonder to me is, how an immense house like this, which has not been occupied for months, should all at once, as if by magic, be warmed, lighted up, & given such a complete air of occupation & comfort. Every thing seems to go on with the ease and regularity of clock-work. We are breakfasting from half past nine, till eleven; each person saunters into the breakfast room as it suits their convenience or inclination, sure to find a vacant place, and at each plate is a little glass cup with water containing two prints of butter—cream— sugar & salt in separate glasses of a sufficient size for one person. The butler pours out the tea & coffee at a side table, which is handed by a servant, and the guest help themselves to cold meat from a side table. Always the last person, is our noble host, who enters with one hand full of newspapers, & the other with notes, letters, &c—which he cast upon the table for every body to help themselves. Some read, some talk, some amuse themselves with the beautiful paintings, which adorn the room. In short, every one does just exactly what his, or her fancy dictates. We either adjourn to the drawing rooms, library, billiard room, or to Mrs. Bowles apartments, which are above stairs, and consists of two sitting rooms, filled with fine paintings, and all the luxurious indulgencies of a boudoir with every appearance of as complete & comfortable occupation as if they lived there all their lives. The gentlemen equip themselves for shooting after breakfast, show themselves, say adieu! and we see them no more until it is too dark to kill a pheasant. Mr. Stevenson has performed wonders, and is the admiration & envy of these Englishmen; seventy three lives has he taken since he has been here. I assure you he has astonished me, and then he bears his honors so meekly. He is reserving all his boasting I suppose until he gets back to you all. As to the ladies, we amuse ourselves in various ways. We have had two days of sun-shine. Oh, the glorious sun! How I enjoyed it. I walked with Mrs. Sullivan & Miss Sullivan all over the grounds—visited the dairy house, quite a large building, with a fine apartment adjoining the dairy, fitted up as a retreat for the family in warm weather —with sofas, tables, paintings &c &c. The dairy looked as nice & sweet as the butter eats. We also visited the gardens surrounded by high walls of great extent. I saw the pinery's—the graperies—the asparagrass, &c, under glass houses. Before luncheon we generally walk, talk, sew or worsted, &c, afterwards, we take a drive. Yesterday Mrs. Bowles with some of the Diplomatique who could not shoot went with me to see Southampton, but the day was dark & murky & I could not see much of the beauties of the place. To-day Lady Anna Marie has got a pile of French & Italian authors around her, & begs us not to talk to her, as she wishes to rest her tongue, and to compose her mind, against the evening. She says she feels the want of mental

(41)

rest. Mrs. Bowles I found busy with her poor, & in works of charity. Heigho! what good works do I perform? What deeds of mercy, or of charity? Conscience, answers—none. Yet I find every English woman has her own pensioners, who look up to her as a second Providence. The higher her rank the greater her power of doing good. The inclination seems never wanting. Mrs. Bowles gave me the most delightful account of the Duchess Countess of Sutherland, (Countess in her own right,) who she says is a little Queen in her own domain, & scatters blessings & happiness around her. This is better than being Queen of England fettered by the forms & ceremonies of life. In speaking of this ladies title which sounded strangely to my republican ears, she mentioned a fact which is curious enough—she says that if a lady of high birth marries a peer of inferior rank to her own she loses hers, & sinks to his, but if she marries a mere commoner, she retains her birth rank. Thus Lady Anna Maria Dunken the daughter & sister of an Earl, has married Sir Rufane & loses her rank of birth which is however designated by her being Lady Anna Maria—instead of Lady Dunken. Lady Gertrude has married Mr. Stanley and ranks as a Duke's daughter still I was surprised to find Lord Palmerston led me instead of this noble lady, but Mrs. Bowles told me I ranked the first peeress in the land. Some are born to greatness & some have greatness thrust upon them—poor me! I know I sometimes feel myself mightily thrust out of my place. But strange to tell—I feel not at all awed or embarrassed by the grandeur or magnificence of the aristocracy of this aristocratic land. I bow only to extraordinary talents or virtue here, as in my own dear native land, and there you know I have had the good fortune to be associated with those who rank among the first in the world. I suppose it is owing to this, that I feel always so perfectly self-possessed. Mr. Rush told me before I left L. he had rarely seen one who bore transplantation so well &c &c. But to return to Broadlands which we expect to leave tomorrow. Mr. Stevenson is threatened with the influenza, & I wish to get him home before he is laid up with it. Today we have some more arrivals from London, & some guests from the neighbourhood, among the number dear Mrs. Nightengale who is one of the most interesting persons I have met with in England—full of feeling & intelligence, and we formed quite a friendship for each other. Her husband is also very pleasing in his manners—very good family &c. They have invited us to visit them in Derbyshire next summer, and promise to show us every thing worth seeing.

Remember me to all my friends—

Your affectionate sister
S C S

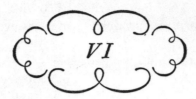

VI

Mrs. Stevenson's relatives in America were already raising their eyebrows at the splendors that had engulfed her in the "decadent" city of London. Their letters questioned the fantastically elaborate life she was apparently leading. Was she not associating with monsters? It looked to some of them as if she had fallen into worldly ways.

But Mrs. Stevenson rose to defend her new-found friends, and in the following letter, it is apparent she was making powerful ones. Of those mentioned here, the Earl of Clarendon was the third of that title, a title which was to pass to his nephew within twelve months. The Marquis of Salisbury, a widower much in demand, was a considerable political and social figure in Britain. Lord Marcus Hill was a palace crony of William IV. Lord Grey was the former Prime Minister, second Earl of that name, known historically as the "Prime Minister of Reform." Edward Ellice was an influential member of Parliament, a great friend of America where he had traveled extensively, and was to become a firm friend of the Stevensons as well. His first wife was sister to Lord Grey; his second, Lord Leicester's widow.

The newspaper editorial that so outraged the Stevensons as they dressed for the King's "Drawing Room" was the work of Frank Blair, editor of the Washington *Globe* and erstwhile close friend of Stevenson's. Blair had criticized the American Minister for daring to comment on the possibility of re-chartering the Bank of the United States which Jackson had "slain" and over whose obsequies Stevenson had presided. To the absent Stevenson's defense rushed Thomas Ritchie, editor of the Richmond *Enquirer;* Sallie Stevenson, as her letter indicates, gave her husband sound advice.

The Princess Augusta was the second daughter of King George III and aunt of the heir apparent, Princess Alexandrina Victoria.

London, April 14, 1837

Believe me my sister no attention, no kindnesses (& we have received much,) can make me cease to sigh for the time when we shall go home. Life in London is like an immense carpet with a black ground, sprinkled over with bunches of red roses. I, dear Bett, pick out the roses & send you. This is right, is it not? As to the morals of the aristocracy—I can only say I have met with none of the monsters you speak of, on the contrary—Sir Robert Inglis & his Lady with whom I have become acquainted are remarkable for their piety & would do honour to any country or any society. The Earl of Clarendon & his Lady to whom I have been introduced are said to be very pious, and Lord & Lady Littleton I am told have prayers every night & morning at which she officiates as chaplain, with all her domestics around her. Mr. Rush was there at Xmas, (the celebrated seat of Hagley) & says it was really edifying—Oh, no! dear Bett I am sorry to say it but there is a great deal more religion here among the aristocracy than with us. The Queen will not receive at the Drawing [Room] any one who has the slightest taint upon their reputation, & I have never seen any one in society on whom a shadow had fallen, but Mrs. Nelson who is scarcely received, and an English Lady, Mrs. Bowles, told me by no means to be inveigled into an introduction to her.

I have but little time for writing and when your letters come I leave all else undone to answer them. It is not now as it was last summer when I bored you to death with descriptions. I think, however, much as you dislike these long stories I must give you some account of a bridal breakfast I have been to recently, but first I will finish answering your letter, that I may not forget any thing I have to say. If my dear Bett you should decide to come to this country, I would give you some hint as to what will be necessary. In the first place then all the money you can conveniently command! Secondly, no servant—colored people are of no value here, they cannot mix with the white servants—in short, it will not do, & you would only have to follow our example, & send them back, which I assure you is a heavy expense. Thirdly, do not give away every thing you have got under an impression it will be useless. I have often wanted some of my old rags such quantities of things are wanted here, & this smoke ruins every thing so soon. Ah! my dear Bett if we could travel about England, Scotland, Ireland & Wales how happy I should be to say—Come—Come—Come—But London is not a home for you, or me—altho' I must bear it, as long as I can. We shall not I think stay long, indeed, we cannot live here, upon the salary more than 18 months or two years. And the Americans a heavy expense. We are constantly dining & teaing and I dare say will be abused from Dan to Beersheba. And now dear sister, I believe I have answered every separate paragraph of your kind & interesting letter. It is always a pleasure to one to know her correspondent is affected by what we write, and in return for the pleasure & amusement you have afforded me I must endeavor to cull a few bunches of roses for you, taken from the black ground of a two weeks confinement with influenza. Before I was well enough to leave the house Miss Blake waited on me to say she had called to ask a favour for her brother, (who is a distant descendant of Admiral Blake) that we would honour the nuptials of his daughter by our presence, as he was from South Carolina he particularly desired to have the American Minister & Lady present at the solemnazation in Church (every body here is married in Church) & at a breakfast given at his house in Grosvenor Square. As I thought it probable I might never be at another, & as it promised to be a very splendid affair, I was very anxious to be well enough to go to the breakfast & determined, if it would be permitted to wear my pelisse

& bonnet, I wrote to Miss Blake who said I might come in any dress I pleased, accordingly I was ready for Mr. S. on his return from St. George's Church (where I dared not venture) to go to Mr. Blake's, when much to my moritification Mr. S. said he could not go with me, & I must venture alone as he was obliged to go to the Foreign Office. I summoned all my courage to the undertaking & went at one. As I approached the door I found the street filled with the rabble thousands collected & the police officer in attendance to keep order. A line of servants received and my name was called from one attendant to another up the grand stair case. Mr. Blake (whom I had never seen altho' he had waited on us) met me at the door, & I found myself in a crowd of ladies & gentlemen not one of which I had ever seen before except Miss Blake the aunt who looked frightened & agitated and when I congratulated the Father he burst into tears so distracted were they both that they left their company to take care of themselves. As I went for the spectacle I was very well pleased to look on un-noticed & un-known. The breakfast waited for the Duke of Wellington whom I had the pleasure to see for the first time, and who handed one of the distinguished relatives of the groom to table, Lord Marcus Hill. 75 persons sat down to table which was covered with all which wealth & luxury could provide, cold meats—jellies—blamanges, creams, fruits, confectionary, &c &c—not only every thing that was rare & curious but every thing that was splendid & costly. I began to fear I should not find a place at the splendid board, when a very pleasing & distinguished looking person offered me his arm, & led me about half way down the table. It was the first time since I have been among these well bred strangers that I have not been led first, however, I felt very well pleased to be overlooked. The company was brilliant, the table magnificent, my companion agreeable, & tho' last not least, the fowl & sallad excellent, & the champagne very exhilarating—my companion remarked to me that he supposed I knew every body. I said, no, I was a stranger. What, a foreigner. Yes, an American. Well, he said with great frankness I will tell you every one you desire to know. Do you remark that fine looking old gentleman who is regarding you so

(47)

earnestly. I looked up just as the person alluded to enquired of his neighbours, "What interesting looking lady that was in a dark pelisse & bonnet". That, said my Diable Bisteaux is Lord Clarendon, the decendant of the celebrated Historian—& the next is the Marquis of Salsbury, & the next Earl somebody, &c, —& the gentleman at the head of the table is the Duke of Wellington, my uncle—&c. After being much entertained by the Duke's nephew & seeing he was curious to know who I was, I replied to his question of how long I should remain in England by telling him I was the wife of the American Minister. The moment I announced myself he exclaimed, "Why you should have been at the head of the table". I said no, I am very well seated. Soon after we rose from table & almost immediately my gallant friend approached with Lord Clarendon & introduced the smiling courteous old nobleman, & in a short time whilst I was yet conversing with the Earl, Mr. Blake brought up to me the Duke of Wellington & I had the honour of a ten or fifteen minutes conversation with the Hero of Waterloo. The man whose fame has spread over the civilized world—yet I was calm, tranquil, & self possessed. Lord Clarendon brought up his Lady who he said particularly wished to know me. Then came other ladies & lords—so that I went home charmed with my breakfast, & boasted to Mr. S. that I did better without than with him. All this would seem very natural in our country but here where introductions are so rare, I certainly had some reason to be flattered—at least I was gratified. The next day they all called & left cards "Field Marshal—The Duke of Wellington" among the first—& the following day whilst confined by the rain, with the Miss Patterson (sisters to Commodore Patterson's) setting with me, Miss Murray called with a Lady Proby, whom she introduced to me as the daughter of the Countess of Carysford, and old lady of 80 who desired particularly to know me, and as she was too old to make visits she had sent her daughter to ask the favour of me to call & see her. Accordingly I went the next day & found the venerable old lady dressed in the costume of the last century surrounded by her books & papers, & she told me she had never used glasses, & showed me her writing which was beautiful. When I remarked upon its beauty & neatness she said, "Yes, it is the hand of a young woman, but I do not say this in vanity, no, that feeling is extinct with me, but with deep gratitude for the goodness of Providence in sparing me my faculties to so advanced an age". She received and treated me with much kindness and invited me to come & spend Saturday evening with her. Miss Murray told me she was the sister of the celebrated Lord Grenville, & that her family and connections were among the first in this country—and yesterday, I was invited to go & see another old lady who came from Norfolk in Virginia & I suspect knew my mother. I cannot tell you what a gratification it will be to me if it is so. By the way, these Miss Patterson's are here, alone, but they have relations among the most respectable English, & a brother who was consul at Antwerp or Brussells. They come very often to see me & appear very fond of me, indeed so far I have been fortunate in making friends among the American's as well as the English, but as old Lady Carysford said, I do not feel vain, but thankful to Him who rules the hearts of all. Sarah Moore is another friend who seems much attached to me. She & her brother who is a nice man & would make the best husband in the world, have returned to America. Do go & see them when you are in New York. Sarah will receive you with open arms. She is an extraordinary person, highly educated, full of intelligence & wit & speaking half a dozen languages she has yet the simplicity of a child, and the most affec & warm hearted being I ever met with. She is connected with Lady Holland & through her means was introduced into the first circles besides the reputation of her brother the Professor, as a man of talents & a writer, gave them some eclat. She is about your age, & we often talked of you, so that she is no stranger to you. The Dudley's are here & a Miss Miller—also the Benny's & a Miss Wallace—sweet girls—the Broche's &c &c. We hear the Americans are coming over from Paris in shoals. I do not recollect whether I told you Mr. Lewis Rogers is staying with us. About a fortnight ago he came in great difficulty and trouble with Mr. Warwick's affairs & claimed my hospitality. He occupies a room in the fourth story, & is certainly as little trouble as it is possible.

(49)

He dines with us when we are at home, sometimes, but not often & comes in & goes out so quietly that no one is disturbed. I fear he is deeply shaken by Warwick, who poor man has ruined himself every way. He is with his wife & children at Brussells, & it said here that he dare not return. I got a letter from her poor Lady! a short time since. The weather continues still very bad, & the old Lady C. told me she had never known such a winter or indeed such a season. I dread the approaching drawing room, cold as it is. It is rumoured the Queen is too ill to hold it, & that the Princess Augusta will receive for her. Most fortunately for me it has been put off once, on account of the sudden death of the Lady De L'Isle, the King's natural daughter altho' this was not assigned as the cause. It is expected to take place next Thursday the 20th. I have procured my dress from Paris, a white satin, embroidered before, & around the tail—the train of maroon velvet, very rich & beautiful, the whole to be trimed with blond, & a little blond ruff a la Queen Elizabeth to cover the neck behind— five feathers one guinea a piece—& the head dressed with bows of velvet & pearl &c &c. Heighho! Lady Wellesley has been very kind, altho' she is still confined to the house, she sent for the Frenchman from whom I procured my plume & made him carry the feathers out to Hurtingham (the seat of Lord Wellesley where she is staying) to see them. And now dear sister I think it is time to say Adieu and yet I have still much un-said. Did I tell you about my introduction to Lord Grey, who is said to be the trump card of the aristocracy, the very pink of chivalry, and I say of courtesy. Before I was ill I dined at Edward Ellice's, an honourable member of P— who married Lord Grey's sister, & who is a man of great consideration here. This noble Lord & his daughter Lady Georgianne dined with us, & he sat by me at dinner. Knowing he was so distinguished a person, I was as these English say a little shy at first, but before the dinner was over I found myself talking away perfectly at my ease. He enquired what part of England I had visited. I named Wiltshire, and said I had been very much pleased in visiting the old castles, that we Americans who had no antiquities, were delighted to visit these venerable ruins over which a thousand years had rolled, that we lived in the future the English in the past. The old gentleman replied to me with that bland courtesy for which he is so remarkable, and added with great cordiallity of manner, "If you like old castles you must come & see me at "Howick", and I will show you all the old castles in Northumberland." After dinner he repeated the invitation to Mr. Stevenson and requested him to let him know when he could come &c.

Now my dear sister do you know I am half afraid to write these things to you, for you & Emily seem so little to estimate my real character & feelings when you talk of being spoiled &c —indeed if you take the bright spots without the black ground you might perhaps entertain such suspicions, but if I know myself I have never felt more humble than since my residence in England. There are many things to make one humble, much as there is to gratify—but I must really close this long scrawl. Say to Mr. Rutherford I hope he has received Mr. Stevenson's mammouth epistle, & also the cheese. Mr. Rogers tells me they went in one of his ships. For fear my letter about Mr. Price's cheese has not reached you I will repeat to you the request that Mr. Palmer would accept it, & present Mr. Sampson a quarter in my name. His letter so kind & friendly has really touched me. I send a thousand loves & kisses for the children. The picture you drew of them was quite delightful to me, & transported me into the midst of your dear circle. Ah my sister, you must leave country & friends as I have done to know how much you love them—my heart yearns towards you all—especially you beloved sister of my heart and how happy I should be to clasp you to my bosom. Think then with these longings after you how generous, how magnanimous I am to tell you any thing which may prevent your coming to me. But now my dear sister, once for all—let me say to you, in all I have said it is your happiness, more than my own I have considered—I have felt it a painful duty to tell you the truth. To come here & not to mix in society is dismal beyond what you can conceive, because you have not here the same resources—you cannot go out alone &c &c. In society, you would feel more painfully your imperfect hearing —but knowing this, if you now come I shall feel the more unallayed pleasure, because I shall feel that you come prepared to meet with that which otherwise might have overwhelmed your fortitude—never did any human being feel more than I have done the want of your sympathy & kindness & I can say without flattery, your judgement. I dare say your advice & counsel would have kept me out of many a domestic difficulty. I know if it could not aid me, your kindness would have comforted me. So now my own dear good sister—do that which your own inclination dictates. Your own heart must tell you. We have only your happiness in view. As to me—my lot has been cast in with another—come weal or woe, I must abide it—I can only try with the blessing of Heaven to do my duty in whatsoever station of life Providence may place me—to keep my heart right in the sight of God—and to be always prepared for the last hour—which comes to all.

But this is treating the matter too solemnly. In truth dear sister, I have instead of a corrupting influence, found my heart here—humbled & purified. But, enough of self—I will not close my letter untill after the 20th.

London April 22d–37

Well, my dear friends—Here I am with my head still on my shoulders, and not quite dead with the influence and what is even worse than influence—the ingratitude & injustice of friends. On Thursday morning just as I was preparing for the Drawing-Room Mr. Stevenson entered with the Globe in his hand & read me from it the attack upon him by Mr. F. P. Blair. I do not recollect ever having seen Mr. Stevenson so overwhelmed, he was like one stunned by a severe blow, the flagrant injustice, & that too from one he deemed his friend—but you will have seen & heard all about it in the papers. The feeling that seemed to weigh most heavily upon his mind was, what course will Ritchie take, will he, "my dear familiar friend", will he whom I love as a brother, & respect as a man, will he too join in this act of injustice & denunciation". Shall I tell

you what I said? "No my husband—never, never—never—
He is too right hearted & clear headed & knows you too well.
Trust me—Ritchie will do what he ought to do. He will do
you justice even against the government papers." & so I believe—or never will I again trust man—or woman either. Mr.
Stevenson was so unhinged that he could not even laugh at
his legs—& made some wise reflections upon life & all its
vanities—but I said, come dearest brighten up, and let us play
our part in this pageant with the best spirit we can assume.

I went first with the barber—such cutting of hair—(I
was astonished to see how well it looked) then came the
mantua-maker to dress me with my maid Dunn as an assistant,
& Jenny the housemaid, & Mary Ann the cook, to look on, or
rather to peep at me, for they are too respectful to come in without permission. At one, I was told our Drawing Room was full
of friends who had come to see me. With Dunn to hold up my
train I decended, Cates threw open the door, and announced
Mrs. S. Then there was such claping of hands, &c. Mr. Rush
steped forward & bent one knee to me. Mr. Duer, said you are
really —— it seems preposterous for an old woman of—to
write such nonsense. Miss Benny said, in her soft tones, you
look like a Queen, & Miss Wallace, how magnificent. Mrs.
Mansfield in her sober quiet way, said—"Your dress is perfect
—it could not have been in better taste"—rouge and all. Lady
Wellesley sent to Paris for a pot of the best. I was somewhat
puzzled to know how to put it on, whether it was to be wet or
dry or how? but they all said I managed it very well, only not
enough so that I had to go back & re-touch. It is, they say,
considered a part of the Court dress as much as the train. At
two we went in the new carriage, yellow with yellow & blue
liveries—in fine taste they say. Now shall I stop—or go on—
shall I tell you how we arrived at the Palace, entered through
files of guards, &c, got without any difficulty into the Entre
room, &c—&c—saw the little Princess Victoria & the Duchess
of Kent enter & pass through to the Throne Room, &c, the
doors thrown open & the Countess Ludoff who presented
Madame Dedel, the Duch Minister's wife & myself passed on,

& we followed, I after Madame who arrived here before me. At the door our trains were taken from us & spread out by a person stationed there for the purpose. The Countess advanced & presented Madame Dedel, whilst I waited, as calm & as self possessed as at this moment, when my turn came, I made my lowest curtsy & the King said a few words to me, "If I had ever been in England before, If I liked it—hoped by health had not suffered from the unusual winter" &c &c. I bowed & curtsied, & passed on—the Royal Dukes stood to his left. I bowed slightly in passing them, & then to the Princess Augusta who represented the Queen & next to her & a few feet off the Princess Victoria & the Duchess of Kent. After the same ceremony with them, the ladies of the Diplomatique Corps arranged themselves so as to form the circle—and there I stood two mortal hours seeing the presentations &c—&c. When it was over, the door of entrance closed & the King & royal family retired through an opposite door, & we were free to depart. In passing through the rooms on Mr. S.'s arm, we stoped to look at the dresses & to speak to those we know. Lady Parke who is very fond of us, said to Mr. S. "Your wife looks so well— you must feel proud of her" and shall I tell you dear sister, I think he was very much pleased to hear the praises of his wife. You know how much dress becomes me, & rouge I can tell you makes me look ten years younger. "All vanity & vexation of spirit". After all tho' I will not be guilty of the miserable affectation of even insinuating I was not highly gratified, because I had grown so thin that I was afraid I should look like a fright or a witch—and I must have been more or less than human, if I had not been pleased to find the dress becoming to me—and be able to make a good appearance before the assembled aristocracy of this great nation. No I am thankful it is well over—Mrs. Bates has just been in & says she saw a flourishing account of me in the papers but I have not had time to look into them yet. If I can venture to cut the government papers I will send it to you. Mr. S. looked very well— indeed you know he looks well in every thing—at least I think so—and now was there ever such a scrawl? I have written without taking time to think or even to spell my words all right —but no matter. Do dear Bett write to my beloved friends & say to them all that you know is in my heart towards them. I have frequently commenced letters to the different members, & then comes a long one from you, & I think I ought to pay my debts before I can afford to be generous. God bless you my dear sisters & brothers & neices & nephews—all—all—Your own devoted

S. C. Stevenson

VII

In Queen Adelaide's Drawing Room in April, 1837, the Stevensons first met the smallish young woman, who within three months was to become Queen of England—Princess Alexandrina Victoria. Victoria was the daughter of Edward, Duke of Kent, who had married Victoire Marie Louise of Saxe-Coburg. The fourth son of George III, the Duke of Kent had died in 1820, the year after Victoria's birth.

Until April, 1837, there was the possibility that if William IV died before Victoria reached her legal majority, eighteen, her mother, the Duchess of Kent, might become regent. Parliament had so defined the dynastic succession, though recognizing Victoria as the heir presumptive. It was hardly conceivable that Queen Adelaide, who had lost her first baby, could ever again become a mother.

To Mrs. Stevenson there was not much "majesty" about the demure young lady, who was so much overshadowed by the feeble King William IV, his spouse, Queen Adelaide, and Victoria's own ambitious mother, the Duchess of Kent.

Although the Stevensons were already winning friends in England, they continued to be attacked by their enemies in America. Always a stalwart defender of her diplomat-husband, Sallie resented the assaults of his political detractors. She was always grateful to those who came to his defense. She says as much in this letter to her brother-in-law, John Rutherford, of Richmond, Virginia.

My dear Brother

    I need not say to you how deeply we feel the tenderness & affection these letters breathe nor our gratitude to you & our dear & excellent friend Mr. Ritchie for your kind & judicious defence of your absent & calumniated friends. It is well for poor human nature there are a few such choice spirits in the world as a—Ritchie—a Lewis—and the last not least in my estimation the kind Brother whom I have known more years than I now care to number & whose heart I have always found in the right place. Mr. Stevenson and myself both like very much your remarks for the Enquirer and also Mr. Ritchie's with one exception—his invoking the tender mercies of the ruthless Editor of the Globe, whom it seems is as willing to tomahawk his friends as his foes. But even in this, the excellence of Mr. R's heart has shown itself. Thank him for me and tell him how my heart warmed towards him as I read his able & dignified defence of his absent friends. You know I said it would be so—and proved how truly and justly I appreciated him. I think you will give me credit for some penetration, or rather—it is a sort of instinct, which I believe most wives possess of knowing the friends and enemies of their husband. You must I am sure recalled what I have always said of the honorable gentleman the Editor of the Globe—but I forbear— lest I should become uncharitable. It is more pleasant to think & speak of the generous and the good than of the evil & malignant. I flatter myself the charges brought against Mr. Stevenson are so preposterous that they must of themselves fall to the ground. I wrote Betsy how much he was at first shocked & surprised but I think now he is recovering. At least, I think he has had enough to revive his spirits in the attentions he has received here. I only wish his countrymen could see the high estimation in which he is held in this our Fatherland. An American gentleman said the other day that he understood no minister had ever been here who was more popular, knew so many people, or would do so much good in producing kind feeling towards his country as Andrew Stevenson. Betsy regrets in her last seeing no English papers. I now send you one giving an account of a great charity dinner in the city at which the Duke of Wellington presided, and you will see my husband was unexpectedly called upon to make a speech. The day after, at the Queen's birthday drawing-room, the Duke passed around the circle and went up to Mr. Stevenson, who stood not far from me, and greeted him most warmly, complimented him on his eloquent speech, and said it had done great good to the charity. He continued conversing with him in so animated and cordial a manner that it attracted the attention of their Royal Highnesses the Duchess of Gloucester and Kent, and the little Princess Victoria, who, I perceived, regarded them with looks and whispers of curiosity. One of the foreign ministers said to Mr. Stevenson "You will have to be our spokesman you speak so very well, we hear you were a great speaker in your own country." As we wended our way slowly through the crowd in the Entre room Lord Palmerston accosted us, and congratulated Mr. Stevenson in his frank cordial way upon his grand success the day before, as did also the particular friend of the Duke of Wellington, Sir G. Murray, the gentleman whom the Duke complimented in his dinner speech. Mr. Stevenson introduced him to me, and he told me, "my husband had delighted every one by his eloquent speech, and especially, the Hero of Waterloo". The Lord Mayor also assured me he had been quite a Lion—and today he received a deputation from the City in which the Lord Mayor rules supreme, to invite him to a charity dinner in the City, urging that the Lord Mayor thought it would so much benefit the charity. Last night he dined with Lord Palmerston at the foreign office a dinner in honour of her Majesty the Queen—which Mr. S. says was magnificent, that they had strawberries, & wines, in profusion, and he longed to bear off a plate to me. To-morrow night he is to attend a dinner at the Royal Academy where I expect he will have to make another speech. These as you know are not political dinners—but I dare say his Countrymen will find something to condemn even in this. Well, I believe after all, the only thing a man need make himself very anxious about, is the approbation of his own heart. If he can "Trust to a good Conscience" the approval of the good & wise will be sure to follow him. I think I shall be acquitted of the charge of not "talking enough of my husband" when your little circle read this, and if they should now accuse me of saying too much, pray, remind them that they have brought it upon themselves, and must take the consequences—but you are all so good in being interested in every thing which concerns us, that I do not fear a very severe judgement upon my wifely effusions. A wife may be excused for praising her husband when she hears him unjustly abused, & calumniated. I may not perhaps be thought impartial evidence, but I must say, no man ever laboured more zealously for his Country, or could be more entirely devoted to its honour & glory—and every day that feeling is deepened in his heart. I do verily believe he would rather have one honest shout from his own dear Countrymen, than all the honours & distinctions which could be bestowed upon him in a foreign land. Ah, my dear Brother, one must cross that vast Atlantic Ocean to know how to value—Country—Home—& friends. Well! I console myself by thinking how happy, how very happy I shall be when I feel myself again in the arms of my dear dear friends. Mr. Wilkins told me when he returned from Russia he wanted to take up the dogs in the street and kiss them. If I live to get back—what shall I do?—as to Mr. Stevenson I dare say he will be as un-philosophically happy as myself—altho' we shall feel deep regret at parting with many kind friends we have made in this Country—among this number is Sir Robert Inglis & his lady, two persons who do honour not only to the aristocracy but to human nature, besides, many others who have treated us with a degree of kindness we should be most ungrateful ever to forget. You will say we have become a very fashionable couple when I tell you I dined at Sir Roberts, a dinner given especially to me, the day Mr. S. dined at the foreign office. It is said one meets more good company at the house of this most pious & excellent man, than any other in London. We sat down to table with a company of sixteen, &

every person at the table was distinguished not for their rank alone, but for something still better with the attainments of an immortal being & notwithstanding the fatigue of having stood three mortal hours at the drawing room, I enjoyed myself very much. Mr. Stevenson went from the dinner, to Lady Allenham's where every body went in full dress, in honour of her Majesty. My republican [word illegible] were so very weary of standing in the presence of Majesty, that I was too tired to drive round, & see the illuminations which were said to be well worth seeing. Poor Lady! her subjects will not in all human probability have another birthday to celebrate as it is whispered her illness must be fatal. The King looks well, & is particularly gracious to the American Minister. I was very much afraid I should forget to say, "Your Majesty" but I believe on both occasions I contrived to bring it in—right or wrong—The Princess Augusta receives for the Queen—she is a coarse vulgar looking person tho' they say very good. The Duchess of Kent is quite a graceful, good-looking woman of forty-five, and the little Princess stands by her side, smiling and bowing and occasionally extending her little fingers to her future subjects. It is a pity she is so small. I am told she regrets it very much herself. Without being handsome, she has rather a pleasing countenance, though nature has certainly not stamped the seal of "Majesty" upon it.—Give a thousand loves and kind messages to Betsy, Emily, & Sally—say I will answer their kind letters very soon, but really I have now so many things to do, & think of—that I have but little leisure. The American's are coming in Battalions, every day Mr. S. comes to me with both hands full of letters of introduction, &c &c. He has now gone to the City in a cape altho' it is raining very fast, & he has a wretched cold, to visit some Americans who have brought him letters from Mr. Van Buren (who by the way writes more letters of introduction than any man in America) & his letters Mr. S. never fails to distinguish the persons by a dinner. Heighho! Well, it is very tiresome—so many come that even to visit all, keeps us busy. Yesterday a whole party came in Mr. S.'s absence, & left a message with the Secretary that the

Minister must carry them to the House of Common's tonight—
and Mr. Secretary was such a simpleton, or so malicious as not
to know that the Minister has no right to take them, & that it
is only through his friends in P——he can get them in—so
away the poor Minister has to go busy or not busy, to see them,
& make arrangements to get them places; I think Mr. Ritchie is
bound in conscience to endeavour to get us rid of this school-
master Secretary for it was our great desire to have W. Ritchie,
and Mr. S.'s resolution to wait till the last moment in the hope
he would be induced to come, that intailed this most disagreeable
& unamiable person upon us—he is a thousand times worse than
no-body—I, in fact, ought to have the salary—Present us very
kindly to all the Ritchie's, I sincerely & fervently hope Mrs.
Harrison may be more fortunate now than in time past. She
should hope for the best, and I believe cheerfulness & hope
would be the surest way of obtaining her wishes. She will have
my best wishes & prayers—Such a lovely gentle creature ought
to leave some copy of herself. Say to Mrs. Ritchie I only wait
to be invited to write her by a single line. You see dear Brother,
the mere assurance from you—that you designed to write me
at some future time has drawn upon you this long letter. I again
embrace my beloved sisters. Oh! that I could in reality. Is Bett
coming to me? I long to see her, but fear to urge her. If my
breast can not stand this climate I am afraid it would soon kill
her, and coming here is like getting married, it is so very difficult to go back. The very idea of the sea, makes me qualmesh
even now—besides all this the modes of life here are so artificial, the hours so contrary to nature & our habits. The con-
ventional forms so strict & so tiresome that I sadly fear she
would not be happy. Still I do want to see her, & have a long
talk. God bless her! & incline her to do what may best promote
her happiness here & hereafter. My love to them—& kiss your
precious little ones for me, do not I pray you let them forget
Uncle or Aunt Stevy. Adieu! beloved brother. Think of me—
love me—& believe me always yours.

Sarah C. Stevenson

VIII

THE DAY BEFORE Mrs. Stevenson began this double letter to her sister she went to a leading London jeweler to have her mother's pearls made into ear-rings. At the same time she ordered a "mock" pearl necklace to match. She explains why.

By May, 1837, every steamer from across the Atlantic brought more harrowing news of the economic disaster that had befallen America. Letters from relatives in Virginia and friends in Washington drew distressing pictures of the hard times. England was appalled. Apparently the sun of the rising Republic in the West was about to set in a sea of gloom.

Poverty walked America's streets. Fortunes melted like snow in a warm sun. Revolution and ruin were freely predicted. British investors in American securities flocked to the American Legation to seek Andrew Stevenson's advice. Would the United States remain solvent? Stevenson's answer was a resounding, yes. Financial England echoed with repercussions of the panic in America, and British bankers threatened withdrawal of American loans. Andrew Stevenson was a tower of strength in this difficult moment. His own supreme confidence in his country went far in allaying British fears.

Americans stranded abroad hurried to the Legation for help. Stevenson and his wife gave every possible assistance, even lending money to some who needed it.

Disturbed though England was, the chariot of royalty rolled on. The Princess Victoria's eighteenth birthday—May 24, 1837—

had arrived. She had reached her legal majority, and England made the day a public holiday. Now she was qualified for the throne, if and when her uncle, William IV, succumbed to his multiplicity of ailments. That night the Stevensons set out in their carriage for St. James's Palace and the State Ball in honor of Princess Victoria.

The Duke of Brunswick whom Mrs. Stevenson saw at the opera was Charles, nephew of George IV's widow, Caroline. There was a possibility at one time of his succession to the throne. His father had been killed just before Waterloo at Quatre Bras. He was a famous dandy and spent much of his time in Paris where he was often seen in a box at the Paris Opera, a man "with a brilliantly painted face, a black wig, and a shirt front and fingers blazing with diamonds."

Giulia Grisi, Emma Albertazzi and Tamburini were top opera stars of the day, and great favorites in London and Paris.

London May 1837

Mr. Stevenson brought me a few days since a pair of beautiful bracelets at 15 guineas, a present which I thanked him for, but prudently sent back because I thought we could not afford it, & besides I prefered spending the 15 G upon the earrings & necklace. I thought when I came here I would not wear jewelry but one looks like an antediluvian without it. O how happy I shall be when the time comes when I shall want nothing but simple garments, & "food convenient for me"— and yet when the sun shines & one feels tolerably well there is much, very much in London to interest & excite, especially, to an American Minister, who is well received by all parties, and if they are fortunate enough "to take" as believe we have, it is impossible not to be pleased.

I believe I mentioned that we had received a "command" to attend a state ball given on the 24th in honor of the Princess Victoria's birthday at St. James's Palace. We left our house at 10 o'clock, and did not arrive at the palace until a quarter after eleven, and some of the unfortunate persons did not succeed in getting there at all, owing to the dense crowd of eager spectators who had assembled to witness the illuminations, in carriages & on foot. In the courtyard of the palace was stationed the royal regiment of Horse Guards, and the King's Guards, dressed in crimson & covered with gold lace filled the inner court, & lined all the passages. The entire suite of state rooms was brilliantly illuminated. The throne-room & the ball-room were prepared for dancing, having orchestras for the quadrille bands in both, supported by columns, the front of the orchestras being ornamented with rich draperies. We found the rooms filled with the elite of the English nobility, covered with diamonds and blazing in all the splendour of wealth & magnificence, and adorned in all the witcheries of the toilet. It was a scene of such gorgeous splendour as the eyes ached to behold, and richer than any vision of sleep. With great difficulty we made our way to the object of attraction, the fair young Princess, who was situated at one end of the room, with two state chairs in the middle. The royal family sat in the centre, and the ladies of the foreign ambassadors and a few of the highest rank sat on each side of the royal family. It was from this elevated station I had a coup d'oeil of all this royal magnificence, and once during the evening a seat by her Royal Highness, the Princess Augusta, who talked to me with such amiable & gentle kindness that I quite forgot she was a princess. Among other things, she said she was "unaccustomed to receive, & felt very much embarrassed." The Princess and her mother were of course the principal objects of attention. Victoria danced two quadrilles with Prince Esterhazy & one of her noble subjects. At one o'clock the banqueting-room was thrown open, where our appetites were gratified by all the delicacies royalty could command, and our eyes dazzled by the sumptuous magnificence not only of the royal feast, but of the banqueting-place. After having partaken of the good things provided for us, we departed with some difficulty, and rejoiced to find ourselves safe at home.

The day was kept with feasting and rejoicing throughout this realm. The Princess having attained her legal majority, in the event of his Majesty's demise, addresses have been sent to her from every part of the kingdom, dinners eaten, toasts drank, and her little Majesty's health most loyally drank by all her future subjects. The illuminations were magnificent. "Victoria" blazed in every part of the town in all the brilliancy of variegated gas. What an interesting situation for a young and innocent creature! She seems gentle and amiable, but not at all majestic—nothing regal on her part. On the contrary, she looks like one of our fresh & ruddy American girls before she has gotten her growth. On the 26th we attended a concert at the Duchess of Kent's, where I heard all the great performer's, saw all the great people—admired all the splendours of Kensington Palace, and after being most fashionably squeezed for two hours, was most happy to escape to quiet & repose.

Mr. Vaux has taken the place of Mr. Fay, untill Mr. Van Buren sends us another Secy of Legation. Of all men living Mr. Stevenson & myself would prefer Mr. Ritchie. We think it is a situation peculiarly suited to him, & our personal attachment to his father as well as to himself would have rendered it particularly acceptable to us. We could then have shown to the son some little of the affection & gratitude we feel for his excellent and noble minded father. From my present experience I know there ought to be perfect friendship & confidence between the Minister & his Secy & even between the attaches, as they can reflect honour or dishonour upon the Legation. Richard Vaux is a treasure to us, and I already begin to feel towards him as a son. He is the only one we have yet had near us worth a straw, on the contrary they have been rather, or, I might say decidedly a dis-advantage. You say my dear Emm you wish I had written something for Mrs. R. Do you know, you & Bett have scolded me so much for sending messages &c that now I am afraid to do so & leave it to your own discretion to say what you think proper to my friends. As to Mr. Ritchie, both Mr. Stevenson & myself regard him next to our own immediate family, and he may rest assured that whether we are silent or whether we write to him, or of him, our hearts must ever be most deeply grateful for the noble & generous stand he has made for Mr. Stevenson in his hour of need. May Heaven bless him and his is the prayer of my heart. I feel very anxious to hear it is well over with Mrs. Harrison and that she has made all who love her happy in a promising heir. I sincerely hope she may live to be the mother of a race as good and beautiful as herself. Pray present me kindly & affecy to them all especially Mrs. Harrison & dear Mrs. Ritchie. Tell the latter I have not seen as young & handsome a grand-mother in England—nor as mercurial a grand-papa. I heard Mr. Stevenson describing him the other day to an Englishman who said, Well, I should like to see this Mr. Ritchie of yours.

I often think of you, and if I had a wishing cap, or a "three legged stool" would soon place myself in the midst of your happy circle. It would be so delightful to exchange the artificial forms of life for nature, truth, & affection, and since I cannot do this, I endeavour to be as happy as I can & to enjoy as Lady Grace says "soberly" all the innocent pleasures of this great metropolis. I have been tempted on a fine day by my kind friends the Morrison's to Epsom races. They went on purpose to show me the spectacle, & I went to see an English race-field, & for the pleasure of the drive in an open carriage with my friends. I have also been once to the opera with a Lady Joddell, who tells me she never saw a stranger who made so favorable an impression upon her—that she loves me, without knowing why, &c &c. She has invited me to go with her to Richmond, to come to her ball, & that I shall have a boudoir fixed for me to retire to & repose, & eat strawberries &c—that she has made a little musical party for me this evening, in short I feel overwhelmed by her kindness, her husband is immensely wealthy & one of the oldest families in the Kingdom. She was the daughter of the Duke of Kingston—but to return to the opera where I saw & heard all the great performers Madame Grisi, Madame Albertazzi—Signor Tumburini &c. The house was very full, & magnificent to my unpractised eye. The Duke of Brunswick with his aide came into the box, but having heard he was on bad terms with the royal family I thought it proper to be very dignified, and play the Minister's lady, especially, as Mr. Stevenson was not with us. He had gone to dine out, then to the Duke of Sussex, & about eleven joined us at the opera. We dine out a great deal, and the dinner parties are generally very pleasant. On last Monday we gave a "grand dinner" ourselves to Mr. Binny his daughter & niece, a Miss Wallace a most intelligent & charming girl. In this country, altho' the entertainments are sumptuous, that is the least care of the host & hostess. It is the company that constitutes the entertainment. The great point is to have distinguished & agreeable people—& invitations are sent out three weeks before hand, as we had only a few days we feared we should not be able to collect such a company as we wished but we succeeded they say to admiration, even the fastidious Mr. Rush declared himself delighted. As to Mr. Binny he thanked us over and over again for the pleasure we had given him. We had titled Lords & Ladies and some distinguished by the aristocracy of talent & worth, among this number was Rogers the poet, Sir George Staunton and a Mr. Kenyon the brother of Lord Kenyon, with whom Miss W. was perfectly charmed, especially when he called the next day and gave her a number of autographs. We had also in the evening, a Mr. Acland a great favorite of mine, the son of Sir Thomas Acland, & Sir Robert Inglis says he is to be one of the first men in England. We had also Mrs. Bowles (Lord Palmerston's sister), Lady Anna Maria Dunken, & General Sir Rufane. She is the Earl of Minto's sister, &c, &c. It must have been a pleasant party as every one stayed untill 12 oclock. The next day we dined at Lady Catharine Boileau's where we were invited to meet Mr. Coke & Lady Anne with some other distinguished guests. We had a gay & pleasant dinner. Lady Anne and myself sat opposite, & after dinner we conversed for an hour and I felt more acquainted with her in that short time than I have done with persons after knowing them for five years. She invited me over & over again to visit her at Holkham & said she would show me her children & flowers. When her husband came up she reproached him for sitting so long at table, saying he had lost so much in not becoming more acquainted with me. He replied that he meant to be compensated when I came to Holkham, &

then added in a low voice "Ah, my dear Mrs. Stevenson, I am the happiest old fellow in the world, & my wife is not only the happiest woman but the best wife that any man ever had". She is the daughter of Lord Albemarle, & is just 50 years younger than her husband. Without being handsome, there is something very pleasing & attractive about her, and she has in her manner much more frankness and cordiality than is usual with the high bred English ladies, to me however she was particularly courteous, said, "How much she had wished to know me, she had heard so much of me that she understood I made a friend whenever I made an acquaintance and that she had requested Mr. Ellice (a person of high tone here) to make up a dinner party to bring us together—all this you may suppose was very gratifying to me from such a person as Lady Anne Coke, and especially when she added it gave her pleasure to tell me that both my husband & myself were the most popular foreigners that had ever been in England, that the Duke of Sussex had spoken in high praise of Mr. Stevenson to Mr. Coke, & how much Mr. Coke liked him &c &c. This old gentleman has numbered 83 years and still looks strong & healthy, his figure is robust, & his face florid, and no one from his appearance would take him to be more than sixty odd. They have five children the eldest fourteen. Mr. Stevenson had seen Mr. Coke before, & brought him up & introduced him to me at Lady Catharine's. They have invited us to dine with them but unluckily we were engaged. England is certainly a dinner eating country, every thing is done by a dinner, if a charity is to be raised, it is by a dinner—an acquaintance to be made, by a dinner, in short, John Bull likes good cheer. I must not forget to tell you one of the most gratifying sights I have seen since I came to England, the annual visit of the Charity children to St. Pauls. The Lord Bishop of London wrote to the Dean of St. Pauls to receive us, & give us a seat in the Bishop's pew. If I was struck by the sublimity of this noble building when empty, how imposing the effect when filled with an immense mass of persons liberally lining the large dome. There were 7000 children and

10,000 spectators. The children of the different schools were dressed in uniforms, all had caps made of white exactly the same shape, but each school distinguished by a different coloured ribbon, or gloves or dresses, and attended by their Rectors, beadles, masters, mistresses, and other parish functionaries, for the purpose of hearing the annual sermon which was preached by the Lord Bishop of Chichester. The service commenced by singing anthems and the fine effect of the hundred of voices in unison with the solemn strains of church music defies all description. The sounds fell upon the ear like a trumpet, and upon the heart like a spell. My spirits felt lifted above the earth, and as I gazed around upon the multitude of little immortals, it seemed like a shadowing forth of Heaven, of that great day when we shall put off the garments of sin & put on the robes of Righteousness. I do not believe their was a dry eye among the spectators, the moral sublimity of the scene affected all hearts alike. The service concluded about half past two, when we with Lord and Lady Aylmer, & about a dozen others were invited to lunch at the Lord Bishop of Landaffs. The Bishop of Chichester with whom I had been acquainted before lunched with us. We found a sumptuous board sat out, with every thing to constitute a good dinner, and only differing from that meal by having every thing placed on the table at once instead of the variety of courses which is usual here.

We have a great many American's here, the Taylor's, the Appleton's from Boston, and a half a score of others, too tedious to enumerate. We have been civil to all & every person bringing us letters have been invited to dine. Some bring letters to me & not to Mr. Stevenson. I am happy to find I have been successful thus far in pleasing my country people.

What a dreadful state the commercial world of America seems to be in, and England too is in consternation. The last accounts from America has depressed our spirits very much. I fear our good friend Mr. Van Buren begins to find himself in the seat of Damocles. He who seeks to be the first magistrate in our country will always find himself involved in "Double, double, toil & trouble". To be the President of the United States is I believe after all—a splendid misery.

June 14th 1837

My dear Sisters—

The packet has just come in—no letters from you. Heigho! One from brother Isaac dated Philadelphia—but some how or other it has not warmed & gladdened my heart. The commercial news which at first appeared to us awful, seems to have been well received here. They say things are looking better—that the crisis is passed, the last agony over & there is to be a new & more healthful state of things. Well, Heaven grant it may be so but I have not yet seen any papers.

I cannot help thinking you and Angelica are coming over with Mr. Singleton and Mr. McDuffie. I scarcely dare to suffer myself to think of it. Brother Isaac speaks of it as possible, but he seems not to know much about your movements. His letter was written I thought in bad spirits & less affec than any I ever received from him, but he says he is out of the habit of writing & has lost his fondness for it which is really a pity for one who writes so well.

My health has improved very much in the last week, notwithstanding much going out, to a splendid ball at Prince Esterhazy's at a quarter past eleven, where we met all the grand nobility covered with diamonds—& crowded to suffocation. The supper is always set in the lower rooms, and the company go down when they feel disposed to partake of the refreshments the sumptuous tables afford, every thing which can gratify the most fastidious taste. A dinner party at Mrs. Bowles and afterwards to a Mr. Remily the son of Sir Samuel, a dinner & evening party at Mrs. Nightengales, a dinner at Sir George Roses, where I became acquainted with a Lady Delafield, who called the next day & left her card with a little packet of lemon drops for my cough with her compliments &c. Now my dear sisters I do not accept one half of the invitations I receive, & excuse myself whenever I can, as the King & Queen have both been ill, I have declined going to Court on the birthday. I wrote a note to the Lord Chamberlain that Mrs. Stevenson regretted illness prevented &c &c (remember illness means here indisposition, want of strength, &c). Of course I would not go in the evening to Lady Minto's court ball. I also declined going to the Littlefields ball, which is said to have been one of the most magnificent things ever seen here, it was given at the opera house, & patronized by the Royal family. Next week we have a ball at Lady Moseley's a musical party at Lady Joddell's a dinner at Lord Bexley's, who is said to be one of the first noblemen in England for worth & piety. A dinner at Mr. Ellice's—a party at Mrs. Mansfields—Prince Esterhazy's &c &c—and on Saturday we are invited to dine with the Duke of Sussex. The King is said to be in great danger, & the Queen's health very bad. This with the state of American affairs are the universal subjects of conversation. Mr. S. is half distracted with these thousand cares & perplexities. No Secy & no prospect of one to help him. Richard Vaux does all he can, but still it is very unpleasant to keep him confined so much, & this is not like a regular Secy. He says he really has had hard luck for nine months to have an enemy in the camp, and as many more perhaps to be without any assistance but what is accorded from friendship & good will. Heigho! What is to become of our dear native land! I hope she will rise like a young giant in her strength.

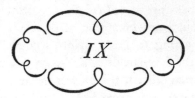

IX

THE KING WAS DEAD! Long live the Queen! William IV had died on June 20, 1837. The court and the Diplomatic set as well were in mourning. Yet, as Mrs. Stevenson put it, "The poor old King is already forgotten".

One of the best friends the Stevensons made in England was Augustus, Duke of Sussex, the dead King's brother and uncle of the fresh young Queen. Many were the Revolutionary gasconades Americans hurled at his father, George III, but what Americans had once thought of his parent made little difference to the Duke, who was born two years before the embattled farmers fired the "shot heard round the world".

The Duke was a studious person. He stood six feet three. Books were his passion, and ladies to some extent. His hobbies were clocks and birds in cages. His palatial apartments were filled with birds chirping and clocks ticking. Negro pages were the fashion of the time in London and the Duke had, or rather owned, a small Negro page whom he called "Mr. Blackman". Presiding over the Duke's domestic menage was "Lady" Cecelia.

The Duke found the Stevensons charming people and showered attentions on them. This letter tells, among other things, of an evening at the Duke's and a little game of cards.

Perhaps, it should be added that the Duke's marriage to Lady Cecelia Underwood had not yet been recognized under the Royal Marriage Act. However, after Victoria's accession, it was recognized and she was created Duchess of Inverness.

Charles Greville said, "They have made Lady Cecelia Underwood a duchess. Everybody considers it a very ridiculous affair."

Sir Charles Bagot and his Lady, who as this letter indicates regaled the Stevensons with Tory tales of Queen Victoria, were high ranking in diplomatic circles. Sir Charles was formerly British Minister at Washington. He and the American Secretary of State had in 1818 negotiated the celebrated Rush-Bagot Treaty that limited armament on the Great Lakes and fixed the boundary between the United States and Canada from the Lake of the Woods as far west as the Rocky Mountains.

London July 12, 1837

My beloved sisters,

You will be surprised to hear that I have been for the last week at Portsmouth and the Isle of Wight and you will be grieved to know that a severe attack of illness was the cause of my going there for a change of air.

Well you know I have always been a little of a philosopher & try to think "whatever is, is best". After a confinement of 10 or 12 days I left home with Mr. Stevenson & our valued young friend Richard Vaux still feeling so ill that I expected to be obliged to turn back. The country air acted upon me like a charm. I revived as soon as I got beyond the smoke of London, and when I arrived at Portsmouth in the evening, 70 miles, I felt completely well and strong and after breathing the pure salt air for one night only I was able the next day, the 4th of July, to dine with Capn Nicolson on board the Independence. I sat on the upper deck & breathed the pure air which revived & strengthened me.

The next day, the 5th, Capn Nicolson came in his barge & took us to visit the Victory, the ship in which Admiral Nelson died. They showed us the spot on which Nelson fell marked by a brass plate, and weak as I was I ventured down, with the polite old Capn to the hold where the celebrated man expired. The very spot where his form was extended is marked out. I thought of his touching & unmanly request, "Kiss me, Hardy"

—but you know Nelson is no favourite of mine. Tho' a hero in war he was a recreant to his domestic duties, false to the woman to whom he had plighted his faith in the sight of Heaven & who was said to have been worthy of him. The splendour of his fame and the brilliant publick actions he performed cannot throw the mantle of charity over the turpitude of his private life.

From the Victory Capn Nicolson took us to visit a royal yacht which was at anchor in the bay. I can give you no idea of the luxurious splendour of this floating castle. It was right royal but what rather a curious coincidence whilst we were gazing on all this royal magnificence, and I daresay some of us wishing in our hearts we too could be Kings & Queens the bell commenced tolling for the burial of William the Fourth (he had been embalmed and kept three weeks) and like the flapper of the Laputians said in language which could not be mistaken "All men are mortal" and when the last hour comes we feel there is but "one thing needful".

In my last I wrote you that all England was celebrating the Princess Victoria's coming of age. Now everybody is run mad with loyalty to the young Queen. Even the Americans here are infected. In all societies nothing is talked about but her beauty, her wisdom, her gentleness, & self-possession. A thousand anecdotes are related to her goodness, and the wonderful address with which she manages every body and every thing. The poor old King is already forgotten, although we are all in black for him. He was ill at the time I wrote you, but it was kept a secret that his life was in danger.

We dined at the Duke of Sussex only three days before he died & he spoke of his situation as being he feared, hopeless, and accounted for the smallness of his party, saying he could only have his friends about him. His Royal Highness has treated us with most distinguished attention & this dinner was given for Mr. Coke, Lady Anne & ourselves. He is considered the most talented & virtuous of all the royal family with liberal principles & a great friend to America. His manners are remarkably frank & cordial. In person he is very tall & large. Having been injured in both eyes he wears spectacles to assist his sight and a black cap upon his head. Notwithstanding there is something noble & commanding in his appearance with a mixture of dignity and playfulness in his deportment & conversation that I confess fascinated me. He led me in to dinner & talked to me as if he thought I had a mind able to grasp even the highest subjects. Then he threw in some pleasantries that made laugh outright. After dinner Lady Cecelia ordered the card tables set. Lady Cecelia cannot take the title of Duchess but in everything else she is his wife. In a note she wrote me she signs herself simply Cecelia. To return to the card tables:

I must now give you an anecdote of myself & how I get on with Royalty. Before the gentlemen came in Lady Anne said, "It is too late to play cards" & when the Duke asked me I began "I am afraid it is . . . ." when I saw Lady Anne making the most vehement signs behind the Duke's back. I caught her meaning immediately that I must not contradict Royalty and changed my speech to "I fear Your Royal Highness will find me a very bad player". He replied I should suit him exactly but Mr. Coke who is very intimate with him said I had promised to play with him. "We will cut for her, if it will please you, Mr. Coke". My old friend & admirer Mr. Coke cut me & I had the honour to win half a sovereign from His Royal Highness. I wish you could have seen my countenance when he laid the money down on the table before me. Involuntarily I said, "I beg pardon, I did not bet" but the old gentleman replied very quietly "The table won it." So my dear sisters when I get back to America (if I live to get back) I will show you half a sovereign won from His Royal Highness— for like my dear old friend Gen Van Rensalaer I will not use money I win at cards.

July 21st

My beloved Sisters—

I began this scrawling rambling letter just after my return from Portsmouth when I was still weak & one of my eyes inflamed, and we found so many invitations &c, awaiting us that

I have been constantly actively engaged, or resting—& now I must still scrawl to be in time for the packet. We have received a very kind letter from Lady Anne Coke inviting us to Holkham (the ladies always do these things in this country,) also from Mrs. Nightengale urging us to come to her at Lea Hurst in Derby Shire. We received whilst at Portsmouth an invitation to dine at Lord Clarendon's where we met some of the high Tories, Lady Bagot, who was in America, & Sir Charles. She amused us with some Tory anecdotes of the Queen, and ascribed to her much spirit & decision. She said, that when the old King was alive it was said to be impossible to get into the Buckingham Palace before Xmas but that this little Queen had accomplished it in a week. She sent for the Duke of Argyle & directed him to have it in readiness by a certain day, when she intended to dine there. He said "I am sorry to inform your Majesty it is impossible". But at the same time said he was not the superintendent. She instantly replied then send him to me, from whom she received the similar answer. She then ordered all who had any thing to do with the Palace to assemble there the next day at a certain hour when they should hear from her. Accordingly these grave old Lords obeyed, & received from her little Majesty a letter written by her own hand, issuing her commands that the Palace should be in readiness for her on the day before named when all the officers of her house hold should dine with her, &c &c. There was nothing left for them but to put all the workmen that could be hired to work, & she moved to the new Palace on the day & hour appointed. So much for a young Queen! Lady Bagot mentioned another instance of her firmness & decision. She ordered her master of the horse to put in training some horses for her use as she meant to review her troops on horseback. The Duke of Wellington ventured to suggest to her Majesty that she had better review them in an open carriage to which she replied, "I shall review them on horseback, as Queen Elizabeth did." This is a Tory picture of her the other side speaks of her as something almost superhuman. That she is an extraordinary person I think cannot be doubted—only imagine, a young creature just 18 brought up in retirement & seclusion suddenly finding herself sovereign of the greatest Kingdom of the Earth. It is said that on the death of the old King, the Queen Dowager wrote her by the Arch-Bishop of Canterbury that she was Queen, & the poor thing was waked up at day break to receive the intelligence. She replied immediately in a letter of condolence & addressed it to the "Queen". The Arch Bishop said to her, Your Majesty has omitted the "Dowager" when she replied with a feeling & readiness that speaks volumes for the goodness of her heart—"I will not be the first to give her that title". On the same day she met her Counsel & behaved with a dignity & self-possession that amazed them all. They say it was impossible for any thing to have been more what it ought to have been than her deportment but when she left the Counsel chamber she forgot that it was a glass door through which she had retired & the moment it closed upon her she rubbed her hand's & skipped off with a step as light & girlish as tho' she had just escaped from her school mistress. Again they say when her Uncle the Duke of Sussex presented himself to pay her homage as a subject she rose, threw herself into his arms— kissing both cheeks, & the same with her governess the Duchess of Northumberland, whom she was told she must receive sitting. She refused to do so, unless the Duchess was informed that she obeyed the laws of etiquette, but the moment she appeared she forgot all laws but those of feeling. She also appointed as maid of honour a young girl with whom she had gone to school. When she was told, this would not do, she had not rank, she replied, "I can give her rank, & will do it". Thus it is she wins all hearts by the union of goodness, sweetness & gentleness, with dignity, firmness & decision. She seems to have turned the heads of the young & old & it is amazing to hear those grave & dignified ministers of state talking of her as a thing not only to be admired but to be adored. She prorogued parliament in person the other day & I was extremely anxious to witness it but Mr. S. thought I was not strong enough to bear such a crowd & heat. He came back delighted (altho' there is something in his man's heart that makes him a little rebellious)

he says she looked beautiful dressed in her robes of state—
crown &c—and that she behaved with ease & a dignity & self-
possession that was amazing & you who know what a nice
judge he is of good reading says she read her speech admirably.

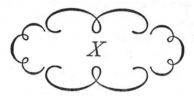

X

IN ADDITION to the palace dinners, balls and other entertainments, the Stevensons found time to pay their respects to those in England still living who had in any way expressed sympathy for the American people in their struggle for independence over a half century ago. Here Mrs. Stevenson records her visit to the widow of Charles Fox, who, with Edmund Burke, the two Pitts and others, championed the rights of America during the Revolution. Fox had, indeed, in the House of Commons worn a coat of buff and blue to match the colors of George Washington's uniform.

Returning to London, the Stevensons found an invitation to dine with the Queen at Buckingham Palace. Henry Lord Cowley, whom the Stevensons met that evening, was the younger brother of the Duke of Wellington. He and Lady Cowley were great favorites of the young Queen.

London August 3d 1837

My beloved sisters & brothers,

Since my last to you of the 22d containing sixteen pages I have been gradually recovering my health and strength and I feel quite well again. I have found an antidote against the dampness of the climate in the use of the warm salt bath and

I have also learnt to keep out of the sun which I find always gives me a fever if long exposed to it, perhaps, from its shining so seldom, the effect is more deleterious than with us.

On the last page of your letter you say Mr. Rives tells you it is impossible to come as Minister to this court without having our "tastes, feelings & habits changed". You say he is more "candid than I am". I can only reply that my letters have been very unfaithful transcripts of my feelings, if they have not proved to you, however changed my habits may be, my heart is unaltered. A change of habits is inevitable even to preserve health, but if I know myself I shall return to those of my early years with the greatest pleasure.

It is certainly a life of great excitement and one is constantly meeting something to amuse & to interest. Still it is not happiness. After a little while the heart pines for the calm & rational enjoyment of an American home. Those who see a great deal of the world, such a world as this, with a Christian's eye, detect its vanity & insufficiency to confer solid peace, and after the novelty has worn off begin to sigh for that "peace which the world can neither give nor take away".

But of all these things we will talk when we meet. In the meantime I know that I shall always have the prayers of my dear sisters and we are told in the Volume of Truth that the effectual fervent prayer of a righteous heart availeth much.

I am sure you cannot complain that I do not answer your letters and having done so I will now give you some account of what we have been about notwithstanding they say "the season is over". And now if you have no objection we will take our departure for Lady Nesbitt's. Richard Vaux and myself in an open barouche with fast horses. We traveled through a beautiful country. I will tell you something of my traveling companion who is without exception one of the most extraordinary young men I have ever known. Mr. Stevenson and myself are attached to him as if he were our son & feel in him the most unlimitted confidence. He has been acting as Secretary of the Legation ever since his arrival in London and made himself very useful to my husband as well as very agreeable to us both. He is a friend who would, I believe, venture his life in our service & one we feel proud to present to our English acquaintances. He is already much known & esteemed here.

We arrived after a pleasant drive at Lady Nesbitt's about three o'clock & was received most kindly by her & her nieces the Miss Wilsons who are her adopted children. Her ladyship's husband is young, handsome & intelligent but is bad tempered and cross as possible. The cottage is very small & everything very plain but kindness & hospitality made up for every deficiency. Richard returned to London after nine o'clock and I spent four days very quietly, two of which it rained so as to keep us within doors all day. The two fair days we were driving about the country, visited the widow of the celebrated Charles Fox. At first she refused to receive visitors. The old butler said she was at dinner with Lord Holland but when Lady Nesbitt told him who I was he hurried back to the house & returned with a request to walk through the grounds & then to make a visit in the drawing room.

I was much gratified by seeing the widow of this celebrated man. She is now 90 years old but still a pleasing looking person with a fine eye. She is very deaf but talked very sensibly and kindly. Thanked me for my visit and when I praised the beauty & taste of her grounds she said they were her own creation, that they afforded her amusement and something to do, altho' now she could only visit them in her garden chair. There were many memorials of her husband in different parts of the grounds. In one beautiful and secluded spot a marble monument was erected on which were inscribed some lines of poetry from his favorite author expressive of the happiness he enjoyed in that retreat & in the pleasures of friendship, but the most beautiful and striking object in the grounds was a temple tastefully fitted up and commanding an extensive view & which was ascended by a flight of steps and underneath when we descended we passed into the most splendid grotto supported by pillars and which bore a striking resemblance to Amen's cave. I beg pardon. I have fairly got into the descriptive vein again. We were met by the venerable old butler & conducted to the drawing room where we spent 10 or 15 minutes and then took our leave after having been invited by Mrs. Fox to repeat my visit.

I also visited a little villa belonging to a Mr. Westmacott an amateur of the fine arts. His house was a curiousity in itself and contained more curious things than was ever before collected in the same space, pictures, statues, busts, antiques, &c. &c. One of his pictures, a Guido, he had refused to take 15,000 guineas for. The best likeness of Walter Scott ever taken and the last he ever sat for. The very pistol of Rob Roy McGregor, ancient armor, &c &c. They were very civil, gave us tea and fruit and carried us through their grounds, made the fountains play for us and showed us everything worth seeing. On the morning of the fifth day Mr. Stevenson arrived after having made a visit on his way down to Mrs. Fox with which he was much delighted. It was amusing to me to see the admiration they all felt & expressed for my husband who was in one of his best moods. We left them the next morning notwithstanding, much persuasion to remain, but as Mr. Stevenson was engaged to dine that evening with the Duke of Wellington it afforded us an excellent excuse to return to London for which I was not very sorry as I did not quite like the young husband's humours. I was delighted to find myself in London.

Mr. Vaux, whom we found in the office, presented us an invitation to dine that evening with the Queen at a quarter past 7 precisely. Mr. S. was obliged to send an apology immediately to the Duke, whilst I went to see Madame Dedel to enquire as to the costume, etc. At 7 I was dressed all to my white crape hat with ostrich feathers, which had not arrived from the milliner's—black silk, with black crape over it, trimmed with crape and black rosettes of berries and leaves, jet ornaments, necklace, earrings, bracelets; & at 5 minutes to the time the hat arrived. And we did not get to the palace until many minutes after the precisely had passed. In trepidation I ran up the grand & magnificent staircase with as fleet a step as was consistent with my dignity, and through the superb suite of apartments, until we reached the grand receiving-room, where all the company were assembled, standing waiting for the appearance of her Majesty. In a short time the glass doors of the next apartment opened, & she came forth in deep black, attended by all her ladies in waiting, maids-of-honor, & her "august mother" (the newspaper language), with her attendants, a goodly train. As we stood in a circle, the little Queen approached us & said something to each person with a calm and gentle dignity, as perfectly self-possessed as if we had all been statues. Her mother followed, repeating the same ceremonious courtesy, & then dinner was announced. She took the arm of Count Pozzo di Borgo (the Russian Ambassador) & led the way. The folding-doors flew open. The band, which was stationed in a marquee below, struck up, and we found ourselves in a magnificent banqueting-room, brilliantly lighted, and the table covered with a service of gold so splendid it dazzled one's eyes to look upon it. The Queen sat midway the table, with her lords-in-waiting at each end. Her little Majesty eat with a good appetite, and did full justice to the rich viands, which were always presented first to her. After the second course, the lord-in-waiting who had led me to dinner rose and drank the Queen's health. All stood up but the Queen.

When the dinner was over, her Majesty rose and passed out first. We followed through the rich and gorgeous apartments, which reminded me of the descriptions in the Arabian Nights, until she reached the grand drawing-room, when she paused and a circle formed around her. No one must speak first to Majesty; accordingly each one waited to be spoken to. Her address was now more in the style of conversation. I told her how much I had been disappointed at not being present when she prorogued Parliament, at which she smiled and looked pleased. The Duchess's civilities always followed her daughter's. While this court of etiquette was going on, coffee was handed to us, still standing, and I must confess I cast some longing looks towards the soft, luxurious sofas and chairs. After the coffee, a folding-door was opened & the Queen, followed by her guests, passed into a magnificent picture-gallery, brilliantly lighted; but she soon returned to the drawing-room, when, feeling my Republican legs about to give out, I glided behind the door and seated myself comfortably.

When I returned to the drawing-room, the gentlemen had returned and were taking coffee and receiving the courtesies of the Queen, who said something to each one. When this was over, she passed out of the room into one of smaller dimensions, where card-tables were set out & new sofas placed opposite to each, with tables and candles before them. On one of these her Majesty placed herself and invited the Countess Pozzo di Borgo to sit on one side of her & the Marchioness of Salisbury to take the other. The Duchess of Kent sat on the other sofa, with the Countess Ludiff on one side, and as I held off, she sent a maid of honor to ask me to sit by her. When she conversed with me very amiably, I took occasion to speak of the deep interest I had felt in the accession of her daughter, &c., and when I alluded to her being the hope and the object of prayer to the whole nation, the mother's heart, I saw, was full, & her eyes, too, but of course I spoke with royal uneasiness. Tea was then handed, & afterwards the Duchess approached a card-table & invited Lord & Lady Cowley (The Duke of Wellington's brother) to play, and also Mr. Stevenson. They drew for partners, and Mr. Stevenson had the honour of playing with her Royal Highness and of winning from Lord Cowley (who was obliged to play with his wife) 14 shillings. Whilst this game was going on, I had full time to look around. The Queen had sent her lord-in-waiting, who stood at the back of her sofa, for Count Pozzo di Borgo, and directed him to place a chair near her for him. The maids of honor had retired to the farther end of the room and taken chairs. The ladies in waiting & the invited guests had found chairs near our sofa, and the gentlemen stood apart, conversing together. As I sat opposite the Queen, I had a fair opportunity of getting her face by heart. It is one of very sweet expression, though not handsome; her eyes are blue & express softness and intelligence, but her mouth, that feature which always gives so much character to the countenance, is not good. Poor young thing! Whilst I gazed upon her innocent & happy face my heart involuntarily offered up a prayer for her future happiness and prosperity. She looked so young so innocent & good, I sighed to think of the time when that fair brow would be wrinkled with care, that light heart oppressed with sorrows, and the joyous laugh be heard no more. At least, if we judge of the future by the past, such will probably be her fate. Who would have thought that Marie Antoinette's bright morning would have ended in a night of such utter darkness?

But to return to Buckingham Palace, in all its light and splendour, & gorgeous magnificence, and to the dullness and etiquette of royalty. When the Duchess of Kent rose from the card-table, the company all rose, too, save the Queen, who waited until we had formed a circle in the middle of the room, when she came forward, spoke again to all and each, then presented her soft, white hand to the ladies, according to their rank, wished us good night, & departed. The Duchess repeated the ceremony, bowing and curtesying instead of shaking hands, and she also withdrew. When we were free to depart, after looking about and exchanging courtesies with each other, we were glad to find ourselves at our humble homes before 12. Now, my dear friends, I have given you a circumstantial account of this royal dinner which I hope may amuse you. I assure you that even here the curiosity to know how these royal enter-tainments are conducted is intense. But here everything this little Queen says or does is interesting to her loyal subjects, & it is amusing to think, with all this outward observance, the Queen has so little real power.

The sovereign of Great Britain is a mere pageant and as an English lady said to me the other day what would England be without the Corinthian pillars of society. It is all very pretty to see now and then but I am very certain I should not do for a lady-in-waiting or a maid of honor, if my pride could stoop to be at the bidding of another to place a shawl, to fasten a bracelet & follow where they lead. I am very sure my legs would not be so obedient to my will. The good Countess Ludoff had to ad-monish me several times the other night "Pray, my dear Mrs.

Stevenson, do not lean against that pillar". Whilst I was on the sofa she whispered once or twice "You are leaning back" to which I replied "And why not, I am weary" but the poor old Countess who has been here some twenty years is thoroughly broke in & thinks to violate an etiquette in the presence of royalty a great offense. I have heard this moment that the packet will be off today. I must therefore close this in a moment without scarcely looking it over. I have a thousand messages to send to all & each, but now they must imagine all that is in the heart of yours & their devoted sister

S. C. Stevenson

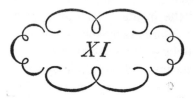

XI

"THE MAGNIFICENCE and hospitality" of Holkham in Norfolk was truly something to write home about. This princely eighteenth century mansion was the seat of Thomas William Coke, Earl of Leicester, and Britain's foremost experimental farmer. In October, 1837, the Stevensons were guests of the Earl and his gracious lady at Holkham.

They left London on a fine October day, posting through the delightful countryside at the amazing (to Mrs. S. at least) speed of ten miles an hour. Their turnout included Attaché Richard Vaux, "Mr. Cates," the Legation butler doubling as Stevenson's valet, and the lady's maid, "Mrs. Dunn."

The "sweet and bitter recollections," to which Mrs. Stevenson refers at the opening of this letter, was the birth of her daughter, October 5, 1817, and her death at the age of five.

Earl Spencer, whom the Stevensons met at Holkham, was the former Lord Althorp, leader in the House of Commons and recently raised to the peerage.

October, 1837

On the 6th of October, the day after an anniversary which ever brings to my heart sweet & bitter recollections, we set off for Holkham that seat of magnificence and hospitality. We left

London after an early breakfast in an open Briska—a carriage which opens & shuts, it will carry four persons inside and two behind, besides the driver's seat, which is not used in posting. It is also very convenient for luggage, (as they say here) imperials, boxes &c &c. Mr. Secretary Vaux Mr. Stevenson and myself occupied the inside, Mr. Cates, & Mrs. Dunn behind. Nothing can be more agreeable or more exhilarating than travelling in England. The roads are so smooth the country generally so beautiful, and the rapidity & ease with which one gets on is delightful—at the rate of ten & twelve miles an hour, for it does not take a minute to change horses, these things are so well regulated here by the time the carriage stops at the post house the ready harnessed horses are brought out—"all right" sounds from behind, & away we go. But for all this, John Bull makes us pay well, but I always try to forget that and enjoy whilst I can. My two beaux were in excellent spirits and beguiled the way with pleasant conversation, and occasionally a song. We often wished for you dear sister, for Mr. Vaux is a great admirer of yours and it is a pleasure to me to talk of you to him. We passed through Cambridge and methought the "Genius of the place" reproached us for posting through it without pausing to admire its venerable alleys where a Milton & a Newton a Burn & Hammond pursued a course of science which enabled them to soar to the most elevated heights of literary fame. Mr. Stevenson, however, consoled me by promising to stop as we returned. The second day was brilliantly beautiful & it felt like an American sun that shone upon us. We stoped for a little while at the village of Brandon and whilst they were repairing something which had given way in the carriage Richard & myself walked before a very good looking house, and a venerable old Lady came out & invited us to enter. She walked us through her garden which was very pretty and gave us fruit. We also passed through New market celebrated in the racing calendar. We did not, however, stop but saw the horses training & the race course. The County of Norfolk is said to present the least beautiful & picturesque scenery in England. It is flat & uninteresting. Holkham is an oasis in the desert, and the improved appearance of the country indicated our approach to the estate of this successful agriculturist. The Park is entered through a grand triumphal arch or spacious portal from which is seen the obelisk or stately column in a vista of a mile & a half—& at some distance beyond the noble & magnificent mansion breaks upon the view. I shall not attempt to give you any discription of this celebrated place, but merely my impression's. We arrived about 4 oclock & was received by the butler or steward of the household a powdered gentleman with a very red face who ushered us into the grand Egyptian Hall with its Ionic variegated marble pillars, its grand majestic proportions struck us dumb with admiration & astonishment. We ascended the steps which led into the saloon. Then through the Drawing room the corridor from which to the right we had a full view of the splendid gallery filled with busts, statues, &c, &c. Then through the classical & manuscript to the grand library where we expected to meet the Countess but the room was vacant & we were glad of a little time to take breath & look our admiration. Her Ladyship soon made her appearance dressed in a calico dress, plaid shawl & straw bonnet, she welcomed us with much cordiality & kindness & after a little conversation offered to show us our rooms. When I was dressed the difficulty was to find my way back. I asked my maid, but she could not help me, so I ventured forth, with my boa wrapped around my throat and soon found myself in inextricable mases lost. Fortunately I met a servant & asked him to show me to the drawing room, instead of the library, where the family meet untill the first of November when they remove to the drawing rooms. Accordingly he showed me to this immense room with one light burning in it, and disappeared. After waiting some time in the cold, I began to think palaces are not the most comfortable residences in the world. In the midst of this philosophical reverie I was startled by seeing a white figure flitting across the room. I hastened towards it and addressed it as boldly as did Hamlet his Fathers ghost, but not exactly in the same way. The lady—for it was no other than a fair & gentle dame (Lady Sherbourne with whom

I afterwards became much acquainted) took pity on me, and conducted me to the regions of light & social enjoyment. I found in the library several guest collected among the number Lady Mary Stephenson with whom I had become acquainted in London. The venerable host Mr. Coke (Lord Leceister) received me with almost paternal kindness and congratulated himself on his good fortune in having under his roof two persons for whom he entertained such warm esteem & friendship, these high bred English never make long speaches and rarely ever make a personal compliment. This excellent old nobleman of natures own making, still preserves all that amenity of manner, that gentle & bland courtesy for which he has ever been distinguished. He led me to dinner and placed me at his right hand. We dined at a round table about 16 or 18 guests. After dinner the ladies adjourned to the library & Lady Leicester sent her little son to her sitting-room for some envelopes which she immediately commenced making into lighters whilst we all sat round the table assisting her, taking coffee whilst we worked. When this was over & just before the gentlemen joined us the servant brought in the tea tray with the urn, which was put on a side table & Lady Leicester made tea whilst we went to the table and helped ourselves, the gentlemen joining us, or not, just as they liked. After coffee & tea the gentlemen played whist with Lord Leicester untill about ten, when a servant entered with a china bowl of boiled milk & bread which he placed beside Lord Leicester, who as soon as he had partaken of it retired. Then another tray with wine, ale, cakes & a silver pitcher containing boiling water for negus. After this we retired to our rooms as we felt inclined, the night candles being all placed on a side table. The next morning which was Sunday I found my way with some difficulty to the breakfast room, where I found most of the family at the breakfast table, every one dropping in as they were ready. The round table was covered with every variety of bread & Devonshire butter, the coffee, Lady L. poured out, the tea was made at a side table & handed, the meat's of every sort at another table, the gentlemen helping themselves. At half past nine the Chaplain retired, and soon after the bell rang for prayers, and those who felt inclined went to the Chapel from the breakfast table. The servants assemble below each one having their own place. The family enter from above the family seats or gallery. The Chaplain commenced by reading a hymn, then a chapter from the Bible, a short discourse, & closed with a prayer. Who that had ever enjoyed the pleasure of social worship would ever forego the blessed privilege. After prayers the family & guests dispersed each their own way, to their own rooms, the publick apartments—Lady Leicester's beautiful sitting room or the grounds. But from half past one to two all the lunch eaters were sure to be found in the dining room. Afterwards the carriage or pony phaeton was brought up, & we drove till dressing time. The Monday after our arrival Lord Leicester invited me to drive with himself & Mr. S. that he might show me some of his improvements. He took us first to the kitchen garden, the only one in England through which one may drive. It was perfect, in neatness & order. The high walls to which every kind of fruit was trained, & over all a net work fastened to protect the fruit from insects. He showed us his pinery's, graperies—&c &c. It was all upon a grand scale. He then took us to the house of one of his tenants, who showed us her dairy—fowl yard &c. This tenant pays him fifteen hundred pounds a year. Then to see his beautiful Devon's, & he stoped also at the establishments of his butter & game keepers. The secret wish arose in my heart that I had such a home in America. He told us an excellent anecdote about one of these places I do not recollect which. It seems some years since before he ceased to shoot, some distinguished frenchmen made him a visit & it was so arranged that Lord Leicester with some of his friends should meet them & take a days shooting before they went to Holkham, and as lunch is a very important meal in England Mr. Coke directed a cold collation to be got ready at the house of one of these his dependents. He says when he invited the frenchmen in they took it into their heads that they were at Holkham, & immediately began to exclaim with french exageration "How beautiful—how magnifique! Mr. Coke says that himself and the English nobles who were with him preserved their gravity & said nothing, but in the evening when they arrived at Holkham and were ushered into the Egyptian Hall, splendidly lighted up, it was amusing to observe their countenances, having exhausted every expression of admiration they had no more superlatives & could only utter with emphatic astonishment, O Mon Dieu! The village to which he also carried us, is extremely interesting. He made the driver take us through the gardens of the villagers, little plots of ground which has been given to the heads of each family & surrounded by beautiful hedges, where as the good old gentleman said, every man might recreate himself with his family after his days labour was over. He also showed us Lady Leicester's schools, and a large building which is putting up upon a very extensive scale for the school, the population of the village having increased so much as to require a larger one. He showed us an inscription in front stating that it had been done by Lady Leicester and added, "Ah, the dear creature, did not like my giving publicity to her benevolent actions, for she would not let her right hand know what her left does, if she could help it". It is delightful to see the affection which exist between these two persons so unequally yoked together. Mr. Coke is just 50 years older than his wife. He is now 86 & she is 36 and he is as much in love with her as a young lover. He thinks she can do no wrong, and that she is perfect, whilst she looks up to him with a feeling of veneration mingled with the most profound tenderness & respect. They have five children four boys the eldest Lord Coke and one daughter the Lady Margaret, a beautiful child of five years old, who has lately sustained some injury in one of her limbs, which has given her parents great concern. The physicians held a consultation on her case a few days after our arrival & alarmed the mother so much that she determined to take her up to London immediately. Accordingly the Friday after our arrival she left us for some of the most eminent of the London faculty to see the limb, we wished to have returned with her, but this they would not hear of. Lord Leicester said with his usual politeness it would make no other difference but the regret his wife would feel in having to leave us. We found no one thought of going but ourselves, & the day after her departure we had an accession of company in the distinguished Lord Althorpe now Lord Spencer (formerly premier of England,) & his brother Capn Spencer. This noble Lord looks as little like a great man as any one I ever saw, in his person he is extremely plain, altho' his countenance has an expression of sweetness & gentleness, and his manners have all the English reserve with more than English shyness. He went out every morning before the family breakfast, with his gun, his dogs & his keeper, & did not return untill it was time to dress for dinner, such is English ease & freedom from restraint. Lord Leicester told me this had been his custom for 15 years that he had spent one month with him annually. During Lady Leicester's absence he enquired of me every day, how I had spent the morning if I had been amused &c &c and made a remark which struck me very forcely, he said, "You see my dear friend, there is here the absence of all ceremony. I never ask any one I do not like to my house—and whilst they are here I do not wish to trammel them with any more attention than is necessary to their comfort & enjoyment. If I wished to get rid of a disagreeable person I would follow him up with great attentions." As Mr. Coke is a person particularly interesting to all Americans from his support of free principles & his constant devotion to our country, I will describe him to you such as he now is in his grand climacterick. It has been said that the man who makes two blades of corn grow where only one had grown before, is a great benefactor to mankind, certainly no one ever deserved this praise more than Mr. Coke of Norfolk, for it is admitted I believe by all that he has done more for agriculture than any man living. In his youth he must have been very handsome, there is at Holkham two full length pictures of him, one when very young, the other in the prime of manhood, which represents him as possessing great physical strength & activity, with an air of much grace & dignity which he still retains, his person is tall & now rather full, but he dresses with great care & neatness always in shirts, his head bald, & wears powder, his teeth are still fine, tho' from having received a shot in his eyes they are constantly red, & his sight much weakened. In his youth he was a great sportsman and won from Lord Jersey 75 guinea's by killing 80 birds at 80 shots. Lady Leicester is not handsome but agreeable in her appearance her manners do not generally please, it is easy to perceive that she has been the spoilt child of fortune, & of an old man, yet she has fine qualities, virtues which render her really estimable. I shall perhaps describe her better by giving you some anecdotes of her, which I heard from Miss D. the daughter of Lord Sherbourne whom we found at Holkham. It seems before her marriage to Mr. Coke the Duke of Sussex who is very fond of "Coke" as he calls him, was in the habit of spending two & three months at Holkham & Lady Ann after a few of these annual visitations got very tired of him so she fell upon an expedient to get rid of His Royal Highness after six weeks stay she said to him suddenly one morning at breakfast "Pray when do you leave us". "Maam"! exclaimed the astonished Duke & when the question was repeated with smiling courtesy, he could only reply really he had not thought of it. Miss Dutton told me that Mr. Coke in speaking of it to her afterwards said, "Only think of the dear creature there I sat wriggling on my chair not knowing what would come next". The Duke it seems took the hint & departed, but on the return of the next Christmas, he was again her guest accompanied by Prince Leopold. Lady Ann was quiet & polite for six weeks again, but then she said to the Duke, "It is always agreeable & convenient to know how long Royal persons mean to stop with us, pray can you tell me when the Prince will leave us?" "I will enquire & let you know Madam". The next morning he told her the day of the Princes departure, and then added, "Perhaps your Ladyship would now like to know when I go". If you please sir. This is one side of the picture. Then again see her feeding the hungry, clothing the naked, & instructing the ignorant, besides many other good works—as a wife she is exemplary as a Mother devoted—as a sister I happened to have proof of her kindness & goodness. One morning whilst I was at Holkham I found her in her splendid sitting room seated on a low stool cutting linen. I took my seat by her & assisted her, & remarking how strong it was in texture she replied that it was not very fine, as she intended it for two nephews whom she had adopted, clothed, & educated, for that her poor sister had married unfortunately, & was very poor, and she allowed her one third of her income. Miss Dutton said some thing about her dress. She replied it was the last time of wearing & then it must go to Georgianna (her sister) for she claimed all her dresses, & she orders me to wear a silk apron with all the gown's intended for her! And you would be astonished to see the work she does, she has worked in worsted a set of chair covers that look like beautiful painting. Such is the Countess of Leicester. On looking over what I have written I find I have omitted an incident which will be discriptive of English manners & customs, as well as of Lady Leicesters peculiarities. About two years ago the Duchess of Kent with the Princess Victoria made a visit to Mr. Coke & Lady Ann at Holkham, and it seems, etiquette requires that the lady of the house should always hand, herself, the coffee after dinner to the Royal person who condescends to visit a subject. Accordingly Lady Ann received the silver waiter from the servant, & on presenting it to her Royal Highness she said something about the trouble, &c—to which her ladyship replied, "If Your Royal Highness does not make haste, I shall drop it!"

I ought not to close my account of Holkham without giving you some discription of Lord & Lady Sherborne & their daughter the Honbl Miss Dutton, as it is possible I may see much of them this winter & they have very kindly invited us next spring or summer to Sherborne a beautiful seat they own in Gloucestershire, near Cheltenham. Lady Sherborne is a sensible, gentle, well bred lady who treated me with much civility & kindness. Lord Sherborne is "every inch a gentleman", as King Lear, was a "King"—and the Honble Miss Dutton is just 20—rather pretty—well educated and sensible, but prides herself upon her English reserve—and her knowledge of phrenology, she & Richard Vaux examined each others heads & hearts too I believe, she seemed to regret it very much when Mr. Stevenson sent him to London on business after a weeks stay. Lady Sherborne & myself drove together walked together, & talked over England & America. There is nothing in the neighbourhood of Holkham worth visiting except the ruins of an old Abbey founded by the Lady of Walsingham, with a very romantic tale attached to it. There is an arch still standing that is magnificent form its height & perfect proportions, also two wells which in the age of superstition was much resorted to by pilgrims as it was said whoever uttered a wish over the waters had it granted. Henry the 8th is said to have visited it. I breathed the wish over its waters which is ever uppermost in my heart—may it have been registered in Heaven —& I ought not to be ashamed to tell it to thee my sister. I prayed that my husband might become a Christian in spirit, & in truth. Mr. Stevenson only went out shooting two days whilst he was at Holkham, and then he beat the noble ex-premier, to his hearts content. I payed for it by the loss of two nights sleep having lost all the skin off his heels he kept me awake with his groans & lamentations. You know he has not the patience of Job upon such occasions. He regrets very much not having brought his gun, if he knew where to direct Mr. R. to look for it he would have it sent to him now & I wish we had brought our little physick chest that I might have had it filled here, the medicine's are so much better than with us. And now dear Sister I think it is time we should take our departure from Holkham. On Monday the 23d we left its hospitable halls.

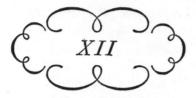

XII

Mrs. Stevenson here records that she had just written an eight-page letter to her niece, one of seven and a half pages to her brother and another of nineteen. Her pages, by the way, many of them, at least, contain three hundred words each.

Yet such monumental letter writing did not deter her from drawing this charming vignette describing the Civic Festival, blazing with light and color in honor of the new Queen.

London Novr 14th 1837

How very good you are to write me so often & so much. I can only evince my gratitude by scrawling to you whenever I have a spare moment. I have this moment finished three letters one to Angelica of 8 pages, another to brother Tucker of 7 & a half and to Miss Cass a well filled sheet—imagine how very tired my fingers must be, and my mind too, but still before the dispatch closes I must scribble a little to you dearest. I hope you have received my letter of 19 pages. I enclosed it to Mr. Lewis, for fear Mr. Forsyth might not frank it, and thinking such a hurried scrawl not worth the postage. There were many mistakes of spelling, &c, &c in it from the haste in which it was written & which I intended correcting but really had not time, however, I console myself by knowing only indulgent eyes will see it. I am truly grieved to hear of sister Coles' affliction but hope it will be only temporary. You are happy my dear sister in your power of doing good, & consoling her in her hour of need. Dear Angelica too! Heaven grant you may be wrong in your conjectures—I have not alluded to it in my letter to her, but endeavored to amuse her. Neither have I done so in my letter to brother Tucker.

Since our return to London the lovers of spectacle have had a magnificent treat in the great civic festival in honor of the Queen. It took place on the 9th day of this month, three days ago, the invitation having been given last summer by the citizens of London to partake of a dinner at Guildhall, the residence of the Lord Mayor. It seems since the reign of Elizabeth, her great prototype, no unmarried Queen of England has visited the municipal corporation, therefore the ceremonial of yesterday was looked forward to with eager expectation. Besides these, there were other circumstances which were calculated to enlist the sympathies of all beholders in the striking destiny of this young, amiable, & lovely Queen, in the morning freshness of her youth and innocence called upon to rule over the proudest empire in the world, to be an object for the admiring gaze of thousands, the mark at which all eyes are aiming, to feel that her glance confers distinction, and to know that her will bestows rank and honours, wealth—nay, even happiness. What a destiny for one so young, so inexperienced! This fair, young mistress of three kingdoms passed along the whole line of St. James's to the heart of the City, a distance of three miles, through a dense mass of her subjects on each side of her chariot wheels greeting her with enthusiastic cheers & blessings, whilst she did her "gracious bendings" first on one side & then on the other, smiling with sweet and gentle courtesy on the innumerable multitude & looking as innocent and happy as a child. Alas! poor girl, who knows what may be written down for thee in the book of fate!

I will not attempt to give you a description of this great national pageant. I dare not even venture to give an impression of its general effect, of the vast extent of the fluctuating multitude which lined the streets and rose line over line to the roofs of every house which afforded a prospect, the general length and grandeur of the procession, the superb equipages, which exceed even our dreams of magnificence. The royal cortege consisted of at least 24 or 25 of these sumptuous carriages, each drawn by 6 noble horses that looked as proudly aristocratic as those they bore. The state coach, gorgeous with gold and the richest decorations,—drawn by 8 of the most beautiful cream-colored horses, adorned with superb trappings,—in which the "Fair rose of England" sat like the enchanted lady in the Crystal Cabinet of the fairy-tale, the "observed of all observers." The illuminations were brilliant & tasteful beyond anything ever seen here before. The whole line of the streets in the Queen's progress back from the dinner presented a dazzling blaze of light. Each side was studded with a brilliant series of crowns & regal initials separately or in multiform combination.

The *woman,* young & lovely & innocent, claimed something from the chivalry, as well as the Queen from the Loyalty of her subjects, accordingly, many devices were employed to show their devotion to her Sex as well as to her station. But 'tis vain to attempt to give you an idea of it, besides, I am too much hurried, and have taken this passage from my other letter to brother Tucker. I suppose one may repeat themselves when they have not time to put the same ideas into a different form.

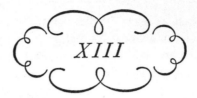

XIII

ALTHOUGH FAMILY and friends at home envied the Stevensons their brilliant life, the situation actually was such as to cause Stevenson to write a friend in America, "Like the galled plough horse I long to get the Harness off, and to roll in the dirt." The brilliance of their environs had not, nor did it ever, dazzle these two common-sense Americans. They formed warm friendships with the right people which, in addition to bringing them personal popularity, helped to solidify the feeling of good neighborliness between Great Britain and the United States.

There is a hint of wifely unhappiness in this letter. Yet, for consolation, Mrs. Stevenson fell back as always on the eternal promise.

The Duke of Cambridge whom Mrs. Stevenson saw when the Queen opened Parliament in the House of Lords was the seventh son of King George III and uncle of the Queen. The Premier was, of course, Lord Melbourne with whom the Stevensons seem to have had little social contact.

Lady "Landsdowne" was the wife of the powerful Marquis of Lansdowne, who, incidentally, like William Pitt, had been Chancellor of the Exchequer at twenty-four. Lady Lansdowne was a great favorite with Queen Victoria. Lansdowne House was one of the magnificent show places of London and the balls given there were fabulous.

London Novr 19th 1837
Sunday Night

My beloved sister

Having spent the day almost entirely in my own room in reading the Book of Books I shall now devote this hour of tranquillity to you. How delightful it would be if I could chat with you instead of write to you. I always have so much to say that I never get half through before the length of my letters admonish me to come to a close.

Ah my dear sister, when you and Mr. Ritchie write about our being spoiled &c &c believe me an American minister and his wife have drawbacks sufficient to keep his and her heart in the right place. Do not be afraid of our staying here too long. It is impossible to live here upon the salary allowed us for any length of time & to go back & starve & beg or dig! You know Mr. Stevenson and you may imagine whether I am too happy. Some persons resemble the bee in extracting of every flower its sweets but not so my husband. He finds only the bitter and turns it all to poison. One feeling keeps me humble and comparatively happy—an entire trust in that kind Providence who has never forsaken me, a firm belief that He orders all things for the best. If the storm comes I bend my head and it passes over me. If sunshine, I bask in its rays and enjoy it with a thankful & a cheerful spirit and endeavor to be anxious for nothing. Never have I felt a more entire reliance upon my Heavenly Father than now for has he not said, "When all others forsake thee I will take thee up". And every day & every hour, nay every minute, I feel His goodness and Fatherly care for me. My heart is full and my tears overflow when I think of His "Loving Kindness" to me and to mine.

I was interrupted last night by a visit from Lady Joddell, a most remarkable person. Her husband is the richest & oldest Baronet in the kingdom and she is beautiful & talented but so eccentric that I am rather afraid to cultivate her acquaintance and she has fastened upon me with so tenacious a grip that I

(*101*)

cannot shake her off if I would—but I cannot waste my paper and time upon her just now.

Last week Mr. Rush proposed our going to the play to see the Queen's reception. He procured a box, and accordingly we went—Rushes and ourselves. It was a most animating and exciting scene even to me, who am neither a queen nor a subject. When her Majesty entered her box there was a deafening burst of gratulation from every part of the house. She answered this ardent demonstration of affection with many kindly obeisances to her loyal subjects, and those near say she wept and trembled. No wonder; innocent young creature, I confess I almost wept myself when the national anthem was sung by the whole vocal strength of the theater, and by its numerous and excellent band, especially at the invocation to the Almighty to "bless the Queen." It is the only thing I have ever envied her. But I will send you the paper containing the description of the scene; or rather my friend Mr. Rush will do it for me.

I saw Parliament opened by the Queen; but first I must tell you a "capital thing." Miss Murray, one of the Queen's maids of honour, offered me a ticket and to go with me. However, on Saturday night some difficulty arose as to the ticket, and Mr. Rush got into the carriage and went with me to the Lord Chamberlain's office; but we were told that it was impossible to secure one. In despair I was about giving up, but not so Mr. Rush. He went home, got his dinner, and came back, to devise some expedient, when Mr. S—— suggested writing in his own name (the Sec'y of Legation) to the great Lord Chamberlain. Accordingly it was done, and the next day we received a very polite note, saying: "It gave the Lord Chamberlain great pleasure to see that a seat should be provided for Mrs. Stevenson, and that no ticket was required; that I was merely to announce my name." Accordingly I called for Miss Murray at 12, so as to have time to send the carriage back for Mr. S. & Mr. R. When we arrived, we were asked for our tickets. I merely announced my name, & again at the next door it seemed an open Sesame, & on we passed. When we arrived at the door of the great Hall or House of Lords as it is called

—Lord Willoughby the great Chamberlain met us & said to me do you wish this lady to accompany you, to which I replied in the affirmative, & he led us to two benches covered with crimson cloth close along side of the Throne, so there I sat by the side of the Princess Gagarini & her daughter, with my maid of honour behind me. Thinks I to myself, fair lady, the tables are turned. In a few minutes she leant towards me & said with a face flushed with pleasure, "What a favour you have done me dear Mrs. Stevenson, indeed I was disinterested when I offered you a ticket". In a few moments the immense apartment began to fill with nobles, lords, & dukes, & beautiful ladies in Court dresses (I had been prepared for this, & was in full dress,). If I could have had the choice of all the seats in the House, I should have chosen the one I had. The Royal Dukes stood immediately by me, Sussex & Cambridge, the latter inquired of the Princess who I was, & immediately entered into conversation with me, (Royal persons dispense with introductions) as did also the Duke of Sussex, & then I was amused by hearing their conversation together which I did, without any breach of good manners. Before the entrance of every Royal person, there was a flourish of trumpets, & when the Queen came it was long & loud with a discharge of cannon. She entered looking really beautiful surrounded by all the great officers of state, Lady Landsdowne & the Duchess of Sutherland—train bearers —&c &c. On one side was the Archbishop of Canterbury & on the other the Premier of England holding the sword of State. Her dress was magnificent, & she looked sweetly placid & dignified. Once or twice a smile flitted across her countenance, but only one as near to her as I was could have perceived it. She first took the oath, which was administered by the Archbishop, & then read with a calm distinct & beautiful annunciation her speech, still seated on the throne. Lord Melbourne whom I was very near, seemed really more agitated than she was. His lips moved & I saw he repeated after her every word. When she had concluded her speech she paused a little, & then arose & retired as she had entered, bowing to her two uncles, Sussex & Cambridge, as she passed. These two noble Dukes stood just before me, or rather more to my side, & squeezed me most Royally, but with all their royal power, both physical & moral, they could not help themselves, and apoligized most graciously. The House of Lords as it is called is not to be compared to our noble Hall of Representatives but these proud English sooth their pride by telling us of the magnificent structure which is about to be erected &c &c.

And now, dear sister, confess I am a good sister to write you such a voluminous scrawl—after all I have written lately. Adieu!

Just as the packet is closing I must say a few more words, altho' I am sure you must be heartily tired of this long scrawl & I write now with Dunn at my head—brushing—combing, &c.

XIV

In her day "Cousin Dolly" Madison had set the pace as mistress of the Presidential Mansion in Washington and Sallie Stevenson had often gazed in wonder and admiration at Mrs. Madison embellished with all her finery for one of her inimitable soirees. Dolly's thousand-dollar turbans, made in Paris, were something to marvel at. The Magnificent Monroes had later invested the White House with Parisian glitter and a welter of gold lace and jewels.

But nothing that democratic America could boast ever approached the gorgeous scenes through which Mrs. Stevenson was passing. "Cousin Dolly" had never worn "at least 50, maybe 100, diamonds in her hair".

There must have been considerable rubbing of eyes in unbelief when this letter reached Mrs. Stevenson's sister-in-law, Julia Coles, at Enniscorthy deep in the Virginia woods.

London Decr 6th 1837

My beloved Sister.

I wrote Betty and brother about my visit to Holkham, some twenty or thirty pages in all, and cannot go over that ground. I believe I gave them some description of the great national pageant, the civic festival to the Queen on the 9th.

Since then she has been endeavouring to cheer the good citizens of London under the dismal darkness of fog and smoke by the brightness of her presence. She has visited the theatres of Drury Lane and Covent Garden in state, which is customary on the accession of a new sovereign. We were at Covent Garden, and it was really an exciting scene. The enthusiasm with which this young idol of a nation's love is received is really enough to turn her young head. I confess I was moved even to tears when the national anthem of "God save the Queen" was sung by the whole dramatique corps assembled on the stage, the audience joining in the chorus. When the line "Long to reign over us" was sung, a burst of enthusiasm broke forth that really seemed to alarm the young creature who was its object; but her calm and quiet self-possession is the astonishment of all who see her in such trying scenes.

At the opening of Parliament she had a much higher part to play, and did it equally well. I was fortunate in being very near her, the seats appropriated to the ladies of the foreign embassies being within a few feet of the throne so that I saw and heard every thing.

Her royal uncles, the Dukes of Sussex and Cambridge, entered first with a flourish of trumpets. They stood just by our seats, and conversed with us while the trumpets and the cannon announced the approach of Her Majesty, who entered, surrounded by all her ministers and officers of state, her train borne by her pages of honor. The imperial crown was carried on a velvet cushion by the Duke of Somerset, who walked a little to her side. She cannot wear it until after her coronation. When she had taken her seat on the throne, the ladies of her household arranged themselves behind her, the Duchess of Sutherland (The Mistress of the Robes), the Marchioness of Landsdowne, Lady Barham, &c. On her left stood the Premier, Lord Melbourne, with the sword of state, bolt upright, and on her right the Lord Chancellor, and the Archbishop of Canterbury, who read with her the oath of declaration, which she signed with her little gloved hand, and then read her speech with a firm, though feminine voice and the most perfect emphasis and enunciation. She neither trembled nor hesitated, nor was her color at all heightened. When it was over, a slight and twilight sort of smile flitted across her countenance, and she looked as if she thought she had done well. Lord Melbourne was much more agitated than she was, and repeated after her (not audibly) every word; I stood so near that I could perceive the motion of his lips. She then spoke a few words to her ladies, and retired as she had entered, smiling, and giving her hand to her two uncles as she passed.

Her voice is as sweet as a Virginia nightingale's, and dwells upon the memory like a spell after the sound has passed away. It is sweet, yet soft; powerful, yet melodious, and it is listened to with a sort of breathless interest, hightened, no doubt, by her extreme youth. Her size is below the middle, but her figure is finely proportioned, and a little embonpoint. Her bust, like most English-women's, is very good; hands and feet are small and very pretty. Her face, though not beautiful, has a look of spirituality, so bright and yet so tranquil that one feels involuntarily impressed with an idea that a good and pure spirit dwells within, which is destined for heaven if earth does not spoil her by its adulation. As yet her spirit has not passed under the yoke of royalty; she has only enjoyed its pleasures, and knows nothing of its pains and penalties; her dawn of life and prosperity has not been darkened by calamity or profaned by sin; but what will she be, when, like her great prototype Elizabeth, she is called to surrender up her trust to Him that gave it?

I dare say now you and Helen and Selina would like to know how she was dressed. It consisted of a white satin dress richly embroidered with gold and trimmed around the bottom with a deep gold fringe; the stomacher studded with diamonds; earrings and necklace of the same; a train of some yards' length of crimson velvet and gold, lined with white satin. On her hair, which is dark brown and always worn without curls, she wore a magnificent circle of diamonds. Her eyes are blue, large, and full; her mouth, which is her worst feature, is generally a little open; her teeth small and short, and she shows her gums when she laughs, which is rather disfiguring. One of her maids of honor told me the other day that she deplores with the most beautiful simplicity the slavery of sitting so much for her picture; that it has been her torment ever since she was eleven years old; that her sister (The Duchess of Kent has been married twice) wrote her from Germany, "Do, Victoria, shut your mouth when you sit for your likeness"; but that her mother said, "No, my dear; let it be as nature made it." She must be an amiable, gentle creature, for all who approach her seem to idolize her, and think her, if not an angel, at least such stuff as angels are made of. She seems to me to possess simplicity with elevation, spirit with sweetness, and wonderful tact and discretion for one so young and inexperienced. She may really be said to have stepped from the nursery to the throne. She still keeps near her person the Baroness Lehzun, who has had the charge of her since she was seven years old, and is said to be entirely worthy of the high trust. The Tories do not, however, think she has either a face or mind of the beatitudes. They accuse her of very womanly propensities, such as extravagance, want of sensibility, &c.; that she gives her hair-dresser 400 pounds a year; and a woman to take care of her diamonds, put them in, and out of their cases, 200 pounds. And an American minister has $9000!

It is so dark at one o'clock that I can scarce see to write. Last night I took Miss Murray, one of the maids of honor, to the palace. She went in to the Baroness Lehzun, whilst I made a visit to one of the Duchess of Kent's ladies in waiting, Lady May Stopford. Whilst I was sitting in her parlor (all the ladies of the Queen and Duchess of Kent have apartments in the palace), there was a tap at the door, and the Duchess entered, wrapped in a large shawl. She conversed with me as any one else would have done until I retired, knowing she must have business with Lady May. When I went out to get into the carriage it was so dark at 4 o'clock that, with all the lamps lighted in the palace yard and streets, and those also to the carriage, we could scarcely get home or see a yard before us. These fogs are really awful; they are so dense and thick that they are tangible, and it seems as if it were impossible to live in such an atmosphere. It keeps me constantly coughing and with a cold.

I wrote you a slight description of a dinner soon after her little Majesty's accession to the throne. This very much resembled it, differing only in being larger and more splendid, and the Queen seemed more at her ease.

We passed up the same grand staircase, lined with liveried servants, who bowed and signed the way (no one is announced at the Queen's dinners), through the same magnificent suite of apartments, to the grand drawing-room, where we stood like soldiers on duty. My republican pride a little revolted at this act, I thought, of supererogation, and I proposed to the ladies of the diplomatique corps that we should sit until the entrance of the Queen. Accordingly we took possession of a sofa, and the peeresses soon followed so comfortable an example; but it was really amusing to see the alacrity with which we all resumed our feet when the mirrored doors flew open to admit Her Majesty with all her attendants. Among them was the beautiful and magnificent Duchess of Sutherland. After passing around the circle, and giving her tiny fingers to be pressed by the ladies, a gentleman-in-waiting (the Marquis of Headfort) whispered the Count Pozzo di Borgo that he was to be the honored person (as ambassador, he ranked all the others). At the same moment a powdered gentleman announced dinner. The band struck up, and we followed after, the foreign ministers' ladies taking precedence of every one but royalty. I was led by Baron Guensloff and seated nearly opposite the Queen, the Baron only between the Duchess of Sutherland and myself. I determined to take a more particular look at everything than I had done before; but when I raised my eyes to look upon all this royal magnificence, the thought occurred to me: "If I gaze about, they will say, 'Look at that wild American, how she is staring at everything! I dare say she fancies herself in one of the enchanted castles of the Arabian Nights.'" So with Indian-like caution I only cast furtive glances around, and endeavoured to bear myself as though it was all as familiar to me as my every-day comforts. In consequence of this prudent determination, I cannot tell you much more than I did before. The room was large, lofty, and so brilliantly lighted that the rich gilding and gorgeous decorations of the ceiling and wall were as distinct as they could have been by daylight. Opposite to me hung two full lengths of George the III & IV in royal robes, and over the table were suspended three golden chandeliers, with twenty-four wax lights in each, and on the table there were ten or twelve candelabra holding 5, 7, & 9 lights in each. There were vases of beautiful flowers, supported by figures of such graceful forms as we may have supposed Pheidias could have sculptured. Thirty-nine guests sat down to table, and there was a servant to every two chairs. Behind the Queen stood two well-dressed gentlemen, out of livery, who handed her all she eat. It might have been ambrosia for aught I know, and that to which she helped herself, and which I thought was port wine and water, might have been nectar. She certainly eat very like a mortal—heartily, but with the delicacy and high breeding which distinguishes all the English aristocracy at their meals. She was dressed in crimson velvet, with a lace scarf light as gossamer, pearl earrings, no necklace. On her head she wore a crimson net studded with diamonds, which confined, without concealing, her hair. The Duchess of Sutherland, so celebrated for her beauty, grace, and splendid dressing, presents in her person a striking contrast to her royal mistress. She is a tall, commanding figure of the most perfect proportions, her deportment graceful and dignified, with a little touch of English reserve; her features are regular, with soft blue eyes; and when she converses there is a brightness in her smile which gives great animation to her countenance. Her complexion, for an English woman, is rather pale, though, like her countrywomen, very fair; hair & eyebrows black as the raven's wing, and blazing with diamonds. She had at least 50, maybe 100, diamonds in her hair, as large as a fourpence & one of a superior size as a fermoir; on one side of her head an ostrich feather twisted to fall in a graceful curve to her face; on the other, a bunch of roses, the leaves with a diamond in each, like a dew-drop, and the same on her bosom; her dress of rich white satin. The evening wound up much as before. We stood, and when the Queen was pleased to sit, we were informed we might do the same. Poor Madame Dedel (the lady of the Netherland's minister) had been ill, and I said to her after the Queen retired, "How do you feel?" "Ah, Madame Stevenson, tres malheureuse! I shall be too happy when I get into my bed. I think I shall be obliged to lay dere all day tomorrow." Poor lady! I presume she survived it, as I have not seen her death announced in the papers. Such, dear Julia, is the penalty to be payed for a glimpse at royalty. She, poor girl, full of life & hope and may be ambition, says she likes to be a queen; she likes business; and I suppose likes to be cheered, followed, admired, and to feel herself the observed of all observers. But age must come—misfortune, for who is exempt, may come, & illness & langour make what now is a pleasure a burden too heavy to be borne. Heaven knows what is written in the Book of Fate for this fair young creature. And now dear Sister, I must bid you an affec adieu. Never was so long a letter scrawled off in so short a time, Mr. Rush has been very good to wait for me pray excuse all mistakes for I have not time to read it over.

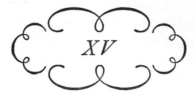

XV

COMPLAINT OVER the inadequacy of the salary attached to the diplomatic posts in foreign lands was raised long before Mrs. Stevenson wrote this letter. As she wrote on another occasion, everything in England was done by dinners. Many an international rough spot was ironed out by catering to the gastronomic fancies of those in high political office. So the Stevensons entertained a great deal. They had to. But the salary attached to the office was only $9000 a year plus an additional one-time $9000 for the Minister's outfit. It meant, of course, that Stevenson was obliged to draw on his none-too-abundant private means to hold up his end socially.

By 1838 the Stevensons' thoughts were turning homewards. They had been in public life ever since they were married and they longed for home and quiet.

Yet all these considerations vanished, temporarily, at least, one day late in December 1837 when a footman in palace livery appeared at the Legation with a missive addressed to "Honorable Andrew Stevenson and Lady." It was a command invitation from the Queen: Victoria wished the Stevensons to spend a few days with her *en famille* at Windsor Castle. It was the most flattering attention they had received since reaching England.

Sallie Stevenson had dreamed of visiting Windsor ever since her foot touched English soil. Now her dream was to come true.

As for the two titled gentlemen who flanked Mrs. Stevenson at the Queen's dinner table: "Ld. Howick" was really Lord Grey,

Viscount of Howick, former Premier of England. "Ld. Albemarle" was one of the royal inner circle, seen often in the royal box at the play.

Lady Tavistock was the leading Lady in Waiting, wife of powerful Francis, Marquis of Tavistock, seventh Duke of Bedford. Lady Tavistock was to play an unfortunate role in the Lady Flora Hastings Affair to come later.

Baroness Lehzun was the Queen's German governess, who had exercised vast influence in her upbringing. "Fraulein" Lehzun was much resented in high court circles. Charles Greville said, "The person in the world she [the Queen] loves best is Baroness Lehzun." Lytton Strachey intimated that Queen Victoria loved Baroness Lehzun much more than she did her own mother, the Duchess of Kent. But the Baroness was to go out of Victoria's life when romance came in. She was ousted from the Palace by the future Consort, Albert of Saxe-Coburg.

Diggeswell Jany 2d, 1838

My dear Sister,

I wrote you just as I was leaving London for this place, a short letter for me, and thought then I would not write again untill my return but as our friends here have persuaded us to extend our visit from a week to a fortnight I think I shall be obliged to write you a few lines, especially, as Mr. Stevenson publick business compelled his return to town for a few days, and my letter will be just in time for the next packet.

I feel the more anxious to write you, dear sister, but you shouldn't be uneasy about my health which I wrote you had been suffering more or less all the summer and autumn. My cough is much relieved since I have been breathing pure country air and I hope another week will quite see me up again. Notwithstanding all we have to make this country agreeable to us and the coldness of our friends at home, I feel my anxiety to return increasing every day & I know my husband shares the same feelings of homesickness with me.

I had hoped ere this Mr. Stevenson's friends would have

(*113*)

made some movement in his favour to bring him home and give him honourable employment, but with his active busy temper to set down and do nothing, especially after the exciting life he has led here, would not suit him, and with his limited means, and I might add his fondness for publick life, he could not become a gentleman farmer to overlook slaves. So my dear Bett, what is to be done? He sometimes talks of going to the far west &c. &c. but this would not do. The English say he is an honour & an ornament to his country, then his wife may be allowed to think him too good for that. He cannot return to the practice of the law, that would be impossible, he would not ask for office, that would be still more impossible to his high spirit and the honourable and dignified stations he has filled with so much credit to himself & his country preclude his taking any low office—entre nous is there any probability of his being made Governor—Senator—Vice President—or being offered any situation in the Cabinet? Van Buren as you know has never shown much disposition to serve him and I doubt his will to do so now, but *nous verrons*——All this is in the strictest confidence and these crude suggestions just made are the result of anxious affection which prompt me to give expression to what is passing in my heart. We should be too happy to return if we had the means of creating for ourselves a comfortable home. As to his debts here, if he has any I do not know of them and I have great faith in his prudence & discretion. Whatever you may have heard to the contrary we have lived with great economy altho' Mr. Stevenson has endeavored to preserve his dignity & that of his country, but the salary is totally inadequate & no one can without ruin remain here long. Imagine for one item, 18 English shillings for a turkey. Mr. Stevenson has certainly succeeded in gaining much popularity here among all classes. Even at the fountain of honour itself he has been honoured.

Nothing could be more gratifying and flattering than our visit to Windsor. Mr. Stevenson was requested every day whilst we stayed to lead her Majesty to dinner, and occupied the seat of honor at her right hand between the Queen and the Duchess of Kent. I have been often struck since I came to this country to see in every trying situation in which Mr. Stevenson has been placed how he has always risen equal to the occasion, and it amused me, who sat opposite, between Ld. Albemarle & Ld. Howick, to observe the progress of his tete-a-tete with these two illustrious persons. At first it was all etiquette, but soon it took a more easy and conversational turn, and before the dinner was over, she had asked him to take wine with her, and conversed without the slightest restraint of manner. Her laugh is to me particularly delightful, it is so full of girlish glee & gladness, whilst her countenance beams with such an expression of innocence & sweetness, so blended with the dignity and majesty of the Queen, that it would be impossible for a person ignorant of her high destinies not to be struck and impressed by her manners and appearance. But Mr. Stevenson has written so much about her to Mr. Ritchie & drawn so just a portrait of her that I must refer you to him. I think it deserves to be published.

We arrived at the castle about half-past 5, too late to see this glorious monument of the olden times & of royal magnificence. The lights, which gleamed from every part of the building, gave us the impression of its immense extent, and I felt an involuntary awe steal over me when I entered this royal residence, interesting not only from its historical associations and its magnificence, but as having been the theme of the historian and the inspiration of the poet. Little thought had I when with girlish delight I pored over Pope's beautiful verses addressed to

> Windsor, and its green retreats,
> At once the Monarch's and the Muses' seats,

that I should ever be an honored guest under its royal roof. But so it was, and I followed the respectful female who met us at the door with a beating heart. She led the way to a beautiful drawing-room, which she said, "Is yours, Madam," then on to a bedroom; "Yours, Madam"; then on to another one, which she said was Mr. Stevenson's with a dressing-room; and on a little further still a larger and more magnificent drawing-room, which she added was for His Excellency. These rooms, it seems, are always appropriated to the King of Belgium and his family, and are considered the handsomest in the castle except Her Majesty's.

We put on our best bib and tucker. Mr. Stevenson was dressed to perfection, and with Miss Murray, a maid of honor, to show us the way, we reached the receiving-room about 15 minutes before the Queen came out, followed by all her attendants. She approached me, and, extending her tiny white fingers, welcomed me to London, then Mr. S., and sent her gentleman-in-waiting to him to say she requested him to lead her to dinner. As she moved off, the band struck up, and it played all dinner-time, and, indeed, at intervals, all the evening. The party was large, although we were the only foreign ministers. All her home ministers were present, and Lord Melbourne sat on her left, and ate as heartily as though he was only seated by a milk-maid.

After dinner, she conversed with me about our friends in Scotland, &c. When the gentlemen came in, card-tables were set, and Mr. S. played at that with the Duchess of Kent. I had a seat near the Queen, and played chess part of the evening with Miss Murray. The parties here are much more informal than at Buckingham Palace. Her ladies all sat by a round table at work, and there was more conversation than in the parties at London. When she retired for the night, she requested Lady Tavistock, her lady-in-waiting, to return and say to me that she hoped I would take care of my cold, and have my breakfast in my rooms, if I preferred it. What charming courtesy and thoughtfulness in a royal woman, who is never allowed to have a thought for herself!

Feeling, however, anxious to see everything, I went out to breakfast, and found a pleasant party of some 24 or 30 persons, dropping in as they were ready. The Queen and the Duchess never appear until after lunch, when they come forth equipped for their ride or drive. After breakfast, Lady Tavistock took us with a large party to see the castle. Of all I saw I shall say nothing here; the castle is open to so many travelers that any one can tell of the windows, of the plate, of the rooms, and pictures, library, &c., but the private life of the Queen of London is a subject of interest and curiosity even to her own subjects of high rank who have not been among the chosen few. At 2 o'clock she came forth, and mounted her beautiful Arabian, and dashed off, followed by her numerous train, Mr. Stevenson among the number. Twenty miles in two hours! But such groaning and twisting for a week after you "never did see." Lady Tavistock (Ld. T. is the eldest son of the Duke of Bedford) and Lady Albemarle (Ld. Albemarle is the Master of the Horse, and I whispered him in private to order Mr. S. a gentle horse) and myself followed in a closed carriage, in consideration of my cold. After following for a little while, we struck off to Virginia Water, and visited the pavilion built by the luxurious George IV.

I had much conversation with the Baroness Lehzun, who always had the charge of the Queen. She says she is a most extraordinary person, and that her heart is as good, as pure, and innocent as her countenance indicates, and that she has a strength and vigor of intellect which is developing itself every day. Whilst we were talking about her on the second night of our stay, she approached and addressed me with an inquiry if I would play chess with her Master of the Household, the Hon. Mr. Murray. Miss M. had played with me the night before, and when I had seated myself near her, I said, "I hope I have Your Majesty's good wishes." To which she replied with the most sweet and winning smile. She said, when taking leave of us, that she was happy to have received us at Windsor, and hoped we would come again. We saw also a stag-hunt whilst we were at the castle, and a thousand other things I could tell you, but write in great haste and with many interruptions.

I have seen the two things I most desired in England— Windsor Castle as a visitor, and Christmas gambles in the country. On Christmas eve we had every sort of Christmas games—danced Jim Crow and quadrilles with the children, played at the "Emperor of Morocco is dead," made a "Knight of the Whistle" of Mr. Sheridan, the son of the celebrated man of that name, cut at the flour pudding, and it fell to my lot to put my mouth and nose in, snap-dragon, loto, &c. We children of the larger growth were quite as happy as the little ones. This is a delightful season in this country. My heart is open to charity, to love, and all the endearments of social and domestic life. Last night we were invited by the children to their school-room, which we found beautifully decorated with evergreens and flower-pots, &c., and a long table with little works made by the children as presents. We, the strangers in a strange land, were not forgotten, and had our offerings presented with such grace and kindness that my heart was quite touched. How beautiful is all this, and how many virtues are cultivated by the observance of this custom—industry, generosity, the forgetful-ness of self, the desire to please and give pleasure! If I had time, I could moralize for an hour upon this subject; but I must leave you for other things, and I dare say you are tired of all this.

XVI

Much cherished, even today, in Albemarle County, Virginia, is the story of how Sallie Coles Stevenson introduced a delicious Virginia apple to the British court, the same story she tells here, following an account of her trip to Paris.

To give background it should be told that on the hillsides around Enniscorthy, and up the flanks of the Blue Ridge, Virginia farmers were then growing a luscious, greenish, tasty apple, the Albemarle Pippin. The orchard at Enniscorthy was extensive.

Without plagiarizing Mrs. Stevenson's story it should be added that so appealing was this apple to the Queen's taste that Parliament, to please Her Majesty, permitted the Virginia fruit to enter Britain duty-free. For fifty years thereafter the Albemarle Pippin was the "Court apple." An orchard, near the top of the Blue Ridge, acquired considerable fame and a name as well, Royal Orchard, because for years it supplied her Royal Highness with Albemarle Pippins she loved so well.

London Febr 1838

My dear Sisters, & brothers—all—

On my return from Paris I found myself more in debt to Edward as a correspondent than any of my other friends. I therefore addressed my first letter to him the second to you,

& this is now my third. I requested Edward to forward mine to him, to Richmond, & to ask of you to do the same to Albemarle, & Carolina. I find, my dear Betsy, my friends to whom I write will do this, for if I am compelled to write to all, my health will suffer from the act of writing so much as I am forced to do, altho' there is not a week I do not write a long letter to some one of my family. This I assure you now forms, but a small item in the account, even to answer the notes in a London life is sufficient employment for one person, and yet I have all to do myself. Whilst I was in Paris, I wrote nothing but notes, and never was better in my life, altho' I was on my feet all day, and at balls, soirees, the opera &c &c almost every night untill one or two oclock in the morning, & sometimes at three parties on one night. Yet I continued well, but as soon as I returned to London & tied myself down to this eternal writing table, I am suffering from indigestion. Now dear sister I am flattered that you prize my scrawls & do not wish to part with them, but you must have the kindness to send copys or extracts—for if you love me as I believe you do, you should endeavour to keep up in the hearts of my dear family & friends those feelings which have constituted the great happiness of my life, and how can they know how I feel towards them now if they do not see what I intend for them. I know—& you know that in America we are very apt to think those who remain long in Europe, & especially in the atmosphere of a Court, may become affected, more or less, by its corrupting influence and a person so situated has a hard part to play. In your last of the 3d of Jany you say from my letters you infer that I am "not happy in Europe". They must have been very unfaithful transcripts of my feelings if they conveyed that impression to you. You should recollect that I have written to you at all times & in all moods—grave & gay, sad & merry— sick & well—& thus it has been with me here, as it would have been every where else—for my experience is, & I believe it will be that of most persons after a certain time of life, that in every situation there will be, as Thomas a Kempis says, "many adversities, and much trouble" that is the "royal way to Heaven". But the letter of mine to which you particularly allude was written at a time which has been to me now for many years one of deep & serious reflection the last of Sepr & first of October in which short space was comprised the happiest and most miserable events of my life. It is the aniversary as you know, of my marriage with the man of my choice, and of my devoted affection—of the birth of our child and of the awful event which took her from her Earthly to her Heavenly Parent, to that God whose very name her pious & innocent little heart had learnt to love & to adore. If you had thought of this dear sister you would not have been surprised that the spirit & tone of my letters at that time should have been more grave & sad than usual—besides, I was suffering at the time from indisposition, which you know always has more or less influence upon the most bouyant spirit—and when to all this you add a little pining after thee, my sister, and the other dear friends & relatives assembled at my mountain home can you wonder that my letters at that time were sad, & spiritless, but my husband soon after took me to Holkham where I again revived to health & cheerfulness and wrote you on my return a letter of 19 pages which I intended for all my family, and another in the same month quite as long describing the festival given in honour of the Queen, which was intended also to be a circular simply because I could write but one. Now, dear sister, I must thank you for all your kind schemes for my return. I hope we shall enjoy together all you have described but we must have a trio. Do you know I think, after your past experience, you are magnimous in your affection to offer to undertake to make me happy 3000 miles away from my husband. No, dear sister the post of duty for me is at my husband side, even tho' I had found it disagreeable, still with my own consent I would never leave him, especially in a foreign country where we are all the world to each other. But you are mistaken in supposing, upon the whole, that I am not happy here, I have had every thing to please and gratify me both for myself & my husband, Providence has raised us up friends, & kind friends too among the best & noblest of the land—and I hear from various sources, no foreign minister, & his wife, were ever so popular, or had

(*121*)

ever received such attentions, notwithstanding, we often cast longing, lingering looks towards those we have left behind us and I feel I should not be content to spend a long period of my life in such a round of gaiety, & in pursuits so uncongenial to my natural taste & to the acquired habits of the last years of my life. I think of you dear Tuti and almost envy you the power of doing so much good, surrounded by a family who adore you, by friends who love & respect you, with the means & the leisure, to dispense blessings & comforts to the poor & miserable. To feed the hungry—cloth the naked—& instruct the ignorant—a fit preparation for that better world to which we are all hastening, and for which we ought all to be prepared, as we know not at what hour we may be called. I was kept awake last night by thoughts like these, it was the Sabbath night, and I had been in my room all day & refused myself to visitors, because I had to dine in the evening at Lord Hollands. After dinner Lady Landsdowne who also dined there, said something about the chime of a clock, & Lady Holland replied, with the most animated look of pleasure, "Well Lady Landsdowne will you believe, I have had the resolution to countermand my clock. Lord Holland knowing my desire to possess one which played a particular chime, ordered it, but I without his knowledge have written to say it must not be sent, & given the money to three parishes in cloths, food, blankets, & fire! & this the act of a woman whom the world calls heartless! True, I would rather have heard it from any one else, still it was told in a manner so easy & unaffected that it touched me deeply—nor did it lessen the value of the act in my eyes when I looked around & saw it would have been a luxury not a necessity. In your letter of Novr 21st which I received in Paris you mention something Wykoff had told you. It was to gloss over some of his misdeeds I dare say. He is a young man of whom we know nothing, except a strong letter of recommendation from our Minister to Russia Mr. Wilkins and a request that he might be attached to the Legation which after some time & some hesitation Mr. Stevenson did, against his will, & his better judgement, just as the kindness of his heart had induced him to do with regard to Fay. We soon found him unworthy of the situation but he was a person who never interested me sufficiently to write about & with whom we never held more intercourse than we could avoid.

I wrote this dear affec brother a long & detailed account of the first two weeks of my visit to Paris & should have concluded to him, but Mr. Stevenson came up & told me it was dispatch day & I must conclude, & as he has every thing to do himself since our return from France, I could not make him wait a moment. Poor Ben Rush has had the small pox dreadfully, & is still confined tho' out of danger. As to Richard Vaux, we know not where he is or what has become of him and I feel very anxious about him. His last letter was from Florence.

And to you my other dear & precious friends on the Green Mountain, I must offer our united thanks for your kind remembrance of us. On our return from Paris we found here three barrels one containing hams which we have tried and found excellent. The other apples, one was good for nothing, the other which was wrapped in paper every separate apple, came in as good a state of preservation as we have generally received them in Richmond, and never did a barrel of apples obtain so much reputation for the fruits of our country. They were eaten & praised by Royal lips, and swallowed by many aristocratic throats. Mr. Stevenson proposed sending two dozen to the Queen, accordingly they were put into a beautiful basket he had given me, and one of the maids of Honour presented them. In a day or two I received through the Countess of Durham the royal acknowledgement and the assurance of their having been much admired—& dining with Lord Durham soon after, he told me my apples had created a great sensation at the Palace, that it had been feared they would have been the death of the Premier, Lord Melborne, who after the Queen retired, had actually eaten two of immense size, & that all who had seen him perpetrate the rash act had considered him as a dead man but lo! he lived unharmed. I said so much for their being Virginia apples. We sent also two dozen to the Duke of Sussex—one to Lord & Lady Sherbourne—½ doz to Lord

Palmerston, & 6 to a score of people not omitting my favorite friend & poet—Rogers—& his amiable sister. After having given them all away we dined with Mr. Ellice (a person of high tone whose wife was sister to Lord Grey) & he asked me if I had one left to send it to him. I was gratified on my return home to find three very inferior which, however, I sent him. As Julia is the only one who mentioned having sent us apples, I presume we are indebted to her kindness for having put them up with such care. I think I recognized Helen's hand writing on the barrel containing the hams. To whoever we owe these kind & acceptable attentions we return many, many thanks. I must not however forget to tell you, the Duchess of Kent took such a fancy to my nice little basket, that she asked permission to keep it, thinking it American manufacture.

I have said nothing to you of our trip to France, because I have been so hurried & occupied this week that I was afraid I should not have time to answer your letters & say any thing about it, but as I have still a few hours, which may be uninterrupted I will tell you what remains to be said on the subject as the letter of 8 pages which I wrote you last week met with an unlucky fate which will prevent your ever receiving it. In a very long one to Edward, I told him of our gratifying reception at Gen. Cass' & of the hospitable ruse he played upon us to get us to his house, of the flattering attentions received from every one, from Royalty down. The Duke of Sussex insisted on giving us a letter to his personal friend Louis Phillippe, and we were much at the Palace, to two receptions— a grand ball, & concert where we had the pleasure to hear some of the most celebrated Italian singers—temporary orchestras were erected in the Salle des Marechaux, (the most magnificent apartment in this truly royal residence) and the royal family with the ladies of the foreign ministers sat in a row within a few paces of the performers, so that I could see every variation in the fine & expressive countenance of Mademoiselle Grisi— Madame Persiani Tachinardi who sang for the first time at Court, and who felt or affected much agitation. Rubini with his powerful voice, & Dupres with his fine thrilling notes. The company was brilliant & numerous and the royal party circulated amongst their guest during the intervals between each piece of music. We also dined at the Tuilleries the finest entertainment I ever saw, the Salle a manger is more magnificent than the Buckingham Palace, and the whole effect was more striking, but of all this I have written already. I also mentioned to Edward the great civilities of the Granduilles, the Thorns—&c &c. The latter took us in his beautiful carriage & four with out riders in royal stile to Versailles. Louis Philippe as you know has restored this Palace to more than its former magnificence and given it the title of the Musée Historique, and dedicated it, "A toutes les gloires de la France". They say it is to conciliate the national vanity, & the national taste of his restless subjects and to give them something to occupy them. Whatever the object the effect is to realize all the splendours of the Arabian Nights. We were between four & five hours going over this superb Palace, without pausing to dwell upon its glorious & touching recollections. We passed through the apartment from which Marie Antoinette made her escape to die with her husband—& where her faithful attendants sacrificed their lives to save her. The room in which the grand monarch Louis the 14 expired &c &c. After traversing countless rooms—galleries, &c, &c, we walked over the beautiful gardens—but I must not leave the Palace without mentioning a work of the princess Marie, Louis Philippe's daughter, who has lately married the Duke of Wurtemburg. It is a beautiful statue of Joan of Arc, executed by the princess' own hand & designed by her own fine taste, but only to think of such a work as this to be done by a woman, & a princess. Col. Thorn took us to a Caffe and ordered some bouillion, or I believe I should not have held out for the remainder of the days work. We stoped on our return to Paris (12 miles) to see the manfuactory of Sevres china, & at St. Cloud, Bonaparte's favorite residence. We got back just in time to make a hasty toilet for a grand dinner at the Gen's to all the Americans. Dont you think I must have gained a great deal of strength for all this, for besides the physical exertion there is so much excitement always in sight-

seeing—The Gen. entertains very handsomely, altho' he had
never given but one dinner untill our visit. He says his salary
gives him his empty house, & carriage & horses, the furnishing
his hotel he told me had cost him 10,000 dollars & he thought
it cheap at that. The ornaments of his table alone, cost 1200 $
besides, the china, glass, plate, &c, I should say from the stile
in which they live that they must be very wealthy. They gave
three large dinners whilst we were there, to the Diplomats, &c,
& a soiree once a week. We found them most amiable, charming,
& hospitable, and our visit was one of the pleasantest we ever
made. Mrs. Cass was like an affec sister to me & her girls devoted—indeed I have not been such a belle since I was gay 18.
The attache's to the Legation are fine young men & young
Cass the Gen's nephew one of the most interesting youths I
ever saw. But I cannot close the account of my visit to Paris
without saying something of the sights of this most interesting
Capital, besides, it will give you some idea of my acquired
powers of endurance, for the Versailles expedition was nothing
to another day of sight-seeing we were fortunate in selecting
the finest days for our excursions, & one of the brightest, &
warmest we felt in France, we commenced at eleven with Dr.
Stewart, (a friend of Edwards, & now attached to our Legation,
and about to attach himself to a very charming wife a Miss
Fisher with whom we crossed the ocean.) At the Bourse, I
believe this is the way it is spelt where the gentlemen got out,
but I had no desire to see the self-destroyer. Then to the
venerable Notre Dame and stood on the very spot, (marked on
the floor,) where Bonnaparte was crowned Emperor of the
French, and where he placed the crown on the head of his
faithful, devoted and—deserted—Josephine—I wrapped myself
in the gorgeous robes worn by him on his coronation, & Mr.
Stevenson sat himself in the coronation chair. We saw the
cushion which had borne his jewelled crown. What a lesson
to the ever-weaning ambition of man is the fate of this most
singular being—whom Providence seems to have sent "To
teach a moral, & adorn a tale"—I dont know why, but I have
always had a feeling of hostility in my heart against this cruel

man, this heartless husband, even in my girlhood, his glory never dazzled me, and when I was in Paris I felt no enthusiasm for him, or for his works; in the Place Vendome I looked with perfect indifference upon the splendid monument erected to his glory—but to return to my day of sight-seeing —from the church we went to the Hotel Dieu, an institution most honourable to the French, then walked all over the Gardin du plants, the museum, &c. This garden resembles very much the Zoological here—from the garden of Plants we visited the site of the Bastille, where Bonnaparte commenced a monument & Louis Philippe is now erecting another—and lastly to Pere le Chaise—I cannot tell you how pleasingly this last home of the French affected me. They have contrived with their characteristic cheerfulness to mingle pleasant associations even with the grave. They ornament the tombs of their departed friends with garlands of flowers and on New Years Day I am told the place is crowded with the friends who come to bring fresh garlands & to renew their tender recollections. We were much affected by seeing at the splendid monument of a son, who had fallen in battle, the venerable father cleaning away the snow with pious care, as a thing too sacred to be done by common hands. We stood by the tomb of Eliza of Abelard, and Mr. Stevenson was guilty of the romantic theft of bringing away with him two garlands from the sculptured figures of the hapless lovers. We walked all over this extensive place, & returned just in time to dress to go out to dinner, whilst Mr. Stevenson was adjusting his french collar, he suddenly exclaimed he had a needle in his foot (five days before he thought he had broken one in his heel) I felt at first dismayed, & thought of poor Dr. Blair, but to the dinner we went, and afterwards Mr. S. accompanied Col. Thorn to the French Opera, I declined thinking I had done enough, but scarcely had I sunk to sleep, when he came in, & you would have thought his last hour had come. I called up my faithful Dunn, & her eyes being the youngest she undertook the operation, whilst I held the candle on my knees. After some cutting & a good deal of picking she drew forth the half needle which had been there for 5 days. I never uttered a more heartfelt "Thank God!" and he has never felt any more inconvenience from it. What a mercy! But truly dear sisters I may say, goodness & mercy has followed me all the days of my life, and especially since most of my earthly props have been withdrawn. My heart is full, & my eyes overflow when I think how His loving kindness has been around me, & mine. I found much comfort in Mrs. Cass' society in this respect, we often met over her fire, or mine to talk over these things which are not heard of in the societies of Paris, and on Saturday nights we stole off together, to hear a Mr. Baird, a sensible pious, & eloquent man who received his American friends up 4 flights of steps & these not short ones. Still it was pleasant & refreshing to hear the Word of God, & feel oneself a little nearer Heaven. We went every Sunday to Col. Thorn's chapel where we had the satisfaction to hear a very good preacher. Col. lives is a palace belonging to Madame Abelard which is truly a royal residence, and he has furnished it magnificently. He loaded us with civilities and kindnesses of every sort & through him the celebrated Talleyrand the servant of so many masters & the present wonder of the age, sent to offer Mr. Stevenson a dinner at his house. To dine with Talleyrand! think of that & to be obliged to refuse, but Mr. S. had heard of the disturbances in Canada, & the United States, and thought it his duty to hasten back to London, where we arrived on the 2d of Feby after a cold and somewhat trying journey to me, and since my return I have had no rest or quiet to recover from the effects of the fatigue. I wrote Edward when I really felt so much worn out with my month in Paris & the journey together, that I could scarcely set up. I believe dear Sall, there was a good deal of bad spelling & writing too, I recollected afterwards several things which I intended correcting but really I had not time nor energy to read it over, when it comes into your hands put it to rights, will you? It will be a good exercise for you. I believe I spelt "Salle des Marechaux" half English half French, but I do not recollect. I find the dispatch does not close untill tomorrow, so that I can add a little more, in the morning, now I must bid you adieu as we are to dine with the

Duke of Sussex today & on Thursday Friday & Saturday we dine out, & for Saturday we have had only three invitations, & on Friday we have not only the dinner but a grand ball at the Russian Ministers, Porzi de Borgo's, and among the diplomats it is considered a violation of etiquette not to go if you are not ill in bed. You see I do not exagerate my engagements, altho' there are a thousand things I have to do, which I cannot even make you understand without too much circumlocution— and this is said to be the dull time. The season has not yet commenced. On looking over this long scrawl I find there are many things I have omitted to mention. I have not said a word about the Louvre that glory of Paris—the Palais Royal, the Palace of the Luxembourge, which contains, besides its fine paintings, the apartments of Mary de Medicis, the wife of Henry the 4th, her bed chamber is gorgeous in its decorations, and the ceiling painted by Reubens whom she patronized. The Chamber of Peers is also in this Palace, but not, I think, as striking in its appearance as our Senate Chamber, and as to the Chamber of Deputies it is not to be compared to the Hall of Representatives. But I do not mean to inflict upon you any descriptions of these things, indeed, I never design to do more than give my impressions of what I see, two of my brothers, I know, will be amused in having these objects recalled to their recollections, and I hope it may inspire the wish to see them in those who have not. I forgot to mention when speaking of Bonnaparte that we saw his sister the ex-Queen of Naples, (Caroline) a friend of Mr. Stevenson's carried him to see her and she received him with marked attention, when he was about to take leave she requested one of her attendants to bring her a little cabinet from which she took a bronze likeness of Napoleon, & presented it to Mr. Stevenson as the representative of a country which had always befriended her family & being therefore the person most worthy to receive the best likeness of Bonnaparte ever taken. Me, she kissed most affecy as the French do upon both sides of my face. She is very like the bust of her brother—But really I must hasten to conclude this long scrawl, altho' I have still many things to say, which I must, however, defer untill we meet. Heigho! how cruelly you have all disappointed me in not coming out! I dare not trust myself to think of it. I had formed such charming plans— now—I know not what we shall do—but I have a presentiment, that it will not be very long, before we meet, if it please God we live—But I try to be anxious for nothing but humbly to resign myself to that wise Providence which does all things well. We often wished for you, my dear Bett in Paris, as indeed, we always do when we enjoy any thing, as to you dear brother John, I can tell you Mr. Stevenson has treasured up some nice French anecdotes for you, which I can neither tell or write. Often in France, he exclaimed, "How I shall make Col John laugh"! Indeed, he has something in this way to suit the taste of all the family—but I think he has murderous designs upon brother John, and "Mrs. Julia". We often thought and talked about you all, in Paris and wished for the Philosophers Stone that we might have bought all the pretty things we thought would be most acceptable to our dear friends at home. Most things are so much cheaper & handsomer in France— we regretted that our friends had not given us commissions. Pray keep this in mind, shoes, boots, glass, &c, &c. We may still have it in our power to serve you before we leave Europe, if you will send your measures. Remember, I address this to all North—South—East—West—and do dear Bett say it to the Ritchie's. Our kind and good friend the Enquirer will be delighted to hear of the honours, which the City of London are about to bestow upon his friend the American Minister. You have no idea what a sensation it has produced here, the English offer their congratulations upon it as something to be very proud of, & the Americans hold their heads at least an inch higher. The diplomats shake hands, & say—"You are the man, Sir". Such a distinguished honour has never before been offered to any foreigner, except crowned heads, and the manner of it is even more flattering, if possible, than the thing itself, for it is offered as a mark of personal respect and esteem. The Deputation was here yesterday, to offer him the freedom of the City, in a gold box with 200 guineas. On his declining to accept, they have resolved to frame the resolutions, & present them to him. The Duke of Sussex thought he ought to accept, upon the condition of its meeting the approbation of the "powers that be at home". He (the Duke) made a most beautiful little speach yesterday after the ladies retired from the dinner table, which Mr. King (the son of old Rufus, & who was invited as Mr. Stevenson's friend,) said, was most friendly to our country, and most flattering to its Minister. Nothing can exceed the kindness of this delightful old man. To me his manner becomes every time I see him more like that of a kind & affec relative—but to return to the box. I should have liked the gold box, would you not, dear Tute? Mr. Stevenson says, Betsy will be delighted! As to Emm, since her beautiful letter four months ago, she has become dumb as the Delphic Oracle. I hope Mr. Ritchie will approve. I am sure he will—it will, I think, be very hard if every body does not. At least he has acted up to the strick republican institutions of the country he has so faithfully—and I say—and the citizens of London say, so ably served. And now I will say Adieu! Remember Sall, you & John are to copy my letters if Aunt Betsy, dear Aunt Betsy chooses to keep them, for I know she is injured by so much writing as well as myself. Write to Mrs. Madison for me dear Bett, and tell her I have written her twice since I have heard from her, and that I love her & think of her most affy, however I shall write myself again as soon as I get time, but when will that be? Also to my dear John Carter, poor fellow! Mr. Tucker of the U. write Mr. S. that all was over with poor Ellen! He has just received the letter by a late packet—two in, and no letter for me. Heigho!!!

XVII

Mrs. Stevenson's letters are flecked with bits of the royal byplay. At this time, in 1838, Victoria's coronation loomed just ahead, two months to the day, and Britain's youthful Queen bubbled with energy. Queen though she was, carefully sheltered by her Duchess mother, Victoria enjoyed the same pleasures as any normal lively young woman of eighteen.

London May 15, 1838

I wrote you, beloved sisters, on the 27th of April, just before I went to Mrs. Marryat's, where I spent four or five days very pleasantly, and returned much improved, but not quite well enough to stand three or four hours on my feet at the drawing-room, so that I was forced to disappoint Mrs. Ludlow, who had her dress all ready for the presentation. I have, however, been dining out occasionally, and ventured out to the Queen's ball on the 10th, which was very crowded and brilliant. We retired before 12, but Lady Lansdowne told me she remained with the Queen until 4 o'clock in the morning, and that the sun was shining beautifully as she returned through Hyde Park about 5, half dead. The Queen danced every quadrille, and said the next morning that she had enjoyed herself very much. She received me very graciously, and said she was delighted to see me looking so well. The Duchess of Kent gave me her hand and said, "Do take care of yourself this cold night," and inquired after my health as if she really took an interest in it.

I can give you no idea of London now. The streets & parks are crowded like the ballroom & I sometimes get jammed up in a fashionable street. Hyde Park is a spectacle to a foreigner, such splendid equipages, liveries &c. &c. so many beautiful women on horseback and dashing beaux. The routs are formidable. Mr. Stevenson goes to them. I do not venture often. The dinner parties are pleasant if they did not last so long. I dined last week at the Rothchilds, the Marquess of Sligo's where I met a very distinguished party & was led to dinner by the Duke of Cleveland and sat between him and the Marquess of Lansdowne.

XVIII

MRS. STEVENSON kept a sort of diary, or running datebook—since lost—in which she jotted down all she did and the names of the people she met. She saw so much grandeur she was afraid she would miss a detail in writing home.

This letter tells of meeting Bulwer-Lytton, the novelist, and Tom Moore, the poet. It comments also on the habits of the ladies in the upper realms of fashionable London.

Lord Holland to whom she refers was a notable figure in aristocratic and political circles. His dinners at Holland House were justly famous.

Thomas Moore whom Mrs. Stevenson met at Lady Lansdowne's rout was the famous Irish poet, much beloved in England, much in demand socially. Forgotten, perhaps, was his visit to America in 1804 when he lampooned President Jefferson, but Moore had long since apologized for this affront to the young nation. His "Believe me if all those endearing young charms" had endeared him to thousands.

Sydney Smith, mentioned in this letter, was the young Canon of St. Paul's. His social charm and ready wit brought him much fame. The Stevensons were to meet him often on many social occasions. Sydney Smith was a "must" at great dinner parties and weekends at famous country homes.

Prince George of Cambridge with whom Victoria danced the quadrille was her first cousin, son of George III's seventh son, Adolphus, Duke of Cambridge.

It would, I am sure, be a sufficient reward to your kind heart, dearest J——, if you could know only half the pleasure you imparted to mine by your most welcome letter of April the 14th which I did not receive in time to answer by the last packet; but I send you a number of the Court Journal, with notes, which would give you some idea of how I am employed in this gay world of London. We are now in the midst of the "Season" as it is called & one must be "seasoned" to it to get through with life—either temporal or spiritual.

My health has been so delicate since my return from Paris; indeed so much so, at one time, that Mr. Stevenson called in to consult with the physician who is attached to the Legation [Dr. Booth] the celebrated Dr. Chambers. Since then, I have been better, and am now almost as strong as ever, altho the life I am obliged to lead here is not very favourable to an invalid.

I continue, however, to save myself as much as possible by being out to midnight routs as little as I can to save appearances, then staying as short a time as possible, although that is not in our power, as it happened to us the other night at Landsdowne House, where we were kept until after three o'clock in the morning before we could get away. We were one hour (some persons two) getting to the door, one more in squeezing our way through crowded apartments to the grand statue-room, where we found Lady Lansdowne and some members of the royal family. Many persons who were there did not see the hostess at all. We were more than one hour in getting from this room to the salle a manger, where a sumptuous supper was provided. The most agreeable incident in the evening was the introduction to Bulwer the novelist. We searched an hour in the unrobing-room for my wrappings, and then waited until it was broad day for the carriage. Sixteen hundred invitations were sent out. And this is pleasure! All this fatigue I endured after being in the drawing-room in the morning,—the birthday, —and the most splendid that has been given. The display of diamonds and jewelry was beyond my power of description. There was a Count Zethy, an Austrian, literally covered with precious stones, and even in that splendid assembly he was gazed upon as a lion. The little Queen looked very sweet, and when I presented myself, she said: "I am so happy to see you. I hope you are better, and took no cold at my ball." She is acquiring a great deal more of confidence and ease of manner, and has won golden opinions from all parties. The wonder is how she can be so discreet—so self-possessed and so thoughtful of others. You saw the account of her ball in the "Court Journal" I sent you. Dear little thing! She danced with all her heart, and said the next day she had been "so happy." Poor Lady Lansdowne, who was in waiting, said she was half-dead. I dined with her a day or two after at the Marquess of Sligo's, and she told us that she had never seen St. Paul's to advantage until the morning after the Queen's ball, when she had admired it from St. James' Park at five o'clock in the morning. We met a very distinguished party at the Marquess'; and Mr. S. and myself became so much acquainted with the Duke of Cleveland that he invited us to one of his splendid castles on the way to Scotland.

I wrote B—— that I had been spending a week in the country with Mrs. Marryat, the Mother of Capt. Marryat the novelist. She owns one of the most beautiful villa's in England, about 10 or twelve miles from London at Wimbleton. Her garden is quite a show place, & it is said she has spent eight thousand a year on it. Indeed the grounds, the house, & whole establishment are perfect in its way. She is an American lady by birth from Boston, & her husband amassed a large fortune after she married him; and with his money & her taste she has made Wimbledon House a little Paradise. She is now a widow, with several children, & lives in retirement, employing herself in good works; and in the pious discharge of all her duties, she finds contentment & happiness. To us she has been very kind. Seeing me so ill & languid, she invited me, altho' almost a stranger, to spend a week with her (for in this country persons specify not only the time but the length of their visit) and after

I entered the house the only ceremony was used towards me was for the lady of the mansion to show me to my rooms. After that, I did as I pleased, took breakfast in my dressing room when I liked, or went down to prayers. I was always sure of finding some of the family or the guests in the library, the common sitting room, & I either remained there, or went to my room, or took a walk in the grounds. I was however, too much of an invalid to do much at that; and Mrs. Marryat had her garden chair brought to the door for me, a delightful little carriage, drawn by a footman, & in which I went two or three miles, around the garden & grounds. I thought of you all dear sisters, how you would have enjoyed it, & how many hints you might have taken in the art of turning deformities into beauties. Stumps & stones into objects of embellishment. Dear H—— what a treasure of knowledge it would be to her.

If you knew dear G——, with what interruptions I write, you would wonder how I could put intelligible sentences together. At this time London large as it is seems too small to hold all the people that are crowding its streets & parks. Hyde Park presents one of the most brilliant & animating scenes. You can imagine splendid equipages drawn by the most beautiful horses, with liveried servants behind & before; beautiful ladies, dressed with the most exquisite taste & fashion lolling in open carriages—& the only signs of animation & life, they give, are an occasional bow or smile to a passing acquaintance; young ladies on horseback, in their peculiar & graceful costume, longcloth riding habits, and little round hats; dandies of all sorts & sizes. & one who is new to this scene is astonished that no accidents happen in such a throng—I go occasionally in our open carriage to look on, but soon tire of the confusion, & order my carriage to the more quiet & rural looking Regents Park. The life of a real woman of fashion here is laborious beyond anything—to rise at eleven or twelve, (but more frequently one or two) breakfast in her dressing room, go out at three to a concert or to the Park, to exhibit their languid graces, dine at eight—& go to the Opera & three & four parties besides until five in the morning! Most horrible! To go to bed when the glorious sun is rising—and that too, in a country where there is so little sunshine! Once since I have been here I came very near it, and it made me so nervous I could not get to sleep & felt as if I had been doing something very wicked. It is amazing how rational beings can so pervert the objects of existence, & change the order of Nature! How often in these dark & murky mornings, do I think of the May mornings of my youth when I stole forth to the dairy & the garden, blither than the birds that carrolled their gay songs around me. Then life itself was new, & the heart promised what the fancy drew; and now, after seeing what may be called the world, & all its splendours, my heart still sighs for the simple & natural pleasures of life— and I must be permitted to repeat what I have so often said to you my sister, that you ought to be the happiest woman in the world, with such a husband, such children, such a home, & health & spirits to enjoy all. What can this world give more? Heaven alone is happier!

Now, dear G—— I am afraid you will think my letter most unreasonably long, but as it will probably find all my family assembled in the dear old mountain, you must allow me to write you all I have to say, & divide it with my dear B—— & N—— who will no doubt be with you, & any other of my friends who may find any interest in my long & rambling scrawls; for scrawls, they truly are—written sometimes from my sofa—sometimes from my knee, & at all times & in any half hour which I can snatch from the bewilderments of a London life. On looking over my diary, I find a notice of a dinner which may amuse you. These are the most agreeable & richerche parties which are given—the aristocratic dinners. They are conducted with such ease, & so little effort, & much pains is taken to asort the company, & to obtain stars, who shine either from the brightness of their wit & genius, or from the splendour of their rank. The one to which I allude was graced by some of the most remarkable men now living, Sidney Smith, cele- brated for his wit & conversational powers:—Rogers, with his mild, bland, & courteous manners, with all his refinement & gentleness, every now & then saying something so brilliant &

piquant, that it is not wonderful his society should be so much sought after. And who else do you think was there? Why little Tom Moore! Never was I more astonished to see anyone. I had expected a little wrinkled old man, when Mr. Rogers brought up & introduced to me this "Sweet son of song", a nice trim looking person, of no particular age, with a fresh & ruddy countenance, and eyes so brilliant, & so joyous, that I should have known they could belong to no common person. He talked to me of America & his reminiscences,—Said he understood it was no longer the same country he had visited &c. At dinner, the topics were all light, gay & pleasant, Sidney Smith said, "Why, Moore, have you seen that, in the life of Wilberforce, they say your eyes have more of joy than sensibility in them," To this Lady Holland (who made one of the company) replied, in her emphatic manner: "Sensibility"! Why sensibility is a very mawkish thing, & who would expect to see that in Moore's eyes;" at which the poet laughed heartily, showing teeth which many a youthful Adonis might desire to possess. Lord Holland is so infirm from the gout that he cannot walk without crutches, & is wheeled about in his chair, notwithstanding he is always the gayest person present, and, as he sat by the grave & sombre Lord Lansdowne, they presented a striking contrast. The latter, however, is not always, like Lord Holland, in the same humour; for I have seen him sometimes grave, & sometimes gay: but, on the serene brow of Lord Holland, dwells perpetual sunshine. His wife told us, after dinner, she had never seen him out of temper but once in his life, & then, she had been the cause: that he arose in the morning, gay as a bird, and that nothing ever ruffled him; & she added, he is not only happy himself, but the cause of happiness to all around him. It is wonderful to see to what extreme old age life is enjoyed here. Lord & Lady Holland, infirm as they both are, never dine alone—that is to say—they have a dinner party every day, altho Ld. H——— dined early & alone; but he always sits at his table & sees others enjoy his delicious viands, whilst he can only enjoy the "feast of reason",—What would you think to see women seventy six years old, dressed in the height of the time, bare necks & arms, feathers, & flowers: yet, so it is. At the Drawing Room, the other day, the Duchess Countess of Sutherland 76—was dressed in a richly embroidered white satin dress, a train of crimson velvet, bound round with a gold band, the width of three fingers, on her head a little velvet cap with gold bands, & feathers, & diamonds of inestimable value; and I assure you, the dress was very becoming, & she looked thirty years younger. At the Queens ball, she wore a white satin richly embroidered, before & round the skirt, with gold, & on her head, a turban of golden tissue with feathers & diamonds. She is however, a nice old lady, & I like her very much.

By the by, I think I must give you some description of a court ball, having in my last letter given you a court dinner. We have been to two balls this season. To the first Mr. Stevenson went with us, and he was in such a hurry to be off we saw nothing; but to the last he refused to go, and Messrs. Rush, Vaux, and Livingston went with me. All of us resolved to see everything and enjoy everything we could; accordingly we found ourselves at the palace gates before they opened at half-past nine. (Royal parties are always early.) We waited until a few carriages of the nobility had passed in, and then we made our appearance at the entrance. We found some acquaintances on the grand staircase, and followed fast behind the Duchess Countess, and her daughter, the Countess of Surrey. The former inquired if the young gentlemen who were with me were Americans, and I asked permission to introduce them. Mr. Rush she had known during his residence here, & was very civil to his son. She enquired, after a little while, if I would like to see the finest diamonds in the world, & when I answered in the affirmative, she introduced me to the Marchioness of Westminster, who had diamonds in her ears as large as ninepence, & one in the front of her dress as large as a quarter of a dollar, besides necklace, & a tiara on her head. On something being said about the fear of losing anything so valuable, the old Duchess jested most amusingly upon the chance of her getting them for me to exhibit in America. We had the pleasure of promenading through the splendid apartments and of seeing all the well-dressed dames & demoiselles, and then we enjoyed the luxury of a sofa until just before the Queen appeared, when all the company formed into two lines from one door of the grand saloon to the other, so that when the Queen entered by the mirrored door at one end she passed down the file of persons on each side. We of the embassy stood together and received her particular notice. When she had passed into the next room, we followed, and saw the first quadrille danced. Her Majesty chooses her own partners and those who are to stand opposite to her, that her hand may not touch that of any one but those she likes. She danced with Prince George of Cambridge, & the Princess Augusta of Cambridge stood opposite, with some high sprig of nobility as her partner. The Queen danced very gracefully & without effort, and her little person appears to great advantage from the perfect taste in which she dresses. She always wears the Order of the Bath over her bosom, which is fastened on the left shoulder with a band of diamonds & looks graceful and royal. Indeed, there is a queenly dignity, a ladylike sweetness in the air and manner of this young Queen that is very striking. She is always attended in public by two little pages, sons of noblemen, who are dressed in the court costume, with swords at their sides; besides her officers of state, the gold stick and the silver stick in waiting. Noblemen of rank, who have rods, which they hold before them, and Her Majesty's Lord Chamberlain always precede her when she moves from room to room. All this seems very ridiculous to us republicans, but royalty, after all, you know, is but a pageant, & take from it the pride, pomp, and circumstance of state, & what would it be? In both the salons de dance there were places elevated for the seats of the royal family, in front of which the Queen stood to dance, & when it was over, she ascended to her chair, & received the homage of her subjects. But I have bought another "Court Journal" to send you, which will give you a better account of all these things. At one o'clock the Queen made a move towards the supper-room, and the band struck up "God save the Queen." At two, immediately after the supper, I made

my escape, after loitering an hour in admiring the decorations
of the tables, wine, &c., and talking to such of my acquaintances
as I met there, among the number Lady George Murray,
dressed in an Irish dress of such brilliant texture that it attracted my attention, in the midst of so much splendor. When I
approached her, & met her smiling, benevolent face, I exclaimed,
"Can this be you!" "Yes," she replied; "I shall be seventy-seven
my next birthday & I have strength and spirit still to enjoy this
scene." Shortly after, I encountered Lady Clarendon, some few
years Lady George's senior, with a figure as good and as youthful as any woman of twenty in the room. But, alas! the poor
old lady is rather blind, & she puts on her rouge in a daub from
her eyes to her chin. So you see, my dear sisters, if you will
come to old England, we shall all become Hebes again. You
cannot imagine how much I have been disappointed at not
seeing any of you this spring. I calculated certainly on dear,
dear B——. I thought she could not, or rather I hoped she
would not, live longer without me, and the coronation presented
so much attraction for us, as we were sure of seeing some of
you. Heighho!—Lord Lansdowne enquired of me, the other
day, if any of my friends were coming over to the spectacle,
and added, he supposed it would have no attraction for us, I
replied, "It was, on the contrary, the very thing to attract us,
as we were sure of not seeing it in our own country." He
laughed & said; "Capital"! I forgot to mention a remark of
Lady Hollands about the Queen, which struck me at the time,
& has remained in my memory. She said "The young Queen
possessed a magazine of thoughts, which was quite astonishing
in one so young and inexperienced! Great preparations are
making for the coronation, Marshal Soult has taken the house
just opposite us, and gives for four or five weeks sixteen
hundred pounds. I really think our government ought to make
us an additional allowance for the occasion, as they send no
one over. It is said the expense of everything will be beyond
belief. The markets have already risen in anticipation to sound
like a fiction in our country. It is however a most interesting
period to be here. I have not only sent messages to you all to

urge your coming, but to say for Mr S— and myself, that if we can do anything for any member of our family, we beg you all to command us. Many things here, are so much better & cheaper than with you, especially cloth & linens, shoes boots & gloves in Paris—Oh! how I did wish for "Midas power", when I was in the midst of so many pretty things. But poverty in Europe is a sad thing—for myself I do not covet so much, but for the pleasure of giving to those I love. I had written thus far, when Mr S—— came up to say that Tom Moore was in the drawing room, & I must hasten down & I have now just returned from a long colloquy with the little poet. He is very little indeed, but his eyes are so fine, & he has quite a poetical mouth & talks very agreeably. We had invited him to dine with us to meet the Ticknors from Boston, & some English persons of distinction, & much to our regret, he came to say he was engaged, & had tried his best to get off & come to us, but could not. He has promised to sing for me at some future time, & says he will get his voice in time especially for me. He looks something like a humming bird. He said, "Old as he was, he still felt nervous as he attempted to sing, and that he could not always command his voice," I wrote B—— that I had seen Southy—breakfasted with him—Wordsworth—Rodgers—Campbell—now, little Tom Moore, besides many more minor poets whose names perhaps, are destined to fill the Trump of Fame.

Mr. Rush has just sent up to say it is dispatch day, & I must make haste with my letter, but I have still a thousand things to say and if I obeyed the dictates of my heart would send a thousand messages to all my dear friends on the old mountain. Dear B—— in one of her letters tells me that little Guy looks every day for London where dear Aunt S—— is. Shall I confess to you this drew from me tears, but not of bitterness—God bless, the dear little Angel. Say to B—— & E—— that I intend this scrawl partly for them. God bless you all dear, dear friends, your own devoted sister

S. C. Stevenson

XIX

AMERICAN CELEBRITIES flocked to London in June, 1838, for Queen Victoria's coronation. Not in generations had Britain crowned a queen as monarch. London resembled a gigantic fairytale brought to life. Visiting kings and princes arrived by dozens arrayed like rainbows.

In this letter to her sister-in-law, Helen Skipwith Coles, wife of her brother, Tucker Coles, of Tallwood, Virginia, Mrs. Stevenson recaptures the brilliant scene. This is perhaps the finest letter she ever wrote.

The American Legation at 23 Portland Place was swamped. Armed with letters of introduction from Very Important People back home hundreds of Americans crowded into the Legation with a single objective: tickets for the dazzling show soon to be staged in Westminster Abbey. Admittance was all but priceless, and the Stevensons were harried to distraction finding admissions for their countrymen who would not take no for an answer.

Irksome, to say the least, was the arrival at this busy hour of John Van Buren, rank-concious son of President Van Buren. This young man had been capering about England, hobnobbing with the elite and the titled. "Prince John" or "Prince Long Shanks," as the Whig rabble-rousers were to dub him in the riotous 1840 election, insisted on being accorded the status of a visiting Prince. Was he not the son of the American President? As such, protocol entitled him to a front row seat at the coronation. Patiently,

Andrew Stevenson took the matter up with Sir Robert Chester, Master of Ceremonies. That functionary apparently shared Stevenson's displeasure at young Van Buren's arrogance, yet he ruled that young John had a princely rating and could therefore accompany the American Minister and his Lady into the stalls reserved for Foreign Ministers. Sallie Stevenson did not like it, and she said so.

Prince Esterhazy, or to be more exact, Prince Paul Esterhazy of Galantha, was the Ambassador Extraordinary from Austria. He looked like a diamond merchant's showcase on parade. His diamond-encrusted hat dazzled even the new Queen. Harriet Martineau corroborated the observant Mrs. Stevenson by saying, "Prince Esterhazy, crossing a bar of sunshine, was the most prodigious rainbow of all . . . covered with diamonds and pearls."

France's special envoy to the coronation—Nicholas Jean de Dieu Soult, Duke of Dalmatia—was a Marshal in the great Napoleon's army. The old warrior created a tremendous stir wherever he went. For the festivities he rented a house directly across the street from the Stevensons'. In a land where ornamented coaches were the order of the day, Marshal Soult's carriage of cobalt blue trimmed with bands of pure silver and gold ran off with the coronation procession honors.

The "Duke's noble mansion," to which Mrs. Stevenson refers, was Apsley House. Over two thousand guests were invited to the Duke's Grand Ball the night of the coronation. Apparently everybody came. Invitations from the Duke of Wellington were worth their weight in gold, and more.

Mrs. Stevenson erred only once in her facts. She gave the number of the Queen's train bearers as six. There were eight of them.

The Duchess of Sutherland, one of the court beauties, was Victoria's closest friend and Mistress of the Robes. This lady, Harriet Elizabeth Georgiana-Leveson-Gower, was wife of the second Duke of Sutherland, George Granville Leveson-Gower.

The incident of the old peer, Lord Rolle, stumbling as he tottered up to the royal footstool to pay homage, is historic. He was Baron Rolle of Stevenstone. Many eyewitnesses have recorded the scene of Victoria rising to help him.

The Marchioness of Westminster was Eleanor Grosvenor,

wife of Robert Grosvenor, Marquis of Westminster. Their home was Eaton Hall.

I have no words to express to you my beloved Helen, how much pleasure your kind and welcome letter of April the 30th has afforded me, It would be impossible for me to give you any idea of the scenes through which we have been passing, such a whirl of splendour & gaiety—such riding & driving—so much to see & to hear, & to do—such noise & bustle, what would have become of me if it had occured two months sooner—but it has pleased Heaven to give me strength & health sufficient for the day. So far, I have been quite well, notwithstanding all the fatigue & excitement—I wrote Betsy just before the Coronation, & Mr Stevenson says he shall write her all about it & send papers, books &c which will give you all a perfect idea of it, but as I promised to tell you what I saw—heard—suffered—& enjoyed, I shall try to make time to redeem my pledge to you. I wrote Sister Singleton & Betsy a very long scrawl giving them an account of events preceding the Coronation, of the crowds of Americans who were here morning, noon, & night, to obtain tickets of admission, &c of the arrival of the Ambassadors, of Mr Van Buren &c,—we took him in our Carriage, which was a great annoyance to me, as it prevented my seeing, and forced me to sit back in a corner, so that my friends complained I would not notice them altho they waved their hankercheifs, & threw flowers at our Carriage and sought in every way to attract our attention as we passed them in the procession—The weather was very propitious it had been threatening some days previously and the morning was overcast, but about 9 it cleared up, & continued fine all the rest of the dy & night as if Nature smiled upon England's Hope—and upon this fair object of all their enthusiasm—we left our door about half past 8—our equipage was thought to be in fine taste. A pale yellow-chariot, with white silk lining hammer cloth of deep blue—brass harness with yellow roses & frontlets, two footmen behind in new liveries, blue coats, with yellow button's & the eagle—yellow short breeches with silk stockings & buckles in their shoes—white gloves, & bouquets in their coats—round hats with the American Cockade & a yellow Eagle—every body had cocked hats, but Mr. S thought it more suitable to his Republican taste & habits to have plain round— It seems our Country people were delighted with the simple and elegant taste of their Minister & he has received many compliments on the subject—Mr Rush, Vaux—& Livingstone followed in a carriage of the same colour & liveries—Marshal Soult is just opposite to us, and when we went out the Street was filled with Spectators to look at his Silver Carriage. I compare it with our Republican Simplicity—after all I must sy ours was the handsomest—as we passed along we wondered where all the people came from that filled the Streets so that we could only move in a snails pace & feared being too late to join the procession, but as all the other Carriages were in the same predicament we were safe—barriers had been raised to prevent the peoples crowding into the Streets (in their carriages) through which the procession was to pass & therefore as soon as we, the priveledged, passed these barrier's our way was unobstructed, but then a spectacle met our view that was really magnificent. The Houses presented almost one solid line of human faces peering one above another, & some such smiling rosy faces, that it looked like a beautiful bed of flowers—for many days previous to the Coronation workmen had been busily engaged putting up galleries for this mighty mass of human beings, & seats sold for several guineas, Van Buren who had not seen any thing of the sort before was overwhelmed with astonishment & admiration, it was indeed a magnificent sight, and much did I wish for those dear friends I love best in the world, to share the pleasure with us. But to return to the procession—when the Queen left the Palace it was announced by the firing of canon & also her arrival at the Abbey, her progress was known by the cheering of the multitude which thronged her carriage—The Streets from Buckemham Palace to the

Abbey were completely filled, except the line kept open by the police for the carriages, and as she moved on, this countless multitude, high & low united in one continued cheering loud & long—and for the whole distance of more than two miles this young creature continued to bow and smile to her loving subjects all anxious to catch a glimpse of her & too happy to have a smile—we reached the Abbey about Eleven and entered through files of soldiers, & men at arms dressed in their gorgeous uniforms & bearing in their hands their badges of office—The Abbey like most of the Old Churches is as you know in the form of a cross we entered at D and at the other extremity was the altar so that on entering we had a coup d'oel of the whole scene of magnificence. Imagine this immense building adorned with the richest draperies of crimson & gold & covered with costly carpeting, & filled in every part with persons in the most brilliant dresses—The peers and peeresses glittering in all the pomp of velvet & ermine, and the ladies sparkling with diamonds, the peers occupying the South, & the peeresses the North transept when the sun shone upon the latter it was realy dazzling to look upon them—It was really a gorgeous scene and one which no eye could witness without calling up in the heart mingled sensations of pleasure and astonishment. Mr Stevenson and myself entered together, Van Buren, Rush, Vaux, & Livingstone following close behind, with the eyes of 1000 persons upon us. My husband never looked better or moved with more dignity & grace. I cannot tell you how many have told me since, that he was the finest looking man in the Abbey, his countrymen & women say they felt proud of their Representative, and even Van Buren & his taciturne friend Mr Clark, speak in high praise both of his appearance in the procession & in the Abbey—we ascended the Tribune, & took our seats Mr Stevenson on the right hand of Marshal Soult, (Duke of Dalmatia) & I just by him—The Ambassadress' were blasing in diamonds & Prince Esterhazy was literally covered with precious stones, it is said he never wears this dress without losing 100 pounds worth of jewels—Mr Stevenson & myself, like our equipage, was handsome & genteel without being fine. he wore a new Coat, which one day or other I hope you will see—I a white Satin dress, with blond, bear neck & arms, a rich scarff, I got in Paris, of blue & gold with a slight mixture of crimson & green, very handsome, on my head a gold turban with a diamond star, necklace, earings & breastpin—Such was the demand for diamonds on that day, that one of the great jewellers told me he had not one left in his shop & that he had hired one set for 25 pounds—our situation was decidedly the best in the house, both for seeing & hearing every thing—The Queen entered with a flourish of trumpets, proceeded by all her officers of State and accompanied by the beautiful Duchess of Sutherland mistress of the Robes, Lady Lansdowne Barham &c and her train borne by 6 young girls of her own age, dressed all alike in white satin with lace over it and bunches of pale pink roses up before, on their heads a string of diamonds with blush roses—these young ladies were of the highest rank in the Kingdom—The Queen advanced up the nave untill she reached the first chair where she Knelt, at her private devotions—The most Striking part of the Ceremony was the Crowning. when the superb crown was put on her head, at the very moment, a roar of canon announced it to her people, by signal I suppose, and at the same instant all the peers and peeresses put on their Coronets, it was really magnificent, but the most touching part, to me, of this great national pageant was when this fair young creature knelt at the Alter before receiving the Sacrement, with her head uncovered looking so young, so innocent, & so helpless, that involuntarily my heart was raised to Heaven in supplication to the great giver of all good, that, the little head which then bowed down in such seeming humility before the foot-stool of His mercy, might at last receive a Crown such as no mortal hands could bestow upon her—She was crowned in St Edwards Chair, which I formerly described in a letter to Betsy, and also related to her the tradition which accounted for its being always used on such occasions—it was covered with crimson & gold and I should not have recognised my old acquaintance in its new dress—In the Center of the Abby immediately under the central

Tower, a platform was erected of a circular form with five steps, the summit of the platform, & the highest step leading to it, was covered with the richest cloth of gold, and in the centre a chair was placed in which she received the homage of the peers—The Royal Dukes first, knelt, kissed her hand & touched the side of her crown, I was struck with the manner of the Duke of Sussex, he kissed her hand repeatedly & when he touched her crown it was more the caressing action of a Father than the homage of a subject—a little incident occured during the ceremony of the homage which created quite a sensation, an old peer, Lord Rolle, vy infirm, in attempting to ascend, the weight of his robe, & his own feebleness caused him to fail & roll down the steps, when The Queen half rose from her seat as by a sudden impulse, & when he was put upon his feet, & attempted again to ascend she rose & met him—The House cheered, & all felt the action as indicative of her amiable disposition, some one in speaking of it afterwards, said, it was the only good action of his life, to tumble down in order to give the Queen an opportunity to show the kindness and benevolence of her heart—It is said she exhibited great sensibility on her arrival at the Abbey when she went into the Robing room on her arrival, that she wept so passionately that her attendants were alarmed lest she should be unable to go through the Ceremony. I remarked when she entered, that she was vy pale, but calm dignified, & self-possessed throughout the whole trying ceromonial—I thought she seemed much effected, when a hundred instruments and more than twice that number of voices united in, "God save the Queen!—Long live the Queen! May the Queen live forever!" The loud anthem, and then the applauding shouts of the multitude of spectators had a most thrilling effect even upon my democratic nerves, & I dare sy drew loyal tears, from loyal eyes. After the Queen retired, the rush to get out was immense, and I thought I should stand some chance of being crushed in the Squeeze when suddenly a Stentorian voice proclaimed, "Not a peer or peeress can leave the Abby untill the foreign Ambassadors have passed out" in an instant I found myself passing quietly along an avenue made

LLIE COLES STEVENSON
m her portrait painted at Lon-
in 1839 by G. P. A. Healy.

iscorthy today, restored birth-
ce and home of Sallie Coles
venson. Partially destroyed by
in 1839, it was rebuilt in 1850.

Photo courtesy of Ralph R. Thompson

Photo courtesy of George H. Barkley

QUEEN VICTORIA
IN HER REGAL ROBES
Reproduced from Thomas Sul
Massive Portrait painted at Lon
in 1838 for the Society of the S
of St. George.

ANDREW STEVENSON
Envoy Extraordinary and Minister
Plenipotentiary to Great Britain
1836-1841. From the Nichols portrait in the Speakers Gallery of the
House of Representatives at Washington.

SALLIE COLES STEVENSON
From her portrait painted by
G. P. A. Healy in London in 1839.
It shows her gowned for presentation at Queen Victoria's court.

Queen Victoria in the year of her wedding, dancing with her husband, Prince Albert.

Lord Palmerston, Foreign Minister, sends two tickets for Queen Victoria's coronation for Andrew Stevenson to give to "any of your countrymen who may not be provided." Palmerston also inquires about General Cass, American Minister to France.

Part of Sallie Coles Stevenson's letter to her niece, Sarah Rutherford, of Richmond, Virginia, describing the wedding of Queen Victoria and Prince Albert in the chapel of St. James's Palace, February 10, 1840.

for us, close along side of Marshal Soult & the procession returned as it had come, the patient Spectators still waiting to behold again the gorgeous show—we got home half starved &
fearful we should find nothing at home to eat, but our tidy and
skilful little cook Elisabeth had us a nice fricassee of chicken,
which revived me so much that after reposing a little while, I
had courage to dress & go to the Duke of Wellington's grand
ball. The truth is, the noise the bustle & brilliancy of evy thing
rendered it impossible to sleep—The whole City was in a blase
of light. Marshal Soult had a brilliant transparency just opposite to us, & we shone forth with the American Eagle—we
reached the Dukes Noble mansion through crowds of people,
on his gate way was a splendid illumination, & the whole house
Lighted up so as to turn night into day—in giving a discription
of one London party, you will have a vy good idea of all, in
approaching in a long file of Carriages you find the Street lined
with curious spectators, (for I believe the English people have
more curiosity than any other in the world.) who are peering
into your carriage as if it contained an orang otang. You enter
through two rows of Liveried Servants, who announce in voices
of thunder "The American Minister, & Mrs Stevenson" which
is repeated all the way up the magnificent Stair Case which is
always brilliantly lighted & ornamented with rich vases of
flowers—Statues &c &c The lady & gentleman of the House
receive you at the door of the first apartment after a curtsy, & a
few words of courtesy, you pass on through suites of apartments, brilliantly lighted, perfumed with flowers, and adorned
with all that art & luxury can supply, and crowded with well
dressed persons of both sexe's, if you are so fortunate as to
penetrate into the ball room, you have the pleasure of seeing
fairy forms whirling in the Walse, or gliding gracefuly through
the mases of the Quadrille to the music of Straus' or Werperts
band—To curtsy low to Royal Dukes & Duchess, & if you have
strength & patience to wait for supper your eyes may be dazzled
by the blase of gold & silver, & your palet feasted with all the
luxuries & delacies of the Season. At the Marchoness of West-
minsters the other night, thy had besides the exhibition of their

(151)

splendid Mansion, the whole garden illuminated with coloured, & white lamps, it was beautiful, as well as magnificent & looked as if the firmament was beneath your feet—And, now dear Helen, I have redeemed my promise after a fashion, but the books & papers we send, give such full & faithful discriptions that it left me but little to sy—What I have written has been by rising early, and denying myself to every one, still I am afraid you will think it very incoherent—(Postscript:) The enclosed letter ought to have gone last week but every body was so busy & so distracted it did not get off—Now I will add a few words to say the—Coronation is over—thank God! Adieu your own devoted Sister

SCS

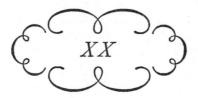

XX

ONE DAY in the fall of 1837, Cates, the ever-efficient factotum and butler at the Legation, tiptoed upstairs to announce a visitor, Thomas Sully by name. The American portraitist's fame had long since echoed across the Atlantic.

The artist had come to London armed with a commission from the St. George's Society of Philadelphia "to memorialize Her Majesty to sit for her picture to Mr. Sully for the gratification and use of the Society".

Could the Stevensons help him? Anxious to be of service, they volunteered to do all in their power at the right opportunity. Everything in England depended on timing, particularly as it regarded royalty. The new Queen—like George Washington after the Revolution—was deluged by similar requests from artists and sculptors of England and America. The Stevensons promised to ask the Queen to pose for Sully.

Time went by. Sully waited patiently. The American Minister took the matter up directly with the Premier, Lord Melbourne, whose influence with the Queen was all-embracing at this moment. He and Stevenson were on most cordial terms.

However, Andrew Stevenson did not stop there. Year end came and the Stevensons went off to visit Victoria at Windsor Castle. During the festivities Stevenson mentioned the matter to the Queen herself. Without hesitation the gracious young ruler consented—as a personal favor to the Stevensons—to pose for Sully. She would let them know when it would be convenient.

Most likely after she had returned to London from Windsor. Lord Melbourne would communicate with them—and so he did.

Came spring, and an improvised studio was arranged in Buckingham Palace, and here, during various sittings, Sully painted the likeness of the Queen's head. He then suggested that he could save her time and patience if she would permit his daughter, Blanche, who had accompanied him to London, to don the ponderous queenly regalia and pose as the Queen for the completion of the painting—a suggestion the Queen acceded to gladly. Thus he finished the massive (58 by 94 inches) and justly famous portrait of the youthful Queen Victoria.

In this letter Mrs. Stevenson speaks, amid a multiplicity of things, of going to see Sully's painting. She made the prediction that it would add much to Sully's "fame and reputation as an artist." She was right.

The Mrs. de Rothschild at whose home Mrs. Stevenson had such an elaborate breakfast, was the widow of Nathan Meyer Rothschild, merchant and financier, founder of the London branch of the House of Rothschild, bankers. Her breakfasts were as fabulous as her countryplace.

Countess "Strogonoff" mentioned by Mrs. Stevenson was most likely Countess Strogoff, wife of the Russian special envoy to the coronation.

The Duke of Devonshire was head of famed Devonshire House in London, a great show place. He was formerly British Minister to Russia. His gorgeous coach outshone all others in the coronation procession save the Queen's and Marshal Soult's. Incidentally, his wife's niece, Caroline, married Lord Melbourne and later became enamoured of Lord Byron.

London July 24th 1838

Beloved Sisters

I wrote by last week's packet letters to Helen and Emily giving them details of all that was going on here in this great world of gayety & fashion.

In my letters to them I told you of my improved health & strength, notwithstanding the severe trial both were undergoing in the progress of a London season the gayest and most brilliant of the last century. The representatives of all civilized nations of the earth (except poor America) have been vying with each other in the magnificence of their fetes in honor of the Queen's coronation. One thing has succeeded to another in such rapid succession that we have scarcely time for the necessary repose of nature. The Queen commenced with a grand ball at which all the foreigners, ambassadors & ambassadresses, shone forth in a blaze of diamonds, & all that was rich, costly, curious, & magnificent in the way of dress that the earth affords, and everything which money, taste, & English pride could do was accomplished in adorning and embellishing Buckingham Palace in honor of its fair young mistress, who passed through the glittering throng, standing up to receive her, bowing and smiling to all, & speaking with gentle graciousness to her august visitors (that's the style) as she passed into the ball-room to the elevated platform raised for her at one side of the apartment, over which was a gilded canopy wreathed with flowers, &c. She dances very gracefully and without effort, & as soon as the quadrille is over, she steps back to her seat, a large arm-chair on each side of which sat the royal family & her attendants, the Mistress of the Robes, the Duchess of Suther-land, Lady Lansdowne, &c. She sends her gentleman-in-waiting to the person she means to honor with her hand, and our re-publican prince Van Buren was, or effected to be, afraid of the honor of being selected; but I suspect he has nothing to hope or fear, as there are so many representations here from crowned heads. The Queen's ball has been followed by one from some of the royal family, which her little Majesty has honored by her presence. The Duke of Sussex's commenced before the arrival of the foreigners, but the Duchess of Gloucester, and the Duke and Duchess of Cambridge, after the coronation,—all very magnificent, but, like all royal parties, very dull and formal. We did not stay to supper at either place, but made our escape as soon as we had made our obeisance to the Queen. The foreign ambassadors and many of the elite of the English nobility are now giving dinners and fetes every day, and sometimes two and three on the same night. But the most magnificent spectacle yet exhibited (according to my notion, but not Mr. S.'s) was a review in Hyde Park soon after the coronation. For three days after, this park was occupied with a fair, which appeared to be the most curious exhibition of everything odd and ridiculous, as seen from the ring; but I did not venture in, as many ladies did. At the expiration of the three days allowed by law, the whole pageantry disappeared as if the wand of a magician had passed over it. I suppose it was all removed in the night. A few days after, the review took place.

I was afraid at first I should not see it, as it was said only royal carriages would be admitted; but the night before, I received a card to admit "Mrs. Stevenson's carriage" (the "s" added to please milady), and as all the gentlemen of the embassies were to go on horseback, I had three seats to offer my friends, no small favor when the greatest duchess in England could not get in. I invited, for Angelica's sake, Mr. Preston, and a Mr. Gibbs from Baltimore, who tells me he is acquainted with all Julia's family, and married the daughter of the rich Mr. Oliver,—she will know whom I mean by this,—and Miss Benett, who came in to pass the evening with me. I should have given the preference to my own countrywomen, but as I could only take one, I did not know how to make a distinction. We went early, at nine o'clock, and got a most excellent situation not far from the place the Queen was to occupy. At eleven the firing of a royal salute from the artillery announced her arrival. As soon as she entered the lines, accompanied by the Duchesses of Kent and Sutherland, the royal standard was hoisted, and the whole of the troops presented arms. After the staff and noble foreigners had paid their respects, she proceeded in her open landau, followed by another carriage containing her ladies-in-waiting, with the whole of the splendid cortege, down the lines, each body of troops presenting arms as she passed, and the immense multitude cheering her with an enthusiasm, as though they would (in the language of the "Journal") have thrown their hearts instead of their hats into the air. It was a most picturesque and animating scene. Imagine 150,000 spectators, who stood outside the lines, and who crowded the balconies and tops of houses and trees, around the park; and inside the lines, a body of 6000 troops from the various military departments, in their splendid dresses and accoutrements; the officers and foreigners in their different uniforms curveting on their graceful and richly caparisoned chargers; the tasteful dresses of the ladies, with their waving plumes. The presence of the great by rank and deed, and the animated question of "Who's that?" and the exclamation of pleasure and admiration, altogether created a sensation of enjoyment and exhilaration I have rarely felt. The gentlemen and Miss Benett were perpetually exclaiming, "How shall I thank you for bringing me here!" Oh, dear Bett, I thought of thee all the time, and if I had had a wishing-cap, or Prince Houssein's tapestry, you would soon have been alongside of me. But to go back to the review. We had a mock battle, which made the earth tremble under the roar of the cannon, and the multitude were so terrified that they began tumbling over each other to get out of the way, breaking scaffolding, and screaming as though they were veritably wounded. The firing along the lines lasted 20 minutes, and was really stunning. The different evolutions were beautiful, and gave an admirable idea of the "pride, pomp, and circumstance of war," without any of its appalling results. We got home about 2 o'clock, tired and hungry.

I invited Miss Bennett up to the drawing room and she took possession of one sofa and I of the other where we rested untill our strength was renewed by lunch when Mr. Stevenson took us out to see Sully's picture of the queen which is said to be the best likeness that has been taken of her and the most flattering. She is in the act of ascending the Throne and her attitude is graceful & natural. It will add no doubt much to his fame & reputation as an artist. And now dear sister in the multiplicity of things I have to write about what shall I select: a breakfast at Mrs. de Rothchilds? the widow of the great banker. It was something so very pretty that I think that I must endeavor to give you some account of it altho' I know you are not particularly fond of descriptions. This fete was given at a beautiful villa about 4 or 5 miles from town called Gunnersburg Park formerly a royal residence. We were invited at 3 & got there about 4. When we reached the grand sallon we found it filled with eager listeners to the thrilling notes of the Italian singers Grisi, Persiani. I penetrated into the room but finding it was warm I passed out through the open window to the terrace where the company was promenading enjoying pure air, the beautiful prospect & the more distant strains of those Italian nightingales. After the concert was over the company strolled about the grounds through intricacies delightful to the eye & the imagination or reposed under the shade of an old ancestral tree enjoying music, sunshine and flowers listening to the transient pleasantries of the merry groups around or their gay flashes of country wit. These English throw off much of their constitutional reserve in their fetes. I suppose it is the influence of nature & sunshine both of which is so little enjoyed in London. At half past 6 a bell summoned the strollers to a magnificent tent on the lawn where tables had been set for 4 or 500 guests and every luxury provided hot & cold meats, delicious viands of all sorts with the most costly fruits & wines. After the repast the company returned to the lawn where carpets with sofas and chairs had been placed & the young people waltzed to the music of two bands who played alternately throughout the day & night and were placed in two marquees near the tent. Nothing could be more picturesque and beautiful. As soon however as the tent was prepared for dancing we removed to its friendly shelter and the ball began in good earnest. Occupied with looking at the dancers and conversation with several agreeable acquaintances I did not look out until the shadows of eve 'gan to steal o'er the lawn when it appeared covered with brilliant glowworms and every bush & shrub & tree sent forth the same bright radiance. It was so beautiful that I started up to go forth & fortunately meeting Mr. Vaux we sallied out and met Mr. Stevenson in search of me. He said he had just been walking around the grounds with the Duke of Sussex and was seeking me for the same purpose. He took me a way I had not seen before, a gravel walk edged with flowers & statuary, all illuminated. In our progress we passed a grotto in which a female figure was leaning over a fountain, the light so dispersed as to produce a fine effect. After ten minutes walk we reached a temple in which coffee was served out to the strollers & on one side was a flower garden illuminated & the other a lake on whose calm bosom a pleasure boat floated from which the merry hum of voices reached us, and gay forms were seen by the illuminations in the thickly foliaged trees which bending their graceful branches over the water reflected a thousand brilliant hues. It was a scene of enchanting beauty, the soft & balmy air, the fragrance which every breeze wafted to us made up a dazzling mixture of sensations which it would be impossible for me to describe. In the fullness of my heart I said, "Oh, if my dear Bett was here!" In joy or happiness I never fail to wish for you my sister. This was a scene you would have delighted in because nature asserted her empire over art and formed by their union a picture of such exquisite beauty as you have taste & feeling to enjoy. When we returned to the house we found a refreshment table delightful to our eyes in one of the large & splendid salloons where ices, lemonade and orangeade &c was served and disappeared as snow in sunshine & at one end of the table that never failing accessory to English comfort, a tea urn.

The Duke of Sussex who occupied a seat at one end of the room beckoned me to one by him & talked to me for half an hour about more things than I dreamed of in a woman's philosophy. American women, I mean. After his departure I strolled through the house and admired the luxurious comfort of everything but I cannot close this long account without an anecdote of Mr. Stevenson's gallantry which will give you good hopes of him. He was in fine spirits, thought himself dressed in perfection (apropos I must tell you presently about my dress) and went determined to please & be pleased as he always does—a happy mood for a diplomat. It seems he was standing in front of the house on the terrace talking to the Duke of Wellington when Lady Jersey & Lady Londonderry, two of the brightest stars in the world of Fashion, approached with Prince Esterhazy. The former exclaimed, "Prince, I am fainting with fatigue. Do get me a chair!" And the Prince, like all royal persons, loves not trouble, and after some little flourish pronounced it impossible when *mon cher mari* with the graceful agility of 18 jumped from the terrace upon the lawn where his quick eye had spied two vacant chairs, seized upon them & returned in triumph. The prince like a veteran courtier as he is, thought to wear the laurels another had won, approached to take the chairs when Mr. Stevenson said, "Oh, no, Prince, having brought them so far I can go the whole" & presented them himself to the fair dames, with his sweetest blandest smiles, whilst the prince cryed out, "That America was always carrying off the Palm," and the beautiful Lady Jersey looked unutterable things & said, "This shall go in the Book". I suppose it will go under the head of "extraordinary proof of civilization & refinement given by an American" 'tho I must say, he has a high reputation abroad, as a polite, accomplished, well-bred gentleman, and always the best-dressed man at every party I'll swear to that—very recherche, I assure you. But to return to myself, that dearest object of human idolatry, (How candid, dr. Betsy) I wore a white figured silk with a blue & gold scarf & a pine coloured silk bonnet & feathers. At these breakfasts everybody wears a bonnet. However light the material it must have the form of a bonnet and every article of dress must be as clean & fresh looking as the flowers around for which my money flies. India muslin & lace over white or colored silk is very much worn, neck & arms covered, of course. The Duke of Sussex told Mr. Stevenson that this fete must have cost 2000 pounds—$10,000. Two days after we were at another breakfast given by the Duchess of Somerset at Wimbledon near Mrs. Marryatt's and altho' we had everything to constitute a beautiful fete that we had at the Duchess of Northumberlands and Mrs. de Rothchild's yet it went off heavily and no one seemed to enjoy themselves. To me it was positively disagreeable.

Mr. Stevenson went with me but had to return to a dinner

given by the Turks to the ministers and ambassadors in honor of her Majesty's coronation so that I had to go in alone to the table with the royal family and all the magnates of the land. Unluckily I sat by the Grecian minister, Prince Soutri who cannot speak one word of English & yet is so fond of America that he is always showing us civility in dumb-show and forcing me upon my small stock of 5 guinea French, (now down to a shillings worth). He says when he can't understand me "Vous parlez francais tres bien, Madame". I was heartily glad when the dinner was over and still more so when Countess Ludoff with whom I returned to town announced her willingness to depart. I should never have done it if I were to attempt to give you an account of all the balls, breakfasts and fetes we have been present at. Marshal Soult our opposite neighbor has given a beautiful ball. The Duke of Devonshire, the Duchess of Sutherland & I wrote Emily a slight description of a ball given in the Russian taste by the Countess Strogonoff. We dined there a few days after and saw the rooms by daylight and enjoyed a luxurious Russian feast. The dinner was so magnificent that it astonished even the dinner giving English. The Duke of Sutherland who led me in spoke in high praise of it. All the ornaments of the table had been brought from Russia.

I liked the Duke much better than his beautiful Duchess. She is the petted child of fortune, a beauty, too fat, and a Mistress of the Robes to the queen. It amuses me to see the air with which at the queen's balls she presents her fan & bouquet to her royal mistress when she returns to her seat after dancing. It is when I witness such things as these I feel what a thorough republican I am. By the way the queen's balls are the most agreeable parties given. There is so much space and everybody goes in their best dresses, best looks and best humour and the little creature seems to enjoy herself so much & looks so innocent & so happy that she imparts a little of her own serenity to others. I've always enjoyed myself more there than anywhere else, made more acquaintances and met more agreeable persons. The ball before the last I was introduced to the Countess of Lovelace (Ada Byron) by her husband whom I knew as Lord King. She is not pretty but her manners are very pleasant, frank, and conversable, with much less of reserve than is usual with her countrywomen on a first acquaintance. It is a singular coincidence that we met at both the last balls in the supper room, exactly at the same spot, took a wing of chicken standing side by side and a glass of soda water and she of wine together & wound up with the same royal strawberries and you know good cheer has a wonderful effect in making persons like each other. At least they are very apt to be associated in our minds with pleasant recollections.

I introduced Mr. Van Buren to Ada Byron who was delighted—also to the beautiful Lady Seymour besides a half score of other fashionables. His position here has been very agreeable & he has enjoyed advantages no other person could as the son of the President of the United States. We have felt ourselves privileged to introduce him everywhere. Whilst it would be considered by these punctilious English as taking a liberty with them to present an ordinary person the son of the President would be received with distinguished marks of favour. Besides he is really an agreeable person although Miss Bennett says very selfish.

. . . . . Neither Mr. Stevenson or myself are now young. (Younger I am by 15 years & never were in feeling) We are not commencing the race of life but approaching that goal from whence there is no return (but far off I hope yet) and we have both passed through the furnace of affliction, which if it has not purified has at least subdued & taught us what a frail tenure all human blessings are held. But for myself I have not relied upon my own strength to preserve me from the temptations of the world or the corruptions of my heart. When I came to this country and began to mingle in the gay circles of fashion and to have my attention occupied by so many new scenes and objects I laid down one rule from which I have but seldom departed which was to pass a portion of every morning in religious reading & in devotional exercises, feeling as my temptations multiplied my watchfulness ought to encrease.

How often, dear Sister, has my tears flowed and my

earnest fervent cry to Heaven been, like drowning Peter, Lord save me, or I perish! And have we not the promise that if we call unto Him, he will hear us—was not Daniel preserved both in the lion's den, and from the temptations of a corrupt court? And yet I will not deny that it is a perpetual conflict between temporal & spiritual, the flesh & the spirit, a warfare from which I would most gladly be released, but shall I like a coward soldier desert the post of duty, because it is one of danger. No, dear Sister, I feel that He whose Providence has placed me here, will remove me when He sees fit, and that I cannot do better than to commit my way—and my husband's way—unto Him, & to be anxious for nothing, but to obtain His Holy Spirit to enlighten, guide, & direct me through the intricate (& too often thorny) path of life, and to receive me, and him whom he has given me as a husband to Himself in his own good time. This is a solemn subject to close this worldly letter with but it is only the more truly descriptive of my life & feelings God knows, but sometimes I think I am very wicked and must be a cast-away from pardon & grace, but then I feel that I love God with a fervour that fills my eyes with tears when I think of all His goodness & loving kindness to me, especially, since I came to this foreign land, and I believe I would infinitely rather be a doorkeeper in the House of my God, than Victoria the proud mistress of this fair realm, surrounded by all the earthly adoration which is offered her, without the heart to love & desire Him above all things. Still the heart is "desperately wicked" & full of infinite delusions and only those who have tried it, know how hard it is to enjoy the world, & yet to live above it. And now, dear Sister, after this frank & humble confession, tell me, is my heart in the right place? I confess my head is a little giddy—but then a good nights sleep will steady that—my mind too, I fear is in as sad a litter as my work box, or my writing table.

XXI

In early September, 1838, the Stevensons set out in their carriage, with coachman, valet and maid, for Scotland by way of the lovely Lakes district of England. It was for Sallie Stevenson, a fatiguing journey but most gratifying to one who loved everything associated with the land of minstrelsy. Andrew Stevenson himself put some store by his Scots background. A trip to Scotland would give him an opportunity to show off his "Scotch pride and lineage." Their destination was Dunrobin Castle where they were the guests of the Duchess of Sutherland.

"Here we are in Caledonia, stern and wild," wrote Sallie Stevenson in this letter to her sister-in-law, Selina Skipwith Coles, wife of her brother John Coles III, of Estouteville, Virginia. With girlish delight she still pored over Scott's fascinating tales; she could repeat verse upon verse of the "Lay of the Last Minstrel" and "The Lady of the Lake." For her the journey was a ribbon of beauty and romance, though tiring to her frail body.

She was also an admirer of the nature poet, William Wordsworth, so the Stevensons paused to pay their respects to him at his home, Rydal Mount, near Lake Windermere. The aging bard was flattered by the visit of the two Americans, and soon after they returned to London—on Christmas Eve, to be exact—he sent them an original verse dedicated to them. Never before printed it was hidden away in the Stevenson Letter Books in the Library of Congress until now. It follows:

There are to whom the garden, grove and field,
Perpetual lessons of forbearance yield,
Who would not lightly violate the grace
The lowliest flower professes in its place;
Nor shorten the sweet life, too fugitive,
What nothing less than infinite power could give.

On went the Stevensons—Edinburgh, Glasgow, then Dunrobin Castle where they spent days enjoying the Highland scenery, hearing tales of the Scottish chiefs, drinking in old legends. As a memento of their visit the Duchess of Sutherland presented them with a small drinking cup, a Scottish quaigh, that may be seen today at the Virginia Historical Society at Richmond, Virginia.

Carlisle Sepr 7th 1838

My beloved Sister & friends

Tired and wearied as I am with a long and fatiguing days journey, I cannot leave the neighbourhood of the Lakes without writing you something about this most beautiful and romantic country, altho' in truth I can say but little having seen it to the greatest disadvantage, through a heavy English drizzle. I wrote you from Mr. Green's and we left it an hour after I sealed my letter to you, the day promised to be fine when we left Whittington Hall, but it soon after clouded up and commenced raining so that we were compelled to keep shut up except now and then at the risk of a cold we had the top put down to enjoy—or rather to look at the scenery which even through cloud's and mist was still beautiful. We passed along the whole length of the lake of Windermere which is considered the largest of the English Lakes being 10 miles upon the water, but measured by the road on its banks considerably more, its greatest breadth a mile, & its depth 40 fathoms, its scenery is very beautiful, diversified by sloping hills, woods, and cultivated ground, with lofty mountains in the distance, its banks are adorned with buildings, and I could imagine with

(*165*)

the sun shining on it, a scene of enchanting beauty. We passed the night at Len-Wood Inn, situated at the edge of the water, a short distance from Ambleside, and the falls of Rydal. Wordsworth lives near the falls, and we determined to make a visit to both. We stoped a few hundred yards from the house, and sent Cates up with a pencilled note to say we should be happy to pay our respects, &c, he soon returned with the poets compliments, & would be happy to see us. We entered a small gate, which disclosed a cottage looking house surrounded by shrubbery and were received at a little low porch by a man servant who conducted us through some dark narrow passages to a small room fitted up as a library which opened into another of the same dimensions & furnished in the same way with books, and many little elegancies which bespoke the presence of the softer sex, but we needed not this assurance of their presence, as two ladies sat at a round table at work. Wordsworth rose from a sofa on which he seemed to have been reclining, & greeted us with cordiality & kindness, he presented us to the ladies, one as his daughter, & I believe the other as his wife. He told us he had been ill with a rhumatic fever, but was then convalescent, as I sat by him for nearly an hour I think I may venture to describe him. Mrs. Turner I know will be delighted to hear what sort of a looking person her favorite poet is, and I owe this to her, as she first taught me to admire his poetry. In stature he is about the middle size, and thin almost to amaciation, his face is long & also thin, with large prominent features. He has lost all his teeth which gives to his mouth a tremulous motion when he talks, his forehead is the only feature of his face which bespeaks the poet or the philosopher, high, lofty & commanding, with a few scattered grey hairs, it indicates the highest order of intellect, but there is nothing in his countenance which betrays the profound feeling which pervades his poetry. He is full of conversation, & converses with ease & fluency notwithstanding the loss of his teeth. When we rose to depart he requested his daughter to take us to a little mound in front of the house where the prospect could be seen to the greatest advantage. It was, indeed, a scene in which a poet might delight to dwell, and which could almost create a poet out of the dullest proser, notwithstanding the murky clouds which threw their shadows over every object it was the scenery of a fairy dream and I felt unwilling to obey Mr. Stevenson's impatient "Come on!" The rain prevented our going to the falls, and I consoled myself with the thought that I had seen—Niagara. We reached Carlisle, this place, just as the sun shone out with a splendour that makes me feel half inclined to turn back to the romantic scenes I have quitted, & only half seen, never to look upon again. As I sat at the window of this excellent Inn gazing upon the last beams of the sun reflected from an opposite house, I cannot help agreeing with the 'wise man', that 'Vanity & vexation of spirit' is stamped upon all earthly pleasures. Mr. Stevenson has left me to walk to the Castle where Queen Mary was confined, and I am endeavouring to beguile the time by talking to you, beloved sister, for whom I wish & pine every day, & every hour of the day. To-morrow I shall think of you, so very much, when I visit Dryburgh, Melrose, & Abbotsford. Heigho! Well, we cannot have every thing we desire in this world, and you, may-be, are happier where you are—for I believe, it is not external good which makes us happy, but the good which dwells in the heart—and who then ought to be so happy as my own good & excellent sister? Still I do so wish you were sitting just along side of me, and we could seek together that "Something which still prompts the eternal sigh for which we bear to live, or dare to die", but here comes, mon cher Man! Adieu!

Edinburgh Sepr 12th 1838

Well, dear Sister, here we are in 'Caledonia stern & wild'

"Land of brown heath, & shaggy wood,
Land of the mountain & the flood"—
Land of the bard whose magic verse,

(*167*)

my muse will help me to nothing more, so I must e'en go back
to plain prose, and tell you in homely phrase how we journeyed
from Carlisle through the most beautiful and romantic country.
We passed through the scene's of the 'Lay of the last Minstrel'
& saw I believe from the road the Castle of Branxholm belonging to the Duke of Buccleuch, a complete ruin, and we
were told, we passed through the stronghold of Johnny Arm-
strong, but we needed no one to inform us that the banks of the
Esk are here romantically beautiful, and the whole country from
Carlisle to the banks of the Tweed, is one continued succession
of agreeable views, nothing struck me as more beautiful than
the Eildon Hills, on which are the remains of Roman Camps.
We approached the Tweed about 5 oclock, on the left bank of
which are the ruins of Dryburgh Abbey, the last resting place
of Sir Walter Scott. We left the carriage at the bridge, and
walked more than a mile, on the romantic banks of the Tweed,
before we reached the ruins. Only one apartment remains entire,
the Chapter, which is kept locked up. The ruins are very extensive, and in an isle of the church is the humble grave of Scot-
lands boast & pride, the immortal Scott whose mortal remains
now occupies a little niche in this old ruin, whilst his fame fills
the world. I felt inclined whilst leaning on the iron rail &
gazing upon the green sod which covers this great & good
man, to ask with the poet, What is Fame? His wife's grave is
by his side, and they now sleep together, "The sleep that knows
no waking in this world". Flowers are blooming around them,
and the birds hop lightly over their graves. I paused for a
moment in the dark damp cell which Scott tells us was the
abode of the poor girl who shut herself up there from the light
of day for love. We passed the night at the little village of Melrose, and visited the Abbey the next day, not by 'The pale moon-
light', but by the 'gay beams of a lightsome day'. I had imagined
this far-famed ruin situated as I found Dryburgh, in the midst
of trees & flowers, &c, remote from the habitations of men,
instead of which, it is in a village; a short walk from our Inn,
took us to the gate, which was opened for us by a talking old
woman. The Gothick towers were seen projecting above the

wall as we approached it, and wore an air of solemnity &
grandeur very imposing, and much as I have heard of Melrose
I was not disappointed, when I stood among its graceful
columns, where beauty seems to have preserved them immortal.
The carving on the columns is inimitable, of fruits, flowers &c,
but the spot which interested me most was the grave of the
wizard Michael Scott. I stood upon the stone which I imagined
William of [word illegible], using his gigantic strength to remove, and just above the grave was a horrible, frightful head
carved in stone to represent the wizard. Under the East window,
so celebrated for its beauty, was the high altar, & here it is said
the heart of Robert Bruce was buried, but the spot is not known.
There are two graves which are said to be Alexander the 2d
who lived in the beginning of the 13th century and who assembled the 1st Parliament in Edinburgh & Douglas who fell
at Chevy Chase—another contrast struck me between Dryburgh & Melrose at the former, all was as still as the decay that
wears the marble of the tombs—but at Melrose we heard the
gay voices, & merry laugh of children who were playing around
the ruins. These pleasant sounds and the bright sun shine have
left impressions of Melrose Abbey in my mind the very reverse
of gloomy & solemn, Our talking friend who had been much
offended at Mr. Stevenson's want of faith in her legends, took
us by way of another trial of his credulity to see the relicks of
Sir Walter Scott which she & her husband had collected to
make money out of her believing victims. Among the number
was the instrument Sir Walter wore in walking. She asked
5 pounds for it—Mr. Stevenson bought some drawings of
Abbotsford to which place we proceeded after receiving a
visit from Sir David Brewster who lives near, or rather, has a
country residence in the Neighbourhood of Melrose. He was
accompanied by Mr. Babbage, as these are names well known
to fame I will not pause to say more about them except that we
declined an invitation from Sir David, and hastened on to
Abbotsford four miles off. It seems preposterous dear Sister,
to write any thing about these celebrated places of which so
much has been said & written, that nothing is left to curiosity

but to see with ones own eyes these stern grey ruins over which Time has thrown such an awful & touching solemnity, that mysterious something, which effects even the most unreflecting mind & has filled mine with feelings & impressions impossible to describe. As to Abbotsford it inspires an interest very different from that created by these time worn ruins. I must, however, confess I was disappointed in the place as a residence. The country around is very beautiful but the situation of the house is entirely shut in, & without any view except slight glimpses of the Tweed through the trees. The publick road runs just above it, & through the trees an occasional glimpse may be caught of the towers, we passed to the right through an open gate with thick wood on each side, & in a few moments the carriage stopt at the lofty & richly ornamented entrance to the yard, or little lawn in front of the house. The housekeeper took us in through the cellars and the first room we entered was the little breakfast parlour, called Anne Scotts room, from thence we went into the dining-room, where Scott died. These apartments were both furnished plainly, but very comfortably, and contained some fine pictures, especially a head of Mary Queen of Scots, taken after her execution, and an admirable likeness of his faithful Tom Purdie. From this room we passed into the armoury or cabinet of curiosities, a small narrow room filled with all sorts of curious things fastened to the walls with labels, Rob Roy's gun, and the one he always used himself which Mr. Stevenson took down & held to his face. The house keeper told us many things had been stolen, even to the labels, so that she was obliged to keep a strict watch. From this receptacle of old & odd things we passed into the Drawing Room, which is a very handsome apartment, & fitted up as a Library as well as a drawing-room, with cases filled with books. Here we saw the chairs presented by George the 4th and also an old cabinet of curious workmanship, a table and vase the gift of Byron &c &c. The ceiling of this room is very beautiful, & must have cost an immense sum. The last and most interesting room to me, was his study, a small apartment with one large double window, in the middle of the floor was the table on which he

(*170*)

wrote all those delightful works which have done so much to raise the reputation of his native land. I sat in his chair for one moment, and wished I could have caught inspiration from its touch. On the other side was another made of the wood of the house in which my favorite hero Wallace was betrayed. On the mantle piece stood the lamp he always lighted his fire with, and in a closet communicating with the study by a small door is preserved in a glass case, the last clothes he wore, a dark green coat, vest pantaloons, &c & on the wall is hung his cane, spurs, boots—hatchet &c &c. This was his sanctum, into which no one was allowed to go uninvited. Around the room runs a narrow balustrade, which is ascended by a few steps and enabled him to get to his books without difficulty and also led to his dressing room above. The Hall is perhaps the most curious part of the house, it is filled with what he called his 'Nicknaccories' all sorts of odd & old things from every quarter of the globe, the wonder is, how the mind of so great a man could be so engrosed by such insignificant things, & how he could have devoted so much time, & wasted so much money, in the erection of a building which has so little taste or convenience to recommend it. To my inexperienced eye, it seems a jumble of all the different orders of architecture and after all looks like a baby-house compared to the fine old Baronial Castle's of England. The sculptured likeness of his favorite dog Maide at the front door was to me a very interesting & touching object as it bespoke the kindness & tenderness of heart of this mighty magician, it represents a beautiful animal in an attitude of repose. The little court before the house is a circle of gravel and between that & the wall turf & shrubbery, on each side of the front door knots of flowers were blooming from one of which I plucked a rose for you, which I will send you if the postage is not too high. I am afraid you will think this a very unsatisfactory account of Abbotsford, but if you saw how I was writing you would only wonder how I could put intelligible sentences together. Mr. Stevenson who is sitting at the other side of the table pouring over a map of Scotland, interrupts me me every moment to ask some question, & pulls & shakes the table so that I can scarcely write legibly. I have asked him to help me out with his reminiscences, but he says, I had better reserve it all 'till we meet. But there are two objections to that, in the first place I may forget, & secondly, I shall never have a chance to edge in a word side-ways, or edge-ways, or any way when we get back, to indulgent listeners. He is surprised you all feel any interest in my stupid scrawl's, & advises me to give over so unprofitable an employment, so that you see, I have my antidote to your poison close at hand, and am in no danger of being spoiled by flattery. His Excellency says, it is time to retire, but before I obey, I must transport you from the lonely & solitary abode of the departed bard, to the beautiful Capital in which he also delighted to dwell. Much as I have heard of the picturesque beauty of this noble City, I have not been at all disappointed, indeed, it has surpassed our expectations. The rocky precipices—the beautiful valleys, & the towering edifices, rising in irregular masses, present altogether a scenery entirely unique as well as most beautifully picturesque. We reached it about 5 oclock in the evening, and took rooms at Wren's family Hotel in Prince's Street just opposite the Castle, and very near Scotts residence, which is in the next St. Soon after we got into our comfortable parlour, from the windows of which we could see the Castle just opposite towering to an immense height above us, Mr. Stevenson exclaimed, I wish Betsy were here! It was an echo to my heart's fondest & most cherished wish—and if wishes could bring you, how soon you would be here, beloved Sister. The next day we took a carriage & went into the old town on our way to Holyrood Palace, and in passing through the Canongate I counted 12 stories to several houses. Holyrood has nothing left of the splendours of the olden times, its glory has departed from it, and it looks as if Old Time was about to consign it to oblivion. The only thing of any interest about it is the apartments of the ill-fated Mary, which consist of four rooms, the first & largest the hall of audience is a good sized room of modern times, with a bed in it which I think the woman told us had been Charles the 2d, some chairs of embroidery, one worked by Mary, and another consisting of two united into one which Mary & Darnley used at their ill stared marriage. Her chamber is entered from this room, & contains a small low bed with its mouldering furniture, a half length mirror she brought with her from France—work table & box, containing her likeness, and a little basket worked by herself, to contain the clothes of her infants. On each side of this room are two small rooms, or large closets, the one her dressing room, the other she was at supper in with one of the ladies of her court when Darnley committed the atrocious murder of her unfortunate favorite. The private stair case is shown by which he & the other assassins entered, & the blood stained floor. Hapless Mary! more sined against, than sinning —peace to thy manes! From Holyrood we went to see the statue of Burns—Calton Hill, which affords an enchanting prospect. I wished much for physical powers to mount to Arthurs seat & look down upon the scenes of the 'Heart of Midlothian' but could not venture. We dined in the evening with Sir John Robison, a very sensible & scientific man. Yesterday the Lord Provost called & took us to the Courts of Session, the criminal court where poor [word illegible] stood at the bar, the seat Sir W. always occupied &c—St. Giles' Church—the University its libraries &c &c. Today we have walked at least 6 miles—think of that! Up to the Castle—& I am tired to death.

HOSTESS TO THE Stevensons at Dunrobin Castle was the aged Duchess-Countess of Sutherland, widow of the first Duke of Sutherland. This lady was proprietress of the greater part of Sutherlandshire, Scotland's northernmost county. Her domain was almost feudal in extent.

A turreted stone stronghold looking out across Moray Firth to the North Sea, Dunrobin Castle dated back almost to the days of the Norse invasion. Getting there was a tedious journey for one so frail as Mrs. Stevenson. The trip up from Edinburgh was hard but fascinating, past Culloden battlefield, Ben Nevis, through the romantic Scotch Highlands until, at last, almost "wearin' awa'," she and her husband came in sight of the towers of Dunrobin.

From Dunrobin two letters went to America—one to "My Beloved Sisters and Friends"; one to her brother, Edward Coles at Philadelphia.

Dunrobin Castle Sepr 19

My beloved Sister & friends—

We left Edinburgh soon after I closed my letter to you, very unexpectedly to me, as Mr. Stevenson had intended the night before to remain one day longer & visit Roslin Castle & Hawthorn-Den, the seat of the poet Drummond, but in the morning he changed his mind, & about 12 oclock we set off for

Perth, which we reached that evening, a distance of 44 miles, having passed through a beautiful & picturesque country. The most interesting object to me was Lough Leven the scene of Mary Stuarts captivity, & of Scotts novel the Abbot, it is a magnificent piece of water, of great extent finely bounded by mountains on one side, and on the other by the plain, & town of Kinross, where we stoped to change horses. There are several islands in this great expanse of water, but that on which the Castle is situated is about the middle of the lake. We could see the ruined tower from the road on which we gazed with deep interest, but not enough to make us think it worth the trouble of crossing over to see it more nearly. The keys which Douglas threw into the Lake have been found some few years since. We reached Perth in time to have a good view of all its beauties —the first glimpse from the hill of Moncrief is enchanting, the prospect from thence, is said to be the glory of Scotland. It affords a variety & richness of views seldom to be met. House of McPherson, the translator, or author of Ossian and nothing could be more varied, rich, & beautiful, than the scenery of this day journey, sometimes we passed through picturesque views of wild & gloomy nature, then entered rich valleys finely wooded & watered by the most beautiful streams, & Lough's which in a a few miles would change to lofty cliffs with their fronts ragged & broken; with flocks of sheep feeding on the short herbiage, the pine seems to be the favourite growth of the soil, and indeed grows out of the naked rock, the melancholy green of this picturesque tree is particularly suited to the wild scenery of an Alpine country. After this day's journey, I do not feel surprised at the love of the Highlanders for the 'woods & wilds' of their native mountains, and that they should fight with such determined bravery for their homes & their "Highland Capes". We reached Inverness about 4 oclock & stoped to change horses, and for Mr. Stevenson to obtain some information about the roads, &c, the inn keeper gave us a letter from the Duchess Countess to say how happy she should be to receive us at Donrobin &c, &c. We stayed all night at the distance of 20 or 30 miles, so as to be able to reach the Castle in time to dress for dinner. To give you some idea of the extent of the Duchess' possessions, the house at which we stayed was owned by her and we understood from the inn keeper that the greatest part of the county is the Sutherland Estate. The late Duke was a great benefactor to the county and did much to emeliorate the condition of his tenants, his memory is held in such veneration that his tenants have subscribed to the creation of a shrine to him on one of the loftiest hills near Dunrobin Castle. It is said to be one of the largest & finest in Europe, & is the work of Sir Frances Chantrey; except two large subscriptions, the whole sum was made up in shillings & sixpences. The Duchess is also very popular, & most deservedly so, for a more amiable kind-hearted person I never knew, she received us with the most frank & cordial kindness, said how good it was in us to come, &c, &c. She went with me to the rooms she had assigned us, consisting in a suite of three, a small setting room, as she said, for Mr. Stevenson to write in, a dressing room, & chamber. She told me she had selected these rooms for us because they looked upon the sea. The Castle is situated on a round hill at a small distance from the sea. The view from the windows is entirely different from any thing I ever saw before. The space from the side of the hill in which my apartments are situated is only a few feet from a precipice. The sides of which is clothed with verdure & ornamented with fine large trees, through which glimpses may be caught of a beautiful garden, and just beyond the broad ocean expands to view. From two of the drawing room windows there is the same view, with the light-house in the distance, and from the other two, a side view of the sea & on the other, lofty mountains, from the tallest of which is seen the statue erected to the late Duke. The house itself is very old, at least 600 & 50 years since its foundation. It wears in every part the stamp of its antiquity in the peculiar form of the windows small with only two large paines, or rather sheets of glass, in deep recesses. She drew up the blind to show us the view of her husbands statue, soon after our arrival, saying it was the finest. We found not many persons staying at the Castle altho' she has every day some one to dinner, a company of 13 or 14.

Lord Francis Egerton her second son is staying here with a Mr. & Mrs. Lock—Sir John Abel Brooke, a great traveler & two or three other gentlemen, but the day after my arrival I was in my own room, and indeed almost all day in bed, by the Duchess command, she discovered the night before that I had a cold & she told me she should prescribe for me and calling up her groom of the chambers, she told him to direct the steward to make up a dose which she ordered, & then turning to me, she said, "You must be good, & take it, you will not find it disagreeable". When I went to bed she accompanied me, & urged my letting Mr. Stevenson sleep in another room, & said she would put him just under me, that I might knock him up if I wanted him, in short, if she had been my Mother, or Sister she could not have been more kind or thoughtful of me, even to having a pitcher of her own barley water brought in for me. The next morning she was at my bed-side to feel my pulse, and bid me 'be good' & lie still, and that I must eat my breakfast in bed. That she was very sorry I could not go out with her as she had planned a pleasant excursion for me, but I must wait till the next day. I felt most thankful to be in such kind hands & such comfortable quarters, & did not get up untill towards the evening when I dressed in a morning costume & went out to dinner—but she would not let me get up to breakfast the next morning, saying nothing was so good for a cold as lying in bed. Yesterday she desired Mrs. Lock to show me the grounds, saying she would join us. We went out through the court a square place open at the top & entered by a large door, it is paved with stone, & in the centre is a well which supplies the Castle with water, in front of this is a green plot of grass between the Castle & the hill which has the earth raised so as to form a kind of parapet on which are placed 6 cannon, pointing out as if for defence. It seems these cannon were spiked in 45 by the rebels & not found for many years after buried under ground. We decended the precipice by a winding precipitous path which landed us in the garden, a pretty Eden looking place which wanted nothing but a bright sun-shine, and an Adam & Eve to wander through its shady walks, to remind one of Paradise, at the bottom of the garden is a stone house with hot & cold baths. The whole garden is surrounded by a stone wall & through a small gate which Mrs. Lock, unlocked, we found ourselves on the sea-shore, a shaded road wound round the outside of the wall & took us up again to the Castle. On the other side of the Castle a shaded road called the "Ladies Walk" took us into the open country winding along the sea side with seats placed at fine points for the view, for such poor walkers as myself to rest. To day I have been out to drive with the Duchess, in her beautiful Barouche & four, with postilions, & an out rider, and a dandy looking footman in the box, she carried me to see some fine views, & to the village, on our return she asked me if I was not tired, if I would like to look at the Castle, and we explored every part of it even to the kitchen & scullery. The stewards & house-keepers rooms are almost as handsome as any in the house—even to sofa's & flowers—but I am sure you must be heartily tired of all this discription, but I have had no incident to write you, travelling all day at night we were too glad to get a little supper & to bed. I must confess I have not enjoyed this tour as much as I expected, my illness & other causes have conspired to prevent its being as agreeable as it might have been and as my fancy painted it would be. But, "Every sweet must have its sour—and every black its white". We shall leave this tomorrow to return to Inverness & from thence by the Caledonian Canal to Glasgow our movements then will depend upon circumstances. We find travelling more expensive than we had expected & fear we shall not be able to see all we wished or make the visits from which I had expected most pleasure. However, I shall not ask Mr. Stevenson to do any thing which he does not feel himself able & willing to perform as I have already seen more than I ever expected to look upon—his health has wonderfully improved & I never saw him look better than he does now. He is fishing & shooting every day & is I think a great favourite with the Duchess, who asked me yesterday if he would not be President, & said, she wished he would sell out in America, & come & live in Scotland that he was a very clever person. I could not help smiling at the idea of his being P—t, & selling out to live in obscurity in S——, she is so clever herself that she felt the incongruity of this remark, & added by way of accounting for them, "That she liked us both so much". But I hear the dressing bell & must bid you Adieu. As the Duchess says, "Am I not very good to write you so much"? It is, however, a wretched scrawl & on looking it over & seeing how much "discription" it contains, I am afraid to direct it to Betsy, of whom & you dear Ned, I was dreaming all night. Do read this & send it on to her to the G. Mountain. Your devoted sister

S. C. Stevenson

Dunrobin Sepr 21st 1838
Eleven at night

Beloved Brother,

As I make it a rule never to send blank paper across the water I will at this late hour say a few more last words to you. I forgot when I was crowding in every thing on the last sheet of the enclosed that there must be an envelope. I am afraid you will think I have become a very careless writer, but you must keep in mind how hurriedly I write. In my last to Betsy I attempted to describe Sir W. Scotts house, whilst Mr. Stevenson was talking to me, & I made the mistake of telling her that the drawing room & library were in one, instead of saying that the D Room was not remarkable for any thing except the chairs presented to him by George the 4 whereas the library is a very beautiful apartment and the one I attempted to describe—however, it is better to write inaccurately & carelessly than not to write at all. I have just taken leave of the Duchess as we start at 8 I cannot tell you how very kind she has been to me, & she said tonight after taking a very tender leave of me that I must write to her from Glasgow as she should be uneasy untill she heard from me. Last night she ordered in the piper in his highland dress to play on the bagpipes for me, & she went with me to the common that I might see him walking about playing

—for the piper cannot play the pibroach setting. To day we have taken a short drive (Mrs. Lock Mr. Stevenson the Duchess & myself) of 18 or 20 miles in her Barouche & 4 beautiful bays, the post boys dressed in short jackets of blue cloth, white pantaloons, a jocky cap & fair tops, as John Randolph would say, 'sweet as my Lady's glove' on their left and they wore a scarlet & black band with a medallion on which was the crest of the Sutherlands & white gloves. The groom on horseback in the livery of the family, & the footman on the box. She is a wonderful person for her age, 73, walks miles, & makes nothing of a drive of 90 miles in the day—never lunches —can fast from half past 9 to 8 at night—& never complains of fatigue or cold. The most kind & unpretending manner —makes a great deal of decisions—but I must to bed for I shall have to be up so early. I am so tired—pray let me hear soon from Sally—again God bless you—Your own devoted sister—

XXIII

Two PLACES above all others—excepting Windsor Castle—Mrs. Stevenson wanted to visit in England: Raby Castle in Durham and Newstead Abbey, Lord Byron's former home in Nottinghamshire.

At both these historic places she and her husband were house guests. The reference in this letter to Angelica's health and happiness was prompted by the engagement of her niece, Angelica Singleton of South Carolina, to Major Abram Van Buren, the President's son.

At Raby Castle the Stevensons were guests of William Henry Vane, second Duke of Cleveland and his Duchess. At Newstead Abbey they spent eight days as guests of "Colonel Wildman" who is chiefly identified as Lord Byron's "school-fellow and friend." But Colonel Wildman was an intrepid restorer. He sought to recapture the glories of this old priory as Byron had known it. The great romantic poet himself referred to it once as "a glorious remnant of the Gothic pile."

London Novr 20th 1838

My beloved friends,

I wrote you a very long letter my beloved sisters and brother, immediately on my return from Scotland by the first packet in Novr which I directed to my dear Edward at Philadelphia. I had so much to say to you in reply to your letters which I found here on my arrival that I had no time, or space to speak of my travels and visits through the North of England, for I do not consider it answering a letter merely to refer to its date. I promised to give some account of my tour and I will comply, however, undeserving you may all be of any more details. I wrote four letters from Scotland, or rather, three from that interesting country, & one from Whittington Hall, Mrs. Green's, in Lancastershire. Lest any of my letters should have miscarried, I will just give you a synopsis of what I saw in our route, of our journey, &c. We left this on the 27th of August by the rail road to Denbigh Hall, then by post to Rugby in Worcestershire and from thence to Birmingham by the rail road, where we spent the night. By Wolverhampton, Stafford, &c to Warrenton to dinner, & to have our carriage repaired, which had been injured on the rail road. By post through Warwick, Newton, Ashton, Yarrow Bridge, &c, to Lancaster, where we stayed all night, & took a walk the next morning to look at the town, and as it was only a short drive to Whittington Hall we got there early in the day. I wrote you of the kind reception, & pleasant time we spent there &c, &c. From Whittington we entered Westmoreland at Kirkby Lonsdale, through Melthrop, Bowness, Windermere, Lenwood where we slept on the banks of the Windermere, and the next morning made a visit to Ridel-Mount the residence of the poet Wordsworth, who lives near Ambleside, from thence we passed through all the English Lakes, the Vale of Keswick—Losewater, Wasdale, & Ullswater, the latter the most beautiful scenery of all the lakes presenting the happiest, combination of beauty & grandeur that the imagination can conceive. Entered Cumberland at Wigton to Carlisle, where we stayed all night, and Mr. Stevenson visited the Castle, now a Barracks for soldiers, the next day we entered Scotland by the Scottish Dike of Langholm to Howick, St. Boswell Green—Dryburgh, the burying place of Walter Scott—slept at Melrose, and visited the ruins the next day by a bright sunshine. Abbotsford—Gallashields, Fashee bridge to Edinburgh

—which after all is the most beautiful thing in Scotland, & those who have travelled more than I have, say it is the most picturesque & beautiful town in the world. We spent four days there very agreeably altho' all our friends & acquaintanecs were out of town—from thence to Perth by the way of InverKetting, Lock Leven, the prison of Mary Stuart, to Kinross through Glenbury the bridge of Earn, the scenery of which is enchanting, passed our friends Ld & Lady Rothven without knowing it, over the Moncrief Hills to Perth—from thence to Inverness through Birnam Wood, not to Dunsnane, but to Dunkirk the most beautiful scenery in Scotland, to Blair Atholl, by the pass of Killiekrankie past the battle-field, & the falls of Bruer, to Dalmacordock, Dalwhinnie to Pitmain where I got my cold in a damp bed, & from thence to Avermore, Freetown and just before we reached Inverness we passed the battle ground of Culloden, but I must have possessed the gift of the seer to be able to tell you more, than that it still looks like "a field of the dead" at the distance from which I saw it, I can only say it had a peculiar look of wildness & desolation. We only stoped in the town long enough to change horses & obtain directions for the road, passed the ferry at Murray Firth where a lady & her maid were drowned a few days after, to Dingwall stayed all night at Stettingham, in the domain of the Duchess Countess, & the next day to Bonor Bridge, Clashmere, Galspie & arrived at Dunrobin Castle about 5 in the evening. We remained there a week as I wrote you and then returned to Inverness to take the steam boat on the Caledonian Canal, through Lock Ness— Lock Lochery, Loch Fortwilliam & stayed all night at an Inn at the foot of Ben Nevis Crinman Canal Loch Fine to Oban, up the Clyde to Grenock & Glasgow, to Ld Belhaven's at [word illegible] Hall, where we stayed three days and then returned to Carlisle by a different route, through Lanark, Chester— Wallace's Cave—Locherby—Gretna Green &c &c by rail way to Hexham & New Castle upon Tyne from thence we posted to Durham stoped at the Castle of Auchland to see the Bishop of Durham, & Mrs. Maltby and then on to Raby—and now dear friends, what can I say of this fine old monument of the olden times which can satisfy your curiosity, or give you any idea of its real appearance it is so very difficult to impress the mind of another with any just sense of objects intended for the sight, that I feel almost helpless in making the attempt—but as one of the greatest enjoyments I have had in sight-seeing has been the hope of imparting pleasure to you I must endeavour at least to give you my impressions of what I have seen, imperfect as they may be. We reached Raby between 5 & 6 oclock a beautiful autumn evening, we were struck as we approached the Castle by the thickly foliaged & lofty trees rising in masses and forming a majestic back-ground to the beautiful & picturesque scenery the park and ornamented grounds around the Castle are disposed with very great taste. The spacious lawns over which the deer sported in wild & happy playfulness, the hills formed a picture on which the eye delighted to gaze. The road cut through the wood decends from hills much higher than the Castle and the beautiful vale beneath opens abruptly upon the noble & massy building, with its towers & turrets, over which so many centuries have rolled, as we approached a loud & sonorous bell announced the arrival of visitors. The Castle is surrounded by an embrasured wall and the remains of the Foss, or moat, the entrance into the outward Court, or area, is by a gate over which was formerly the drawbridge, & the remains, or marks of it are still visible. This outward gate is guarded by two square towers and flanked with a parapet ornamented with turrets, another gate or immense folding doors admits the carriage through an arched passage into the inner area, or quadrangular court yard surround on all sides by the walls of the Castle. On crossing this another folding door is opened, & the astonished travellers find themselves in a magnificent Gothic Hall, the carriage way passes immediately through it, the roof of which is arched and supported by 6 pillars—on each side of the carriage way which is of stone, there are two fire places, and when the Hall is lighted up by 4 large and brilliant chandeliers, it is impossible to conceive any thing more striking or imposing than the coup d'oeil. The carriages & horses (for a long train of carriages may set down, without any inconvenience, as they pass out through folding doors on the opposite end of the Hall,) with innumerable liveried servants, headed by the groom of the Chambers, the lights the splendor, & above all the novelty, is quite bewildering, & makes one almost fancy themselves in an enchanted Castle, from the carriage a satin slippered dame may put her foot upon a soft carpet which leads to a flight of 5 or 6 steps extending the whole width of the Hall and opens into the presence Chamber or Saloon a circular room furnished with gorgeous magnificence. The Duke met us in the Hall and welcomed us with all the warmth & cordiality of high bred courtesy and soon after the Duchess entered, & was too happy, &c. After a little while she offered to show me my apartments, and I cannot give you a better idea of the extent of the Castle than by taking you with me through the intricate mazes of the broad gallery & the Hunters do &c. Her Grace led the way with my cloak on her arm, up a flight of steps when she turned to the left, and we passed through a gallery which she told me was occupied by his Royal Highness the Duke of Sussex. I counted 5 doors all of which she said were his, about half way we turned to the right and I thought there would be no end to this gallery, but at last I found myself in what appeared to be a drawing-room a fine fire with sofa's pictures &c &c on looking round I saw 4 doors which I found afterwards led to different suites of apartments but I never found out the use of this room unless kindly intended for poor wanderers to warm themselves in their weary peregrinations—but to return to my own—the Duchess passed on through one of these doors, and on, & on, we went untill at last my weary pilgrimage was ended, and I found myself in a spacious and magnificent bedroom with its state-bed reaching to the lofty and highly decorated ceiling and surrounded by satin damask curtains, the sofa's & chairs to correspond. The Duchess begged I would feel myself at home and directed my maid to ask for what I wanted & then left me, as she said, to repose before dressing time & kindly added, she would send her page to show me the way down to the reception room. After her departure I was induced to extend my observation to Mr. Stevenson's room, which was quite as splendid as mine. The cost of the parian marble chimney pieces in these two rooms, would build a comfortable house for a poor gentleman in our pleasant land. When Mr. Stevenson came up he was quite as much struck with admiration as I had been & he found many things which I in my weariness had overlooked. We were both surprised on drawing aside the damask drapery on one side of the room to discover recesses to the windows quite as large as small rooms surrounded by sofa's of silk damask, and looking out upon the beautiful lawn covered with deer that frisked & frolicked about in every direction giving beauty, life, and animation to the picturesque scenery that surrounds this time-hallowed Castle. But I must not forget the little page who waits to play the part of Ariadne, a youth of 16 covered with gold lace, and buttons, as necessary an apendage to every fine lady as her lap-dog. I was a little annoyed on entering the grand Saloon to find all the company assembled & waiting for me, it is the etiquette always to be before a Royal guest, who enters to the company, and they pay him, or her the compliment to rise & stand untill bidden to sit, or their Royal highnesses are pleased to be seated themselves—a little at war with our republican principles, you will say! But the Duke of Sussex is so amiable, and so little exacting that every one seems to take a pleasure in showing him this courtesy, & he is careful not to make it burdensome. I will not pause to describe the gorgeous magnificence of the Salle-a-manger, or dilate upon the sumptuous splendours of the festive board, where we had both mirth & good cheer, & not less than 28 & 30 guest every day whilst we stayed there. The table was resplendent with gold, & covered with all that wealth, taste, & luxury could supply. The Duke of Cleveland led me, & his Royal Highness desired I would sit by him, saying good-humouredly to his host, 'That he must forgive his selfish monopoly'. When the ladies retired they amused themselves with coffee—tea—& chit chat. I must however, do the English ladies the justice to say, there is nothing of scandal or ill-natured remark in their conversation, in high-bred society the harshest censure I have ever heard of an absent person has been the exclamation—How odd! How very odd! Generally their minds are as highly cultivated as their manners are polished & refined and they make things not persons the subjects of their conversation; whilst at Raby there was a lady Elizabeth Hope Vere a very intelligent high bred woman but she had the most insatiable fondness for telling ghost-stories or tales of chivalry & romance, she is a Scotch woman, & lived near the great Magician, so that his mantle may have fallen upon her. She certainly related her tales with all his graphic elegance, and much of his eloquence of language. We were delighted to form a circle around her, and draw her into the relation of those tales of other days, but when the gentlemen entered the scene changed. After they had taken their coffee & tea the Duke sat down to cards, and those who liked music went into the next apartment, fitted up in the Chinese fashion, and brilliantly lighted up. The communication between these rooms, is very curious, it seems to have been made in the wall and such is the immense thickness that it forms quite a passage which is lighted by a Chinese lamp, imagine walls 9 feet one inch thick, it is not wonderful therefore that they should have stood the shock of time, before which all things fall sooner or later. Just before the hour of retiring a servant here, as in all English houses, brings in a tray and places it on a table, with refreshments & when every one has helped themselves, they take from another table a night candle & retire after being informed by the hostess that their hour for breakfast is 10 oclock and in religious houses their hour for prayer is also named to the guest. Nothing can be more unceremonious than a breakfast in an English house you can either take it in your own room, come at the beginning or ending of the meal, without exciting the least observation. The breakfast table at the D. of Clevelands was the most magnificent thing I ever saw. The whole table was covered with bright & burnished gold, at the plate of each guest numerous as they were, was placed a gold sugar dish, a little vessel for cream, of the most beautiful and classic shape. Salt & an egg cup all of gold—& the middle of the table filled up with gold baskets, containing different kind of cakes, cold but not sugared. The hot cakes were brought in covered plates of the same bright metal—but I shall never have done if I dont get on a little faster besides, I am getting tired before I have fairly began. But next to having you with me dear sister is the pleasure of telling you what I have seen in the hope of amusing you some long winter night. I think of you always dearest, but most when I am pleased & gratified. Alone—in crowds—serene or sad—in shade or shine—I think of Thee—my sister—and often—often did I wish for you & Angelique and imagine how you and my dear romantic Cas would have enjoyed it all. The day after our arrival the Duchess' neice Miss Russell took us all over the house to the different suites of apartments which are numerous and more modern in their proportions and distributions than one could easily conceive in so ancient a building. Those appropriated to our use were decidedly the handsomest in the Castle except the Duchess'. The saloon is the most gorgeous both in its furniture & decorations. This with the Chinese & billiard room form a suite to themselves on the other side of the dining room is another beautiful D Room filled with fine pictures by the old masters this room the family use in common but the part of the Castle which gives the strongest impression of its antiquity is the Old Baronial Hall in which 700 Knights were entertained, it is 90 feet long 36 in breadth, and 34 in height. The roof is flat and made of wood the joist ornamented with shields of arms of the family of the Nevilles. The present Duchess has converted it into a Museum and filled it with all sorts of odd things. After looking at all the inhabited & uninhabited parts of the Castle, we decended to the kitchen, which looks as if it had been built to prepare feasts for 700 hungry Knights fresh from a tournament. It is a magnificent and lofty square and has three fire-places, one for the grate, one for the stoves, & the 3 for the great cauldrons, the top is arched and a small cupola lights it in the centre, on the sides are five windows with a gallery passing all around, from which tradition says, the dames of the Castle in former days, ordered the feasts. We assended a narrow stair case to the head cooks room, which is so constructed that he can hear the slightest whisper from his subordinates below, thus keeping a vigil with his ears when his eyes are away. The larder would have made an epicures mouth water, and the pastry room my good sister Singleton coveteus, could she return to the days of her merry youth when she was want to rise with the sun, to make our dear Father cherry-pie (at least three times during the cherry season) with her own delicate fingers, singing all the while merrily as the morning lark. The wall was of Dutch tile looking so nice & cool, & the fixtures for the dough so complete. The places for the flour— butter, &c, &c and, on one side a receptacle for ice. The dairy with its milk troughs so fixed as to enable the dairy-maid to take of her cream without losing a particle, cheeses of every size, shape & age, with presses to make them. The bread-room adjoining with its vast vessels of dough & the fiery oven with its yawning mouth. The Still room—the butler's & house-keepers rooms and lastly the stewards parlour where all the upper servants after dining in the servants hall took their wine & fruit much to the annoyance of some of their fair mistresses who in vain rung their bells to call up the bells from below (Richard Vaux you see has infected me with his punning mania). The servants hall is an immense apartment, containing a table at which from 75 to 100 domestics took their meals, at the head of the room are two figures representing peace & plenty, here the upper servants sit, and at the other end, where the ale is served out, are two more figures with the words, "Waste not, want not!" Miss Russell pointed out to me a door, that led, she said, to a subteranean passage which extended to Staindress a town a mile off and opened there into the Dukes family vault. To give you some idea of the immense antiquity of this Castle one of the towers called Bulwars was built in the time of Canute—but I am sure you must be tired of all this, and wish to hear of our departure—but for brother Walters amusement I must just say a word about the Dukes hounds horses &c. The day before we left the Castle he took us to his stables. Oh, if Mr. Singleton could see them! Showed us his beautiful hunters, and the Duchess ponies half made me wish to be a Duchess. The most perfect little things that ever bore the form & semblance of a horse, she has 4 two of which she drives in a poney phaeton & the other two her grooms ride after her. From the stable he took us through the gardens—very pretty—& by the servants establishments, the very head-quarters of comfort, with their nice trimmed walks & gardens. The dog-kennel is an ornamented gothic building with 4 walled yards, he first took us to the eating room—then the cooking room with boilers for the oat-meal & the bouillion, & then to the yards one half of which was paved & the other of soft turf with shelters from the sun, before he went into the yards he put on a long linen gown & took a whip in his hand, & when the keeper opened the door out rushed 80 hounds, sleek, & nice & well-fed they looked, but I confess I was glad to get out of their way—much did I wish for my dear good brother Walter, & Mr. Stevenson spoke aloud, & said, "My wife has a brother that would be delighted with all this"—and then away went my thoughts, & wishes across the wide waters. The Duke has been a great sportsman in his day and has some splendid trophies of his victories on the turf—he is not at all literary, but is very high bred & elegant, & has no doubt been very hand-some in his day. His Duchess has been a Helen of Troy and still preserves the remains of great beauty. Her age is past finding out. I saw very little of her as she was confined almost the whole time of our visit with a severe cold, but 'Rumour with her hundred tongues', has whispered that like the fair Helen of Troy, she has been as frail as fair. Ld Clarendon told me there was a shadow upon her fame, but at the same time gave me advice which was so kind as well as so sensible that I think I must take time to repeat it. He said, "As a stranger I had nothing to do with the private scandal of English society, it was sufficient for me that persons were visited and received into good society". That if I refused to visit those who were gen-erally received, it would be like casting a censure upon those who received them, &c. What a singular disgression from a dog-kennel to English morals. I can only say of the D. of C. that I found her very kind & civil. She issued every day from her beautiful boudoir directions for my amusement. She requested her neice "a nice girl" to take me to see her bath-house about a mile from the Castle a natural & very bold spring of water which has been made into a bath, & over it a Gothic Temple built with two rooms one for the bath the other as a dressing or tea room, or whatever use fancy or caprice may put it to—around this building the grounds have been improved & adorned with an expense which we poor American's would be too happy to have the power of bestowing on our residences. A little rural cottage with its garden, &c has been erected near for an old woman who stays there as guardian of the grounds, & keeper of the key. These magnificent old Baronial establishments which overshadow the land I must confess rather shock my republican prejudices and are sadly at war with my principles of 'equal rights' notwithstanding I must confess it is all very beautiful to look at, and must be very delightful to the owners, especially, to those who have not only the power, but the will to do good, & to be to their dependants a second Providence. I was much struck with this at Dunrobin where the amiable & high-souled Duchess Countess of Sutherland reigns over her splendid domain like a beneficent sovereign dispensing joy & happiness wherever she could, and ameliorating the condition of all. I am told the Duke of C. is also very kind to his dependants & does much good. I regretted very much it was not in our power to go to Alnwick; the Duchess of Northumberland wrote to us at Dunrobin a very kind and cordial invitation and I should have been highly gratified to have seen this celebrated place, and still more this amiable Duchess in the performance of her works of charity & love, for even in London she appeared to me to be all that was good, gentle, & graceful in woman & those who have been to Alnwick, say it is delightful to see her with her straw-bonnet, & little basket on her arm, tripping along to her schools dispensing smiles & kind words to all she meets, and entering the cottages of the poor & the afflicted to illumine with the light of her benevolence the gloomiest depths of despair & misery. This is what I envy the rich & great, I would not take the pride, pomp, & state, of the rich, if with it I must also take a cold selfish & unfeeling heart. I am afraid with all these digressions you will think I shall never get a way from Raby in truth our visit there was extremely interesting. I saw much that I shall always recollect with pleasure. The Duchess requested Mrs. Murcheson, a literary lady with whom I had been previously acquainted & whom I found at the Castle to take me to visit the places of interest in the neighbourhood. We gave one whole day to 'Rokeby' rendered classic ground by the magic pen of Walter Scott. It has much beauty independent of the romantic interest shed around it by Scotts poem. We traversed all the scenes so minutely described by the Poet, followed the flight of the ghost, & stood by the tomb at which it disappeared—looked at the ruins of the old Abbey &c, &c, and tho' last, not the least appreciable part of the days adventure, lunched, with the very identical 'Minne' of Scotts Pirate—and admired a splendid painting of the two sisters, lovely as the 'poets' dream. But the living moving reality before us had not a trace of beauty left, there was nothing in the pale, wan, & sickly looking girl before us, which even my imagination could invest with romance— but time the destroyer, had nipped this fair blossom, & disease has also committed ravages on what might have been a fair & delicate complexion—she gave us, however, a very comfortable lunch of which we partook with most un-romantic appetites, after our long & scrambling walk. Mr. Stevenson affected to be very much out of humour with being made the sport of anothers imagination, but he took care to obtain from one of the ghost walks a reminiscence in the form of a stout walking stick—to help his steps when a few more revolving suns have made a staff necessary. We also visited Barnam Castle which like Raby is rendered interesting from its historical associations, but unlike it, in being now shorn of its glory, this once stirring scene of human pomp and power is now only an immense ruin. We saw other places of less interest, but I will not detain you longer with discriptions of these monuments of the olden times. The day of our departure the Duchess sent her compliments to request the honour of a visit in her Boudoir. This room had an air of the most refined luxury. The walls were adorned with blue satin damask and mirror, put in alternate strips of about half a yard's width from the ceiling to the floor, the damask in rich folds. The furniture of the same, & the room filled with objects of taste, virtue, or luxury. To give you some idea of the immense wealth of the English nobility I will mention a little circumstance which took place on this visit. When I entered the Duchess had a jewel case in her hand, which she was showing Lady Cecelia, who had requested to see a broach, or what we call a breast-pin—it was as large as the palm of little Helen's hand, a saphire set round with large diamonds. I wished very much to know what it cost & was glad when Lady C. asked the question. She replied that the Duke had given—10,000 pounds for it, as a bridal present 50,000 dollars! A watch in the case at 4000, and a bracelet—one remember—at 2000 pounds—now when you take into consideration that this was only a small part of her Grace's jewelry, that one single little case contains 80,000 $ worth, what must her diamonds be worth!!! We reached York the night we left Raby, having gone a little out of our way to see the celebrated Minster the most glorious work of art in all this glorious little island, it is indeed a fit Temple in which to worship the Supreme and impresses the beholder with a feeling impossible to describe. The mind is dazzled, awed—confounded—It is in art, what the falls of Niagara is in Nature—unique—in grandeur and sublimity. From York we found it an easy days journey to 'Sandbach', the Earl of Scarborough's where we arrived in time to prepare for dinner. This is a modern house, but all is elegant, appropriate splendid, yet useful. The most fastidious admirer of simplicity could not find one object which he could denominate gaudy, nor the lover of grandeur one thing which indicated deficiency. The house is very large & admirably conducted, altho' the Earl has no Lady we found a small but agreeable company there which I was rather glad of as I was not well enough to enjoy much company. Lord Scarborough is immensely wealthy and owns only 3 establishments Lumley Castle in the North and Rufford a fine old place about 19 miles from

Sandbach, and is said to be a fine specimen of that peculiar stile of building half convent half Castle which remains as a monument of the feudal times. Mr. Stevenson went with a party from L.S.'s to see it but I was not well enough to venture so far in one day. After spending a week with the Earl we went to Sheffield to see the manufactories, Mr. Rogers took us all over the establishment, showed us the machinery &c. We saw them making those celebrated knives & rasors which are considered the best in the world. Mr. Rogers was very civil to us & made me a present of a very pretty ivory paper cutter with knife in it and a painting of the place where the grinders lived. I bespoke for you a very pretty & useful little article which he promised to send to me in London but which has not yet arrived. We went on in the evening to Newstead Abbey, now owned by Col. Wildman, who gave 100,000 pounds for the ruin & has spent 200,000 in repairing & renewing it. I have visited no place in England which has excited deeper feelings of interest than this celebrated old Abbey, consecrated not only by its historical associations but by the genius of Byron. As we approached it, I looked out upon what had once been the noble forest of Sherwood and thought of the days of Robin Hood, of his 'merry men', & of all the legendary tales of the olden times. The Abbey is situated in a low and sheltered spot and the approach to it is rather circuitous; the coup d'oeil is very striking, when the first glimpse of the lancet window covered with ivy met my eager gaze, I involuntarily thrust my head out of the carriage and was only recalled to the proprieties of Indian stoicism by a whisper from my husband. Col. Wildman & his lady received us in the library with a warmth of hospitality which made us feel ourselves among friends instead of acquaintances, he was one of the hero's of the field of Waterloo and is in all courtesies and elegant accomplishments the model of a cavalier. Mrs. Wildman is one of the most amiable and interesting persons I ever knew, and the most extraordinary. She is afflicted with a kind of jerking or nervous twitching which would render most women useless to themselves & disagreeable to others, but by the force of her talents the sweetness of her

temper and the cultivation of every agreeable and useful accomplishment she seems to have forgotten herself and to make
others forget her infirmity. She plays and sings delightfully—
dances gracefully—and can do more worsted work in a day than
any one I ever saw could accomplish in a week and when it
comes from her hands it looks like a beautiful painting—and
tho' last, not least, she has never been seen out of temper in her
life. We intended staying two days, and were kept eight by the
hospitable kindness of the kind host & hostess, and those whom
we met as scarcely acquaintances we parted from as attached
& devoted friends. We found there a large and pleasant party
I should have spent my time perhaps too agreeably, but for my
indisposition—my husband enjoyed himself very much, more
than I have seen him since he came to England, & indeed, notwithstanding my occasional illness, I was highly gratified &
delighted with my visit, & half in love with the gallant Col.
who among all his other excellencies is the model of a husband
and blends as Miss Speare would say the 'softness of the dove,
with the perspicacity of the eagle' to me he was as watchful &
kind as one of my own dear brothers could have been. For a
discription of the Abbey I must refer you to Byron if you can
venture to look into that naughty poem of his 'Don Juan' &
to Washington Irvine tho' neither of them can give you any just
idea of the place as it is now. The hall of which Byron & Irvine
speak as a mere lumber room is now one of the most magnificent
apartments in Europe & is so strikingly beautiful in its taste &
finish that the stranger guest on entering involuntarily pause
with an expression of admiration and delight, the rooms which
Byron occupied have also been renewed & finished off in the
most beautiful taste. Like the Duchess of Cleveland she has
three for her own use, chamber—dressing room—& boudoir
all opening into each other the latter is a perfect little Bijou,
the sealing is highly ornamented, & the walls composed of the
dark oak highly polished, & mirror, in alternate strips from
the ceiling to the floor, in which one sees themselves reflected a
thousand times I stood upon the very spot in which Byron
composed 'Child Harold' and looked from the window at the

oak he planted with his own hands. In the Col's sanctum is the furniture he used at college, his sofa & his chair &c &c. I also saw his bed and the one in which Oliver Cromwell slept and dreampt of Empire. In short I saw every thing from the garret to the cellar. The cloisters where the Friars used to walk, the Chapel in which they offered up their prayers, & which has been repaired for the use of the family—examined the tapestry in the state rooms and the curious mantle pieces described by Washington Irvine—looked out upon the quadrangular grass-grown-court, & admired the lofty and fantastic Gothic fountain whilst Col. Wildman recited the beautiful lines of Byron describing it—walked over the Abbey gardens, & through the Devil's wood, & upon the broad terraced walk the favorite resort of the monks. The scenery around is very much embellished & enlivened by large sheets of water, which has been divided into ponds for fish. There is one which is called the 'Monks Stew' where the fish were deposited by those luxurious old gourmands for use, it is a dark pool overhung with cypresses. I also visited with Mrs. Wildman the monument erected by Byron to his dog on the very spot where the high altar formerly stood. The epitaph is the severest satire ever written on Man. From this place he obtained the famous scull which he had converted into a drinking cup, & which the Col. now keeps in a curious old fashioned cabinet, & on high occasions brings out, & circulates it around his festive board—he thought my husband's visit such an occasion—but I refused to taste—the very thought was horrible. My husband must tell you what he did. One can scarcely wonder at the wayward destinies of a man who scrupled not to desecrate the holiest things, and whose stormy passions and ungoverned temper made him an oppressor and tyrant to the hapless being who entrusted her happiness to his keeping—yet, such is the omnipotence of genius that we admire the poet whilst we can not but dislike & condemn the man. Col. Wildman cherishes his memory with all the warmth, & affec enthusiasm of friendship, and extenuates his errors with all the charity of a Christian. He pities him for having had such a Mother to watch over his childhood, and blames Lady Byron for many of the excesses he committed after marriage—he says, if instead of a rival genius, and a 'slattern blue stocking' he had found her an affec and sympathizing friend she might have moulded him to what Nature intended him to be—a glorious creature—but as Byron has himself said, it is difficult for a third person to form a just judgment of the mutual wrongs of husband & wife. There is a sacred mystery in that tie which cannot be solved. Col. Wildman took me to Hacknall Torchard where he is buried, an old county church, venerable with age about four miles from Newstead. I stood upon the flag stone that covered his mortal remains and thought of what value was his genius to him now, but as he had used it for the good or injury of mankind—he has gone where neither fame or flattery will reach him more. On the outside of the church as near as could be made to the object of her idolatry is the grave of the little White Lady, whom Col. Wildman with his usual benevolence had buried there. I heard from Mrs. Wildman some very interesting anecdotes of this poor little unearthly creature's adoration for the poet, the man she had never seen. When the housekeeper was showing her the house she asked on a slate which she always carried about her to see Byron's picture, and then stood before it with her hands clasped like one entranced untill roused by the housekeeper, when she requested to be taken to see his bed, & throwing herself upon her knees she kissed it repeatedly with passionate devotion. Strange power of genius o'er the human heart—or fancy We found at Newstead a Mrs. Joy, she a *belle esprit*—Mr. and Mrs. Fisher he an eminent barrister & she highly connected. Gen. Sir John Gardiner, & his Lady the sister of Col. Wildman, Sir S. & Lady Graham Sir F. O'Donnal & his Lady besides sundry other Ld's & Ladies who came to dine or spend the evening. Sir F. O'Donnal amused us with tricks of legerdemain & showed us more conjuration than Edward or poor Cary Nicholas ever dreamed of in their days of necromancy, and the night before we left Newstead, we danced a quadrille, I & Col. Wildman to his Excellency & Lady Gardiner—think of that! Mr. Stevenson dancing! his first appearance on that way, & really doing it in fine stile—he gained so much confidence from this first effort, that he proposed a waltz but I hinted that his head tho' pretty strong might be turned, & his heels tho' light, might perchance, unused to such rapid & sudden twirling, play him false—and like a good husband he hearkened to those prudent suggestions. I wrote you of the honours the Nottingham people were disposed to show him, & what a 'Lion' they made of him—of the stile in which we payed them a visit & of their presenting me with a beautiful lace dress & three scarfs one of which I have put away for thee, dear sister &c &c &c. We had not been in London many days before we received an invitation to Fulham Palace, the Lord Bishop of London, where we spent several days very agreeably but really I am so tired of scribbling that I cannot now go into any more details and I am sure you must be equally wearied with all these nothings. Decr 7th—This letter was written to go two weeks ago, but I kept it in hopes of receiving something from my friends—but not a word. I have neither been well or in spirits. These November fogs have had their usual effect —given me a dreadful cold & cough. I feel very anxious to hear from you my dear Edward & have thought much of my dear Angelica & sister Singleton. I was dreaming all last night about them. Say to Angelica we drank health & happiness to her on the 27th and that she has had my earnest prayers for her happiness here & hereafter. Adieu! A long Adieu—may Heavens blessing rest with you all is the prayer of your affec

S. C. Stevenson

Mr. Van Buren is still in Ireland from last accounts feasting & enjoying the hospitalities of the good people of the Emerald Isle, his health quite returned—he will be here in Decr if he don't change his mind.

XXIV

THOMAS JEFFERSON's granddaughter was in London, and Mayfair received her with open arms. Even though sixty-odd years had elapsed since the celebrated American statesman defied King George III, a certain awe still invested the name Jefferson.

This young lady, Ellen Wales Randolph Coolidge, daughter of Jefferson's beloved Martha, was newly wedded to Joseph Coolidge, Jr. of Boston. She had been a favorite of the patriot. To her and her husband, indeed, Jefferson had presented a most unusual wedding present, the small lap desk on which he wrote the Declaration of Independence. Now the young lady was in London, guest much of the time of the Stevensons. In this letter to her niece and namesake, Sarah Rutherford, daughter of her sister, Emily, Mrs. Stevenson, first, points a moral: the virtues of the "delightful art" of letter-writing.

London Feby 23d 1839

My dear Namesake,

You ought to think it very good in me to take this large sheet to write you when I tell you it is my second essay to thank you for your most welcome letter by Mr. Heth. I wrote you a long letter by the last week's packet which I am sorry to say was destroyed through an accident and now, not withstanding a thousand engagements and a multiplicity of things to do and think of doing I have sat down to write you, Miss Lazy Sall, who can only find time or inclination once a year to indite a short epistle to me, the poor exile of almost three years. Well I have sighed and cryed myself into philosophy and patience.

But to return to your letter. What a charming flatterer you are, my sweet niece. You tell me so prettily that my letters are delightful and yet you so seldom take the trouble to thank me for them that I am half inclined, not withstanding my self love, to doubt your sincerity. I am very sure of one thing that if you would practice a little more and write only half as much as I do, you would be infinitely my superior in this charming & good-natured accomplishment. It is one so peculiarly suited to our sex and for which most females have a natural talent that it is a pity when it is neglected. To woman "whose noblest station is retreat", it is a never failing source of agreeable occupation to herself and of pleasure to her friends. You know, or perhaps you do not know, as it is a forbidden poem to such young eyes as yours, what Pope says, "Heaven first taught letters for some wretches aid, &c &c—and my dear mother taught me among my first lessons that whatever was worth doing at all was worth doing well. Therefore, dear child, let me impress upon you whilst you are young to cultivate your talent for letter-writing and you will soon like it when you find by constant practice you do it with ease & elegance. There is no subject however trifling or insignificant in itself which may not be rendered agreeable by the pen of a ready writer—and besides, is it not the bond which unites the absent? "They live, they breathe, they speak, what love inspires"—warm from the heart, even at the distance of three thousand miles. I could go on to the end of my paper in praise of this delightful art, if by so doing, I could inspire my friends with the love of it but alas! they have the power, I the will—as I am proving at this moment when I write amidst a thousand interruptions.

Mr. Van Buren and Ellen Coolidge literally live here & come in upon me at all times & all hours. Ellen has rather taken here. The desire to see Mr. Jefferson's granddaughter extends to all classes, Tories and radicals. I whisper around, very like him—educated by him &c. &c. She seems very grateful to me for the trouble I have taken for her which has been not a little. To get even Mr. Jefferson's granddaughter into society here, without any letter, or aid but what I have been able to give her has been the means of taking me out much more than I should otherwise have gone. She goes to many of the places without Mr. Coolidge. She seems very much at her ease. She has the repose of manner which is so English & great self-possession with an air of modesty & sweetness which is very becoming. She comes to me for everything. I often laugh and ask her how she thinks I have got on without anyone to tell me anything. One of the strongest feelings of pleasure I have had in my success with Ellen is the assurance of my own strength. I feel now I can present whom I please, for many have said when I asked permission to present the granddaughter of Mr. Jefferson "If she is your friend, Mrs. Stevenson, that is sufficient". Thinks I to myself I will try your courtesy my Lord, or my Lady, next spring if it please God I live to see the dear and precious ones that are coming over to me!!!!

The season is already beginning, dinners & soirees without end. A few days since we dined with Hallam (the author of "The Middle Ages") and met there the Lady Davy, the widow of Sir Humphry, and a Lady Coke, the contemporary of Samuel Johnson & the "blessed Hannah," as she called Hannah More. She is all intellect, and at 94 her faculties are in a tolerable state of preservation and her conversation is really very agreeable, but you can imagine nothing more odd than her appearance, her little shriveled person clothed all in white mumbling under her white bonnet such witty and sensible things that one could almost imagine her a spirit. I maneuvered a little to get a seat near her at dinner that I might see how this antidiluvian eat, and learn a lesson in longevity. She began with a sago pudding made on purpose for her, but she soon branched off upon chicken patties, &c. She told us at dinner that Boswell had called on her to obtain anecdotes of Johnson, and that she "had told him a great deal, but not one word of truth, and that he had put it all down in his book." She told us that she was present on one occasion when a lady flattered Johnson to such an excess that he was disgusted, and turning to her, said: Madam, you are more than sweet: you are luscious." Of Hannah More she told innumerable anecdotes all going to prove the piety and uprightness of her mind. It is a pity she could not have cast her mantle upon her witty and talented contemporary who has so long held a contest with the grim tyrant, death, for I am told she has looked as she does now for years past. This is a wonderful country, I must say, where women never grow old!

XXV

THE GRAND DUKE Alexander of Russia, "heir to all the Russias," was assuredly somebody to write home about, and that was precisely what Sallie Stevenson did the moment she could take up her pen and paper. This Russian youth had come to visit Britain's new Queen who, it seems, was quite taken with him. After dancing the Mazurka with him she confided to her Journal, "He is a dear delightful young man. I am quite in love with the Grand Duke." The future Czar brought along a trunkful of diamond inlaid boxes and enormous diamond rings which he distributed to elite ladies and gentlemen of the Queen's entourage. Mrs. Stevenson met the Grand Duke but does not record being so favored.

As fate would have it the famous Bedchamber Crisis broke over England during the Grand Duke's visit. This petticoat imbroglio—almost as devastating as the Peggy Eaton Affair during President Jackson's administration—aroused much curiosity in two continents, and won admiration for Victoria's ability to hold her own, auguring well for the future.

This fiasco developed out of the Queen's refusal to part with the Ladies of the Bedchamber at the insistence of Sir Robert Peel, who, it seemed, on Lord Melbourne's defeat in Parliament, was about to succeed to the Premiership. Peel informed the Queen that if he took the Prime Ministership she must give up her Bedchamber Ladies, who were hostile to him and his policies. Chivalry was considerably strained to say the least.

The Diplomatic set, of course, were agog over this bed-chamber muddle, which forced the temporary fall of the Melbourne cabinet. Moving spirit in Parliament against Melbourne at this crisis was powerful Lord Brougham, who was apparently proud of his role, as Mrs. Stevenson found out when sitting opposite him at a magnificent dinner for the Grand Duke of Russia.

London, May 11, 1839

London is even gayer than this time last year. The presence of the Grand Duke of Russia has given rise to fetes and parties not only at the palace, but among the nobility, and at the Russian embassy. On Thursday evening we were at Ashburnham House, at a magnificent soiree, to meet the future Emperor of Russia (Alexander II). All the royal family were present except the Queen herself. I was taken up by the Countess Pozzi de Borgo, and presented to him. He addressed me first in French. I answered in English, and said I did not speak French. He then conversed in tolerably good English with me about a few royal questions—how long I had been in this country; if I liked it &c. Wished I would go to Russia, &c. He is in appearance about 22 or 23; graceful and symmetrical in person; a full face, though not very intellectual, with a small, well-shaped mustache on his upper lip. His manner is dignified and kingly, though silent and reserved. I think him rather handsome, but I find the English will not admit that he has any claim to be thought so, and say that his g.father was infinitely his superior in personal appearance. The Queen received him with great distinction, sent 4 state carriages to take him and his suite to the palace for a private audience, and gives, on the 13th, a splendid ball in honor of his arrival. He entered, it is said, the House of Lords, just as Ld. Melbourne tendered his resignation. It must have been an interesting scene for him. By the way, her Majesty has been in great trouble. She accepted the resignation of her ministers, and sent for Sir Robert Peel, who insisted, if he accepted the office, that she should give up all her ladies, especially the Baroness Lehzun, who is every thing to her—mother, nurse, friend, companion. In short, the poor little girl I suppose, would feel lost without this early friend and faithful attendant, who has declined all honor and distinction but that of being near her beloved pupil. It was a cruel situation for this young and innocent creature, but she met it with Jacksonian firmness—refused to give up her ladies, and re-installed her old ministry. The night of her ball it was made known, and Ld. Palmerston himself told me that he was still Minister for Foreign Affairs. I told him that I rejoiced, and that I knew Mr. S. would still more. He said that whatever change might take place, that he (Mr. S.) would never have a firmer friend or one more inclined to yield whatever he could both to himself and his country. The Queen looked happy, and danced away with the Grand Duke as if no sorrow had crossed her path. Indeed, it would be a pity that tears should so dim those dovelike eyes or sorrow cloud that innocent face. It is said she wept a whole day when her cabinet was dismissed, or rather, in parliamentary phrase, when the ministry resigned. What makes me feel more for her, is, that there is no doubt she is not on such terms with her Mother, as Mother & Daughter ought to be—& from what I can learn the Duchess of Kent is to blame, however this is all entreneus—I say 'entreneus' because of my husband's excessive caution. For fear Mr. McDuffie will not tell you I must give you some account of a very pleasant party we had a few nights before his departure, and of a dinner at which we had many distinguished for their talents—learning & rank, besides a host of Americans —amongst whom were Mrs. Van Buren & McDuffie &c &c— and in the evening we had quite a brilliant party of Americans & English and it was remarkable that every English person in the room was persons either of high rank or extraordinary for some thing either wit talent poetry or philosophy. Baron & Lady Parke, Baron & Lady Alderson, a sweet beautiful creature, Sir John & Lady McNeil, he is remarkable for talents, & had been ambassador to Persia. Babbage Senior—Ld Jeffrey who dined with us Mr & Mrs Grote at the head of the radicals and she a person of really wonderful acquirements, very eloquent, and talks like a man—& a philosopher—Milton a poet, whose name must be known to Fame. Heyward the translator of Faust (& sent me his work the next morning) Mr. & Mrs. Sydney Smith. The Rev. Sydney is considered the first wit in the world, & has said more good things than any man living. After the company dispersed, all to about a dozen, Mr. Stevenson & himself got upon the subject of canvas back ducks & he said so many brilliant things, that it was talked of at the clubs the next day. In short, my dear Brother, I succeeded perfectly and was really astonished at my own success, and as to Mr. Steven-son, he looked round in wonder, & thought I must have used some witchcraft to have collected so many agreeable persons in so short a time for here they have to give invitations two and three weeks before hand but I am exceedingly gratified to find how eager the English are to come to us, & several whom I have not named who were here late in the evening, had come from dinners & other parties, to me, & some who came early said they had declined to other places after accepting to enjoy one of my pleasant parties &c, &c. These soirees are much more pleasant than dinners. A little tea, ices and lemonade is all that is offered in the way of refreshment, and persons meet for in-tellectual enjoyment, & not to eat & drink. By the way, I recollect in one of your former letters, asking me about Lock-hart. I will now tell you all I know of him. He was to have been with me the night of my party, with Rogers, & Words-worth, but they sent apologies, saying they dined in Belgrave Square & it was midnight before they could get to our door, & then they thought it too late to come in. Lockhart, lost his wife soon after our arrival in England, & has not been much in society untill lately. He is about the middle size, very slender, in person, with rather a distingue air, & manner, but owing to a little deafness he is very shy. His countenance without being handsome is pleasing, & indicates talent & genius. His fine dark eyes, sparkle when he is excited by any feeling, but it is impossible to describe one accurately, whom you have only seen in mixed assemblies, or at large dinner parties. I sat by him one day at a large dinner with Ld Brougham vis a vis, and he conversed with me, but did not at all join in general conversation. By the way we were at a large party at his house on last Tuesday evening, to meet the Grand Duke, & the Royal family. It was a very brilliant soiree, and Ld Brougham seemed to be the happiest person there. He said to Baron Parke—"Well, Baron you know the ministry are all out, and I did it".

May 15th

Well, my precious sisters, my beloved A has arrived, I have seen her, embraced her, & shed tears of joy over her. But ah! how different is her feeling from mine. She just from the bosom of her family the pet of all, comes here to bestow upon me a calm kiss of kindred kindness. It is very natural it should be so and I ought to have known that she could not feel as I do, who have been pining in absence from all I have most loved for three years—besides, my heart has always been my torment, and I have wished sometimes I were a caterpillar. No, a butterfly, and had none—Heigho!—Well thats my last sigh—and now for a narrative of events. It has been one of the most trying weeks I have passed since I have been in London, for with constant going out, I have not had my usual repose in the morning, & the idea of seeing A. has kept me awake at nights. On Monday the 6th went to grand soiree at Countess Porzi di Borgo's, and a ball at Lady Parke's—Tuesday the 7 dined at Mrs. Greens—and went afterwards to Ld Brougham's —Wedensday—heard of A. arrival in England, so excited, had the hysterics, laughed & cryed, until, not fit to have gone out, and if I had not previously declined a grand ball at the Russian Ministers I should not have left my own room. On my return I could not sleep, thought of you, my own & best beloved, ill, disappointed, and prayed that you might be restored & spared to me, & find your happiness where it is only to be obtained— "At the fountains of living waters" and not where I am—at "broken cisterns"—but to return to my diary which I have open before me—dined at Ld Cheif Justice Fendal's, and went afterwards to a concert at the Duchess of Cambridge's, poor Mr.

Rush! he went with me, after a most elaborate toilet, full dress —shirts—buckles—&c no doubt it had been two mortal hours work for him, and I was so hard hearted, or rather so physically worn out, that I elbowed my way through the crowd made my curtsy to the Duchess, worked my way out again, went to the cloak room, waited half an hour for my carriage, & then home to bed. Friday—went at 10 oclock to the Palace to a grand ball, an hour getting there, stayed until two in the morning—saw the Queen dance with the Grand Duke, smile & bow to all, and look the triumph no doubt she felt—talked to a thousand & one persons, stood on my feet until I was ready to drop, eat some forced strawberries, at about 2 shillings a piece, & then home to bed, & to get such sleep as I could—Saturday— dined at a Mr. Justice Erskine's the son of the celebrated Lord of that name, met there a sweet creature, Lady Teingmuth so pious—so gentle & good. When we parted she said, do go home & go to bed for you must be worn out. But when we got to the carriage, James the footman, said Mrs. Van Buren has arrived, as they had written to take apartments at the Brunswick Hotel we hastened there & were directed to another, but they were not there, & we lost sight of them & were obliged to return home when we found two notes from her she having received a very affc one I had left the day before at the Brunswick for her, but as it was then 12 oclock, it was too late to go, & we went the next morning & found them in bed, Angelica, however came out in her dressing gown & we stayed with them an hour being Sunday I wished to have a few hours to myself as we were engaged to dine at Mr. Ellices to meet some of our particular friends a small Sunday dinner. I however, asked Angelica to come up after 3 & she did so, & stayed with me untill it was time to dress for dinner, at a quarter past 7 oclock. The next morning Monday 13th instead of spending the morning in my own room as usual putting my heart & head to rights I went as soon as I could get the carriage to A., & took her to all the shops dressmakers &c, &c returned home half dead with fatigue after 5 oclock. Rested a little while, dressed & went to Ld & Lady Lovelaces (Ada Byron) to dinner, to meet a distinguished party Ld & Lady Pitman (one of the Queens ladies,) the new Ld Clarendon &c, &c, immediately after dinner we went to the Palace to a concert, which tired as I was I enjoyed. The grand saloon was brilliantly lighted & the piano placed at the upper end with seats in rows, leaving an avenue up the room to the circle formed around the instrument, on one side of which sat the Royal family & the Grand Duke, with their attendants at the back—& on the other side the great dignataries. I had modestly taken a lower seat, when one of the gentlemen in waiting came to me, & said I was requested to go on the other side, where I found myself by the amiable Duchess of Northumberland, who made me a sign to come to her side. The old Tory Duchess of Richmond behind me, & the Duchess of Somerset a little in the rear, so that I found myself in the midst of "The Graces"—I made good use however of my proximity to her grace of Northumberland to obtain an invitation for my friend—& her husband which I managed I thought with considerable address and also from my little favorite Miss Wynn the Duchess' neice the young lady I chaperoned to the Marchioness of Sligo's ball, & who I told you presided at the head of her Fathers magnificent establishment. I told her she must also be kind enough to send me a card for my nephew Mr. Singleton which she promised to do—so that I think that was rather a good nights work. The next day Tuesday, we put aside every engagement & asked Angelica her husband Mat—John V B friend Clarke—Col. Thorn & his son —Mrs. Howe her daughter & son & a party of 12 to dine en famille. In the morning Angelica kept me waiting for her. A. and her husband wait for me now, which must not be, as the word wait is in no ones vocabulary here, except a coachmans— So adieu dear ones—

Your Sister S C S

XXVI

THE ARRIVAL of Angelica Singleton Van Buren at London was a source of great pleasure to the American Minister's Lady. Of rare beauty and accomplishment, Angelica was the daughter of Mrs. Stevenson's sister, Rebecca, wife of Richard Singleton, large landowner and planter of Sumter County, South Carolina.

In 1837, Angelica, just twenty-one, was introduced by her kinswoman and matchmaker par excellence, Dolly Madison, to President Martin Van Buren at a White House reception in Washington. Soon handsome Major Abram Van Buren, the President's eldest son and graduate of West Point, was paying ardent attention to the charming girl from South Carolina. Abram Van Buren was an attaché at the White House and private secretary to his President-father.

In November, 1838, after what might be called a whirlwind courtship, Abram Van Buren and Angelica Singleton were married at Hills of Santee in South Carolina. The bride and groom soon sailed off for London on their wedding trip to visit Angelica's "Aunt Sallie" Stevenson. She was the only member of Mrs. Stevenson's family ever to do so.

Apparently, shortly before the arrival of Angelica, one of Mrs. Stevenson's sisters in Virginia had written her a scorching letter on the subject of President Van Buren whom Mrs. Stevenson referred to as the "wily chef." But the lady in London was too tactful to reply in kind. She did, however, say what she thought of Van Buren's sons, both of whom were now in England.

With considerable pride Mrs. Stevenson made plans to present her beautiful niece to the Queen. Not only did she show off the attractive American girl to the Queen, but she managed to introduce Angelica into the charmed "court circle" where she met, among other royal and titled persons, the Grand Duke of All the Russias.

The Marchioness of Londonderry, the diamond-studded lady of this letter, was celebrated for her jewels. She was Frances Vane-Tempest, second wife of the third Marquis of Londonderry. Creevy called her "Young Lady Londonderry."

London May 1839

My beloved Sisters,

Altho' I sent you yesterday a volume by the great Western, yet I cannot resist the desire I feel to continue my scribling to to you, today, indeed, I can truly say I am never so happy as when I am holding a little chat with you and Emily, in the only way that is left to me, and now that I have given up all idea of seeing you here, I feel it a duty as well as a pleasure to devote to you every spare moment. During the last season I gave all my mornings to you, & to devotional reading & exercises—now, I am afraid I shall not be free always to do this as Angelica will have claims upon me, but I shall be a miser of my time for your sake. In my last, long as it was, I did not reply to yours on the subject of the Pt. We both feel beloved sister, most deeply your affc interest in what concerns us, and your warm zeal in our service, we only fear, it may perhaps carry you too far, or that the wily chef may think you have been prompted by Mr. Stevenson. These politicians & diplomats are two edged instruments to deal with, and we innocent, single tongued women are no matches for their cunning & address. I have found that out in my own case—and I dare say you will some of these days. With Gen Jackson a woman might venture to talk on these matters of high import, he hath the simplicity & single-mindedness of a woman & used his tongue as He who gave the power of speech, intended it should be used, to express his thoughts & not to conceal them. But I trust our destinies are not in the keeping of any man, & that a higher power will so order events as to restore us, and that soon, to our country & friends. The Major was here yesterday & Mr. Stevenson spoke of the course of the administration towards him, in the matter of mourning &c. I saw evidently from his (the Major) countenance that he thought we had had hard men sure dealt us, but he replied in a deprecating tone "But Sir, to have granted it would have ruined the Administration"—so it seems to render common justice to an innocent man, struggling to perform his duties, & to keep up the honour & character of his country, (indeed, to preserve his windows from being broken to pieces by the mob,) is to ruin the administration. The fact is, V.B. would not risk in the slightest manner his popularity, to do an act of common justice to a man who had stood by him in his hour of need, regardless of consequences—Mr. Stevenson also spoke of the immense tax it was to him the number of persons sent to him by Mr. P. & the Secy. The Major said he was obliged to do it to avoid making enemies. Mr. S. replied, "Sir, he forces me to make enemies, for if I were to multiply myself a thousand-fold & had twenty times the salary given me, I could not meet all the claims which your father & the members of the administration give persons upon me". The Major seems very amiable and we like him very much—he is very different from Prince John, who resembles his Father in using his fellow men as a ladder upon which to mount & when he is up, kicks it down, & without any scruples of conscience denies he has had any aid—Well, I am tired enough of it all, and wish some happy turn of fate—no Providence, would place us in an honourable retirement with peace, health, & competence, where we might spend the residue of our lives in such pursuits as would prepare us for that Eternal world to which we are hastening—I have no words to express how intensely I long for retirement, nature—beautiful nature! friendship & affection—It seems to me the air of London kills & withers up every thing that comes within its baneful influence. All here is so cold—so artificial so meretricious—that my heart sickens

& turns from it. And now one more word upon this ungrateful subject and I have done. I wrote you that I had been able to procure for Angelica an invitation to the Duchess of Northumberland's grand ball, which had been prevented by the death of her father an old man of 86—John Van Buren persuaded her that he had procured the invitation for her, altho' I assure you he had never been introduced to her, and had asked me to present him which I had had no opportunity of doing, and again when Mr. Stevenson wrote to Ld Palmerston he ask as a personal favour that I might be permitted to present her at the Birth-day drawing room he told them he had spoken to Ld Palmerston & made all easy, now all this is very provoking having had so much trouble with him, that he should now, not only take credit to himself not his due, but give these young people false views of their position here which may induce them to think we neglect our duty to them, whilst we are doing every thing in our power to assure their enjoyment—however, it is natural perhaps that the young man should wish to recommend himself to his new sister in every way he can, but I wish he could have done it without injustice & ingratitude to us—notwithstanding all this I still like him very much. There is such a mixture of good with all his faults that I regard him very kindly, & besides he is so amazing—he took your trumpet, & wrote his brother, to tell me he had taken it on erand under a roar of cannon, I don't know what he meant but I am sure he will take care of it.—& now a word of Mat—It was I fear in an evil hour when his parents thought of sending him to Europe, & he is like a wild-man he dined with us with his sister, but when we asked him again on the Saturday after he neither came nor sent an apology & yesterday he was invited to dine at the Bates' with his sister &c, but no Mat nor no apology. Two days ago Mr. S. got a note in a card to say he had bespoken his court dress & wished Mr. S. to give orders &c for his presentation. When he came Mr. S. showed him his instructions or rather what was expected at this court "That none but distinguished foreigners were to be presented"—we laughed heartily at his nonchalance—however, he goes tomorrow with

Abraham—& the Bishop of Vermont. I wish them all well through with it, the day after we go to the Drawing R. Angelica's dress will be blue watered silk trimmed with blond & silver, the under dress white satin & blond over it trimmed to correspond—mine green velvet train—with satin & lace dress a present from manufacturers of Nottingham—with a trimming of gold & green leaves, for which I have to pay some 3 or 4 pounds. Heigho! Well it cant be helped—& must be endured. I have tried to do it as economically as possible but there are no short cuts here, the "Ambassadors lady must be well dressed" everybody says—but then I say, I am a poor ministers wife—still all the others are so gorgeously dressed, especially at the Birthday D Room. Angelica & myself get on very well since our talk on the etiquette of England & America. She has too much good sense, and right feeling not to feel and act as she ought upon the subject. I cannot imagine what could induce Mr. Forsyth who has been abroad to give her such erroneous impressions.

May 17th

I had written thus far a week ago, & since then I have not had one moment to give to you without neglecting higher duties, & I consider but one higher than writing to you—but what with note writing, making calls, dining out & evening parties, I have been overworked the last week has been even worse than the week before.

On Thursday we attended the drawing-room. Angelica looked very well—sweet, pretty, and lady-like. The Queen received her very graciously, asked her the usual questions—How long she meant to stay? and inquired after the President. And the Duchess of Kent, to whom it is not usual to present strangers, said to me (after a little conversation in which she reproved me for my imprudence in driving in an open carriage), "Is that your neice?" I replied it was, & if her "Royal Highness would allow me, I would have the honour to present her," which I did, & also the Duchess of Gloucester, who made a sign as though she wished it. Her Royal Highness of Cambridge, who is very proud, made no sign, & we passed on to my place among the ladies of the foreign corps. I kept Angelica by me, which is not often permitted, but I did it upon the ground of her being a person of distinction. The drawing-room, being the first day, was crowded, at least 2000 persons, & no one presented but Mrs. Van Buren & a lady attached to the corps diplomatique. Angelica was delighted, and dazzled by the blaze of diamonds. It seems to me only necessary for one to go to the drawing-room once to get a surfeit of jewels, especially diamonds. The Marchioness of Londonderry was literally covered with brilliants. but the coup d'oeil was nothing like as magnificent as the last season, when all the foreign ambassadresses were here, but to a republican eye sufficient to be very dazzling. We did not get back until ½ past 4, when I had to put Mr. Stevenson upon my sofa & put him to sleep for having a bad cold & to go to Ld. Palmerston's to dinner. He required a little nursing. At 7, he took the carriage & went to dinner, & at 10, Angelica & myself went alone to a grand party at Lansdowne House, where the gentlemen joined us. I took her on my arm through the splendid suite of rooms and presented her to every one I knew that I thought it would profit her to know, amongst the number, Lord Lovelace, the husband of Ada Byron, who had sent me an invitation for the following Monday evening, and as I thought it would gratify Angelica to know the countess, I introduced her, and accordingly I received a note from Ada inviting them the next day. On Friday night, the Queen's ball, which perfectly enchanted Angelica. Mr. Stevenson left us before 11, & I should have been glad to have gone, too, but I stayed to introduce Angelica, until after supper, and got her, by a little management, into the court circle at the supper-table, where she saw the Queen take her strawberries, &c., and the Grand Duke his champagne, & all the royal circle make their bows of recognition & courtesy to those who ventured to approach, or had the right to do so. The tables were placed around the room, and at the upper end, where the Queen sups, all the royal plate is exhibited on the sideboard behind the table & lights so placed as to reflect a degree of brilliancy beyond the light of day. I left Mr. Rush with them, & got home by ½ past 2.

XXVII

IN THE SUMMER of 1839 disaster struck Britain's idolized Queen. Buckingham Palace was enveloped in the thick fumes of the scandalous Lady Flora Hastings Affair that dimmed Victoria's popularity and made her an object of censure.

Flora Hastings, unmarried, in her twenties, attractive, aristocratic, was Lady of the Bedchamber to the Duchess of Kent, Victoria's mother. The supposed scandal began with surreptitious giggling over Lady Flora's slowly distending figure. Palace gossip had it she was with child. But whose? Fingers pointed to a gentleman of the court circle who had, it was alleged, traveled with Lady Flora from Scotland in the same chaise.

Inevitably, the gossip seeped through the palace walls. Victoria heard it. She apparently gave credence to it by listening. Such a charge against a young woman in high life in those days was devastating. It was an era when virginity and an unblemished reputation were of supreme value. Charles Greville wrote of it, "though such things sometimes happen in the servants' hall . . . they are unprecedented and unheard of in good society, and among people in high, or even respectable, circles."

The Queen's physician, Sir James Clark, examined Lady Flora and pronounced her pregnant though he was forced to withdraw his diagnosis immediately. In the midst of the furore the luckless young lady died, leaving a note requesting an autopsy that revealed a malignant growth and the falsity of the charge against her.

With infinite propriety Mrs. Stevenson wrote her family of a visit from Lady Tavistock, one of Victoria's ladies in waiting, who led the palace pack in spreading the canard that Lady Flora was *enciente*.

London July 29th 1839

My beloved Sisters, and
My dear & precious Edward
& dear name sake—

I have just received your kind letters, and thank you a thousand times, for your kind and unceasing remembrance of the poor exile. I only wish I had more time to repay you as I ought for your long & most welcome letter, which came to me like manna in the desert. I think sometimes—my heart will break—or that it is broken, and wonder why I still live on in this tiresome world away from all who have ever loved me, or cared for me save one, who is truly, "Job's comforter"—without the hope beyond the grave, what would become of woman, helpless, hapless woman? When this world cannot fill & gratify the warm & glowing affections of her heart to what can she turn for peace & consolation, but the promises of the gospel, which can save from despair & anguish the wounded broken spirit that has nothing on Earth to rest on—and whilst it supports & raises the afflicted bruised & broken, above the storms of life, it has also the power to subdue the proud, the arrogant, & the prosperous & to teach them by what an uncertain tenure they hold the best gifts of Providence—I ought not to send you this effusion of un-spirit, but I feel much depressed today and greatly at a loss to know what to do. Betts letter urging my return, and the melancholy account she gives of her health, alarms me and creates a conflict in my mind which has rendered me very unhappy. I have been praying for direction and in the fulness of my heart I have written. Duty—I think requires me to remain here, for many reasons, and inclination—yes—an intense longing to behold my family again, and the fear, that if I tarry much longer we may never meet again in this world, impells me to return. But then comes the recollection of my last parting with my husband—the hope deferred—the sickening apprehensions & then the frightful certainty when I knelt at his sofa & saw him as I feared on the brink of the grave it seems.

We have declined almost every invitation to dinner and evening parties since our return from the country, we are so thoroughly tired out. On Sunday week after being kept up by a party of Americans over night, we arose at half past 6 o'clock and went to Mrs. Marryats to breakfast then to church to hear the Bishop of London deliver a most admirable charity sermon, for which we had to pay 15 shillings—lunched, & came home in time to dress & take a family dinner with Mrs. Mansfield. I am sorry to say she has borne the death of her good old Father, too well, her daughters did not keep out of society a week, & she herself not a month. They are selfish & worldly, tho' with many excellent qualities, and have been very kind to us and I believe feel as strong a sentiment of regard & friendship for us as they are capable of feeling for any one. But here no one mourns long for any body, or any thing. The world has too many attractions for those who knew no happiness out of it. Mrs. Mansfield is a devoted wife & mother, and I am therefore the more astonished at her not feeling more poignantly the loss of such a parent. I took the Porcher's, Marions friends, to Wimbledon and they were delighted with the garden—house, & grounds—and very grateful for the few attentions we had it in our power to show them. I am sadly afraid, the invalid will never recover if he does not take more care of himself, sightseeing is very trying to a delicate person. We have been invited to several places in the neighbourhood of London, to spend a few days. The Countess de Salis—Lady Hamlyn Williams—and a Mr. & Mrs. Cook about 7 miles from London—to the latter place we shall go in a few days—and I regreted their invitation came for the same time as Lady Hamlyn's, who has taken a great liking to me, and says I am "The most natural person she ever saw, and that I had captivated her at first sight by my unaffected good sense, and right feeling &c, and she added, "This is not flattery Mrs. Stevenson because every body says so, and that you have remained now for three years in close contact with the great world without being at all changed" —I write this not from vanity dear Julia, but to comfort you, and in reply to your ominous dreams—now my Sister we are told, & I believe it, "That our hearts are desperately wicked." & that we none of us know ourselves. This also I believe— But I think I am more humble than when I left my native land —& I know I do not deserve any credit for it.

On the 24th we attended a fete at Wimbledon given to her Majesty by the Duke and Duchess of Somerset at their villa near Mrs. Marryat's, who invited us to go to her & sleep and remain the next day, which we did. From the extent of the preparations and the Queen's presence much was expected, & indeed it was considered as the affair of the season. The marquee, or temporary tent, was very beautiful. The roof was supported by 12 columns, and the interior lined with crimson stripes decorated with wreaths, festoons, and various forms in natural flowers. It was said to be 180 feet long & 40 feet broad, and 480 persons sat down to the tables in perfect comfort. At one end of this magnificent tent the military band was placed, who played "God save the Queen." The illuminations were extremely pretty over the Tuscan portico, which looked upon the beautiful lawn, "God bless our Queen," in large letters surmounted by a crown. The grounds were also partly illuminated. At the entrance into the park, which was lined with curious spectators, a triumphant arch of evergreens and roses had a beautiful and striking effect, especially when illuminated. The Queen arrived about 6 o'clock and promenaded the grounds, where the company had generally assembled, on rich carpets, with sofas and chairs. Here also were stationed the Tyrolean minstrels, who sang their national airs; the Russian dancers, who exhibited their national steps; also Alpine singers; and Highland pipers in their national dresses, the tartan and the bagpipes. What amused me most was the old dowager Duchess of Richmond, who is most loyally aristocratic and by whom I chanced to stand. When the bagpipes struck up a Scotch air, she began to shuffle away like a girl of sixteen. Imagine a fat old lady upwards of 70, dressed in a lilac satin with a lace dress over it, attempting to dance! The fact is that no one grows old in England, and if I stay here much longer, I shall live back to gay fifteen. But as yet I have made no step backwards. I wish I could. The old duchess made many, and not content with this exertion of her own strength, she insisted when the Queen came out that I should stand. I had half a mind to tell her my republican knees refused such hard service, but I rose at her bidding, knowing the old lady meant it kindly. Lady Lennox, who married the younger son of the duke, said, "Her Grace thinks it high treason to sit in the presence of royalty." After dinner (our party at the table consisted of Ld. & Lady Surrey & daughter & Ld. & Lady Tavistock), there was an accession of company and the ball commenced in the tent. As soon as we could make our escape we did so, & found Mrs. Marryat at prayers with her family. A contrast, you will think.

The Queen, sorry I am to say, has lost much of her popularity since the sad affair of Lady Flora Hastings. The papers I suppose have informed you all about it. Mr. S. and myself have both sent papers to Philadelphia & Richmond which I hope you have received. It was noticed on the day of the fire by a person who had not been in England since her coronation the change which has taken place—then the air was rent with acclamations—now, she is received with a silence almost unbroken. I think I mentioned to you in a former letter that the Marchioness of Tavistock, the first lady in waiting, & the future Duchess of Bedford, had requested me to allow her, (that's the phrase,) to call and show me her statement of what part she had in the affair. In this statement she says, "That on the first of Jany when she went into waiting—Lady Flora's situation was the general topic throughout the palace, that her own impression was that she had been privately married and her first impulse was to speak privately to Lady Flora—but circumstances prevented her doing so, and she then felt it her duty to communicate what was passing to the Prime Minister she being in charge of the palace, &c. Accordingly she had asked for an audience of Ld Melbourne & stated the fact—and for this she was responsible." Of the Queen she says nothing—and it is this mystery which has inflamed the publick mind. Everybody infers the blame must be with the Queen that she ordered the examination which condemned this innocent & highminded maiden to a humiliation which ultimately caused her death, together with the constant exertion of appearing in publick when she ought to have been in her bed—and then her not dismissing the physician who gave so false an opinion on her case and acted with an indiscretion that has deprived him of the practice of every one save the Queen, who still retains him as Court physician. Sir James Clark is the name of the unfortunate man whom not even royal favour can sustain. The Duchess of Kent dismissed him immediately—and added to all this, is the little harmony which exist between Mother & daughter. Rumour, who you know is always busy about such things, even ventures to give conversations as well as facts to prove their disunion—for instance it is generally talked of that after the death of poor Lady Flora, the Duchess resolved to leave England, & to prevent her executing her intention the Duke of Wellington, who seems to be general pacificator, was sent for & he said to the Duchess, "She must remember altho' Victoria was her daughter she was also her sovereign" and to the Queen that the Duchess tho her subject was still her mother and for the sake of each other and the publick weal they must bear with each other & continue to live together, as to part at this time and confirm all the rumours afloat &c &c. During the last illness of Lady Flora the Queen issued tickets for a ball which she afterwards recalled—but the head policeman told a friend of mine, that had the Queen persisted in having it, there would not have been a riot, but that every street leading to the palace would have been baracaded. It is the etiquette in court that no corpse is permitted to remain in the royal palace, but the Queen dispensed with this rule of etiquette and ordered it to remain untill removed to its last resting place, and also had the shutters all closed as a mark of respect. I am really very sorry for all this, for independent of her being a Queen,

I like her as a woman. She looks so innocent & helpless, so gentle & dignified that when she takes my hand in hers to shake, my heart yearns towards her—and then she is so considerate of others. On perceiving tears in the eyes of one of her ladies in waiting she asked the cause, and when told her nephew had broken his leg, she said what can we do for him? Oh, I will order a watch at 30 guineas for him to amuse himself with! I only hope that adulation and the glittering pomps of this world may not corrupt her heart and turn her little head, before she can find out what a heartless pageant it is—certainly as yet, she seems very little injured by what would have perverted the hearts or turned the heads of half her sex.

I have received two notes from Angelica since her departure one from The Hague with an old fashioned Dutch fan and the others from Brussells. She says she has been very little, indeed, not at all in society. I hope they have had better weather for sight-seeing than we have had here, it is now almost as cold as winter & constant rain. She wishes I had accompanied them, but I doubt a little her sincerity, as she, nor the Major, ever spoke of it untill a day or two before their departure, however, it made no difference as I should not have gone, unless Mr. S. could have accompanied me. The Vanderpools are with them. Mat is still here acting as attache and I hope it will be of service to him. Mr. Rush is very kind & treats him like a younger brother—he is very fond of his Uncle and myself—and very obedient. I take special care that he shall not get his head turned as a certain young gentleman of our acquaintance. Mr. Mat is I assure you a much more prudent and sensible youth than I had thought him, but for his bad health which has prevented his making the best use of his time he would have been a very remarkable person with his present advantages. I treat him exactly as I would a son, and altho' his Mother has given me no authority—I exercise it as far as I think is for his good. I do not think he quite likes my adherence to the republican Princess as he calls her, & thinks me a very gullible person— but I had rather be deceived than not to trust, & to tell you the truth this is what I like least in my nephew—however—Time will show who is right—To me there is something so tender & so holy in the tie which binds brother and sister that I must confess I would wish to see them more blind to each others faults—to say the least of it—It is painful to me even to think of, therefore I feel unwilling to say more on paper. Angelica says she shall not be able to get back as soon as she expected, but that they hope to be in Paris early in Septr—I think from her note's to me she must have had a very dull time of it, independent of sight seeing, which after all is more pleasant in the retrospect than in the enjoyment—or the endurance. I have just put down my pen to see a poor American woman who has come to me to get her into service here, & having written her a note & sent her off, I have returned to finish this long scrawl. You would be surprised to know how many applications I have of this sort. To get my country-ladies English maids, & my poor country women English places I am always too happy to do either, remembering always how limitted are my means of doing good. Mr. Tucker arrived in the last steamer, and dined with us yesterday, he tells me he saw all my Albemarle brothers in Charlottesville a few days before his departure but not one sent me a letter, or even a message by him!!!

August the 18th

This is my last day, and I must give you a few more last words in reply to your last letters. It was very good in you my dear Edward to write me such a long kind letter by Mr. Coxe's which I must say a few words in reply to altho' my time is now so limitted. You scold me so pleasantly & good humouredly that it reminds me of auld lang syne, and as in days of yore I must still plead, "Not guilty". Mr. McDuffie told you how many parties I went to, but he did not tell you how many I staid away from, or how difficult it is to say in London society, "Thus far will I go, and no farther". I will venture to say, however, that no one refuses so many invitations or stays so short

a time as we do, we often go, & show ourselves, & retire just
as every body in the fashionable world is making their entre
—but I have nothing to say in defence of the rationality of a
London life, it is all sad work for me—still, whilst I am here, I
must go out—& get on as well as I can, what with English
society, English popularity, and our duties to the thousands of
our compatriots who come over in every steamer & packet
loaded with letters. I assure you we have our hands full. As to
the Markoes I wrote you about them, & my letter must have
miscarried. We were on the most friendly footing all the way
over, and when we arrived at Portsmouth Mr. Stevenson took
a parlour, and invited them to use it as their room, which they
did, & parted from us most excellent friends. They did not
come to London, & we have not seen them since. Mr. Markoe
gave a letter of introduction to some one, but whom I have
forgotten, this being such an every day affair—so that I must
believe they can have no unkind feeling to us. I do not understand your allusion about Angelica in which you say you suppose Betsy has written me all about it. She has told me nothing
except in reply to my letters she said she knew she had come
here with the most extravagant expectations & to my letters to
Betsy I must refer you for every thing on that subject, (I hope
she became sensible of the unreasonableness of her expectations
before she went away, but it is very difficult to awaken one
from such a dream as hers, and woe unto the unfortunate being
whose duty or necessity it may be to give the rousing shake)
—and now dear Brother I must take my leave of you with a
thousand loves & kisses to Sally and the dear children. My love
to Richard Vaux, but it is truth to say, dear brother, that you
do us injustice when you say we spoilt him—"Thou art the
man"—The active steps you took to make him Secy of Legation
had a great affect in turning his head & destroying the equi-
librium of his mind—his visit to the continent had also a most
pernicious affect upon him, he never was the same person after
his return, the change was so obvious that I told him he ought
to go home—In short—I tried to do a mothers part by the

youth—warned him against the indulgence of some very pernicious habits, but in vain—especially that of exaggeration, & telling the thing that was not, in jest—If the homilys I preached to him could have been collected & printed I dare say (vanity apart) they might greatly benefit the rising generation. I used to tell him that all the quantity of hair he wore on his head & face I was sure made him so "hard headed"—notwithstanding all his faults I loved the merry youth, and still feel the deepest & most affc interest in him—& wish you would try your transforming powers with him—especially in the sense of a strict & rigid adherence to truth in the merest trifle—It is the foundation stone of all excellence. I have been persuading Mat to take a master on several branches of education, above all—a writing master to teach him a good & bold hand writing & secondly, to make him a good accountant for his Fathers sake—I give him books—religious & of a lighter character, that he may have light topics for the girls—My dear Julia! I really thought I had a sheet & a half for messages & thanks to you Emma Sally & Mr. R. but here I am on the last page and I am determined not to take another sheet, I shall send this by a private opportunity to Philadelphia to my dear Ned, and must beg of him to enclose it to Mr. Lewis or Forsyth if no private mode of conveyance offers to my sisters. It is a wretched scrawl to send but the best I can do. Many thanks to you my dear Betsy & Sally for your letters. I did not think my dear sisters as affc as usual, but it might have been fancy! I feel very uneasy dear Bett about your health. Angelica tells me you are very imprudent in eating— that you eat a most imprudent dinner at the P—l's, &c, pray be cautious and who knows but you may see old England yet, for those steamers annihilate both time & space. I write in great haste—& many interruptions—4 gentlemen to breakfast with us tomorrow morning. It is breakfast, dinner & tea. I shall send your things now by the first safe opportunity. You will scarcely believe me when I tell you I have never been able to get one day for shoping since the season commenced but we shall be more quiet now. I don't know what we shall do this summer yet —very hard times obliged to economise in every thing—I should like to go to Ireland & Wales—but shall not propose it. If my dear Bett was with me it would indeed be a pleasure. Mr. S—— said the other day I do wish Bett was here—I kiss you & embrace you with my whole heart—Your devoted

Sister
S. C. Stevenson

XXVIII

In the summer of 1839, Daniel Webster, with his wife and daughter, journeyed to England. The mighty Expounder of the Constitution traveled "in a private character," not as the powerful Senator from Massachusetts. He was desirous of meeting British higher-ups, political leaders especially.

Webster, one of the Great Triumvirate in the Senate, had not only helped defeat Stevenson's first appointment to the London post, but had unsuccessfully opposed the distinguished Virginian the second time President Jackson sent his name to the Senate. Yet no one could have been more courteous and attentive than the Stevensons were to the Websters on their London visit.

Mrs. Stevenson did not record at too great length the doings of the Websters in England, but she listed the celebrities to whom they presented the Senator and his family. The festivities included dinner *en famille* with Queen Victoria where Stevenson, and not Senator Webster, was invited to lead the Queen in to dinner and where she, Mrs. Stevenson, sat between two massive lions of the British hierarchy, Lord Palmerston and Lord Holland.

> Worthing 50 miles from London and
> 9 from Brighton on the English
> Channel August 20 1839

My beloved Sister's.

You will be surprised to receive a letter from me dated from this place, but since my last voluminous dispatch which I directed to "Garlands Store" I have not been well, and my good husband has brought me to the sea-side for the benefit of the air, & bathing—my indisposition has been caused in a great measure by anxiety & grief at the sudden death of one of my country-women, Mrs. Minnie Robinson of New York, the sister of Mr. John Duer, and one of the most amiable persons I have ever known. She came over with her husband & two daughters for his health about two months since, and as their lodgings were near us we saw them very frequently in a family way, to tea &c & the girls attached themselves to me particularly; Matt we thought was a little smitten with the youngest, Fanny, and during our absence at Black Hill gave a dejeune, at his rooms, & it seems poor Mrs. Robinson partook freely of all the varieties of fruit & drank champagne, the consequence was a violent cholera which terminated her life on the 5th day, her family were not aware of her danger untill the day before her death. But such a death! Ah my sisters, it is better so to die than to live, never may I lose the recollection of it—cut off in the prime of life—of health, & enjoyment, she met her fate with a firmness & calmness that seemed almost supernatural. She took a tender & affc leave of her family, who were with her, and sent messages to all that were absent, remembered & provided for all her poor pensioners in New York—and then taking off her wedding ring she placed it on her husband's finger, saying, 'wear it for my sake' she sent for me about 5 in the morning two or three hours before her death—pressed my hands in hers, saying, "God bless you", and, "I thank you for all your kindness", twice she repeated this—and commended her weeping daughters to my care. She often spoke of her trust [word illegible] & repeated over & over again "How [word illegible] to a dying sinner". There was a moral sublemity in all she said & did, that would have converted an infidel, and compelled him to acknowledge there was a reality in the Christian's faith, not to be doubted, when a weak woman naturally timid & afraid of death, could give such proof's of courage & fortitude. Her last words were, "Oh how bright and glorious"! as if, in the language of Revelation, a "door had

(*229*)

been opened in Heaven" for her departing spirit to catch a glimpse of its glories whilst it yet lingered on Earth. Her remains were deposited at Kendal Green Cemetery, about 8 or 9 miles from London a sweet & quiet place. Her husband & daughters had fortitude & resolution to follow her even to the vaults of the chapel, where the service was performed. Susan the elder leant upon her Fathers arm, the younger, Fanny, on her Uncle Duer's, & when the poor girl looked upon the coffin in its little narrow cell her fortitude forsook her & she uttered one piercing shreik, & fell into the arms of her Uncle, who was scarcely less agitated than herself. Susan who looked like a statue—said, to one who stood near her—"Tell her to remember our Father"—in an instant she was calm, & said, "How could I forget him"—It was a heart-rending scene—but one I would not have been absent from, both for my own sake, & the poor motherless girls, who cling to me as if I could fill the place of her they had lost. Her family have been very much sustained by the remembrance of her happy death yet still in a foreign land & away from all their friends it has been a severe trial. I exerted myself to be a comfort to them and my health suffered from anxiety & the sympathy I felt in their sorrows. Since I have been here I have recovered my usual health which is never as you know very strong, the quiet, pure air—exercise & salt bathing, has restored, even in one week, [illegible] to my system. We were persuaded to come by Lady Elisabeth Hope Vere, who is here with all her charming family—the daughters are charming, the two eldest, twins, are the most amiable & accomplished creatures full of goodness, sweetness, grace, & one of them, Hannah, who is really a Hannah, plays and sings almost as well as Grisi, and is yet so humble and unaffected &c unconscious of her beauty and extraordinary acquirements for to her musical talent she paints & draws beautifully—takes minature likenesses better than most artists—understands several languages & what is more extraordinary than all this, is as simple & affc as a child. We ride the donkeys together with Sophy, the other twin to take care of us, who is, next to my dear Bett, the most un-selfish of all human beings—indeed she reminds me of her not only in this beautiful trait but in her love for her twin sister, whom she seems almost to idolise—Heigho!—Well after all, there is nothing on Earth so beautiful as family love—and where that exists in such force there is always virtue & goodness. The Humes are also here, and I am expecting Mrs. Hume every moment to take me a drive. I am delighted with this place and often think how happy I should be if my dear Bett was only with me. I had, however, a great [word illegible] yesterday in hearing of the illness of my dear brother's little boy Edward. I hope it will please God to spare the dear little fellow whom I love most tenderly altho' I have never had the happiness of seeing him. It appears to me, I think of you all more in the summer than at any other time. I imagine you assembled on the Green Mountain receiving & confering happiness—every face is before my minds eye—methinks, I see brother Isaac's brilliant smile of cordial welcome, and dear Julie looking so gay—so happy—& so funny—and brother Tucker with his look of mild benevolence, distributing his elegant hospitalities, and Helen, sometimes I see, on horseback sometimes, on the bed—& oftener with that indefatigable needle—but always smiling kindly upon me as to Selina—not one line—or little word of message in more than three long years—as to my dear brother John—his merry laugh often rings in my ears, and I see him on old Blacky slowly .pacing up to the front door, to bring the news—and I am sure he will ask with eagerness [illegible] pleasure any thing about his dear absent [word illegible] warm hearted & laughter-loving friend, & brother.

Mrs. Hume broke in upon my family party before it was half assembled—Dear brother Walker & sister Carter with all their appendages—neices, nephews, & grand neices & nephew's with the addition of the foreign Corp's. The Singleton's—Rutherfords—Baltimoreans & Skipwiths. When shall we—all —meet again—in peace & happiness, I hope—But Heaven will be done——I must, now dear Sisters, go back to where I left off in my last letter—as I make it a point to keep you informed of all my movements. I think my last concluded with an account of the Duke & Duchess of Somersets breakfast to the Queen, very regal & very magnificent. After that we spent two or three days in entertaining our country people Mr. Tucker & others. We then went to Black Heath & Lord Bexley's about 10 miles beyond at Firth Cray one of the most beautiful places I have seen in England. We were absent only three days and returned in time for another dinner to Mr. Tucker at which we had some distinguished English, the Earl of Scarborough—Babbage—&c &c. The Earl gave us a most kind & pressing invitation to visit him at [word illegible] one of the most magnificent seats in England. We have been very civil to Mr. Tucker but I don't know whether he will think so. Our first dinner was en-famille, the second was to introduce him to persons he wished to see & know. Ld Brynham was asked, but engaged, also Hallam of the Middle Ages.

We were also at a very pleasant party at the Queen's, a dinner to which Mr. & Mrs. Webster were invited. I never saw her little Majesty so gracious and so agreeable. Mr. Stevenson was invited to lead her to dinner, at which she talked and laughed with him in a manner more free and easy than I have ever seen her indulge towards any one else. I was given the seat of honor opposite to her between Lds. Palmerston & Holland. After dinner we had a select ball, at which no other foreign minister was invited but ourselves. We have also dined twice with the Duke of Sussex, a luxurious dinner, to which he invited the Websters, whom he had met at our house, and again en famille at a grand concert at the Duke of Wellington's, to which the Robinsons were invited. Poor lady! it was the last time we met in public. We were at several other small parties, and declined going to many more, also to the country to make a visit to Lady Hamlyn Williams, the lady who commended me for being so very natural and unspoiled.

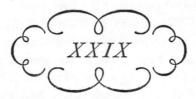

XXIX

LORD DURHAM—John G. Lambton—was a commanding statesman and social figure in England in the 1830's. Because of his advanced ideas, Britain's populace dubbed him "Radical Jack." As former Governor-General of Canada he had come in direct contact with the United States, and thus he and the Stevensons were to find much in common.

In the fall of 1839 the American Minister and his wife spent a week at Lambton Castle that was not without its touch of comedy as Mrs. Stevenson indicates in this letter to her brother, Edward Coles.

This tour—for such it was—included a stopover at "Lord Scarborough's," Lumley Hall. The Earl—Sir William Lumley—was Groom of the Bedchamber to Queen Victoria. The Stevensons also visited celebrated Alnwick Castle, an ancient architectural pile famed in song and story, seat of Algernon Percy, Duke of Northumberland.

Lambton Castle Octr 28th 1839
The seat of the Earl of Durham

My dear Brother,

You will be astonished to hear that you have been the cause of my losing my breakfast this morning, in consequence

of which I have hurried up stairs to inflict a letter upon you—
but you will have to suspend your curiosity untill I have told
you something of our movement in case my letters to my dear
Bett should not have been received. I wrote her from Lord
Scarborough's and again at Mr. Beaumonts, which letter I
took with me to Wentworth and sent off the morning after
my arrival there, since then I have been too busy to write much,
but I have sent Mr. Rush a short account of our proceedings
with instructions to send the letter to my dear Sisters lest they
should be uneasy about my health, &c. And now to return to
the cause of this sudden letter. The Duke of Cleveland who
has been for years a martyr to the gout, is here on a visit, and
the sudden deaths of the Dukes of Bedford & Argyle his con-
temporaries has so frightened the Duchess that she has persuaded the Duke to consult a very celebrated physician who is
also here on a visit & it was my good fortune this morning to
sit by the Duke & his physician, and unavoidably I overheard
much of their conversation, but fearing I might not be perfectly correct, I ventured under the protest of apologizing for
my involuntary rudeness in listening to conversation not intended for my ear, to make the Dr repeat to me all he had said
to the Duke and thinking how valuable it may be to you, my
dear Brother I hasten to put it all down on paper & send it to
you earnestly praying I may be the humble instrument in the
hands of Providence of doing you good & ridding you of this
horrible scourge to man. "He, the Doctor—says—altho' a certain relief is a dangerous remedy as it often brings on paralisis,
and is therefore to be avoided. That magnesia with the smallest
possible mixture of Epsom salts taken a tea spoonful every
morning as soon as the patient awakes, has been known, indeed
has never failed, to cure if persevered in, & that far from doing
injury to the constitution is on the contrary very friendly &
beneficial in its effects, that when the fit is on the dose is to
be encreased & then gradually diminished again, that he had
known a case in which the patient had been considered as past
hope and this simple remedy regularly administered had restored the sufferer to health & long life. He said much about the

causes of gout, &c, &c but with this I have nothing to do. It is certainly well worth the trial, and my dear Emm's busy fingers & persuasive voice must get you to swallow the dose every morning. The doctor says a new mode of preparing the magnesia has been discovered, in which it is made as pure as possible. No doubt it can be procured in Richmond or to the North. If not, let me know, & I will send you some. A cure has also been discovered in France for the dispepsia, & Mr. Stevenson has sent for the article, it can scarcely be called a medicine, for our precious Bett it is very costly, but he said, "I would freely give my little finger, yes, put it down and let it be choped off for our dear & kind hearted sister, who I believe would do any thing for me". By the way—I must tell you, who are a dreamer, of one I had this morning, & you must send me the interpretation. Methought I found myself suddenly at home, and that Betsy & Emily approached me on their knees whilst I also was in the same position all weeping & embracing each other. Then a 'change came o'er the spirit of my dream' and methought we were at a dinner table, and no one would give me any thing to eat—and it was your house in which I suffered this inhospitality. Then I saw the children—Emily a great girl, and little Helen with a cape of two colours—chattering away as saucily as possible &c &c and lastly—my dear Bett, looked thin & sad—but Emily was rosy—& certainly not one of the lean Kyne. Heigho!—Well, you see, these splendid and great people cannot draw my thoughts or wishes from auld lang syne. This is a magnificent place. The drawing rooms filled with gifts from the Emperor of Russia, King of Sweden, &c &c beautiful vases—tables worth their weight in gold formed of the costly Malekite. I believe that is the way to spell it. It is a rich & beautiful green. The whole house is filled with objects of art and finished & furnished with great taste. They have been very civil to us, and sent an invitation to meet us at Raby Castle. By the way I wrote you how very kind the Duke & Duchess had been to us, sent their four horses, with two or three servants in the rich Cleaveland livery to meet us a stage off. The Duchess spoke very kindly of Angelica. I thanked her for her civilities to them. She said she had been happy to show them for our sakes at first but that when she knew her she liked her for her own, that she had so much sensibility & had wept so much at parting with her it had quite touched her heart. &c &c. We leave this tomorrow for Alnwick Castle the Duke of Northumberlands, & have promised on the 4 of next month to be with the Ld Bishop of Durham at Auckland Castle to spend a few days—then back to Raby—as the Duke & Duchess say they will not forgive us if we do not go back from thence to the Earl of Tetland. Then to a Mr & Mrs Herbert—where we shall consider where next, but there is scarcely a day we do not get some new invitations—commencing with "seeing from the papers" &c and besides this long letter I have scratched off to you this morning I have written two notes—to a Mr & Mrs Davenport—& the Greens have also written besides others of whose names you have never heard. Say to my beloved sisters if I live to get back to London they may expect a more detailed account of what I have seen.

A large party to dinner. After the gentlemen joined us, when the Duke of Sussex, Lady Durham, and myself were sitting together and forming a social trio, Lord Durham came in with his imperial air and said, "I do not know whether your Royal Highness objects to cards on Sunday evening; for myself I think there is no greater harm in playing on that night than any other." "Nor I," said the Duke. "If it is wrong to play on Sunday, it is equally wrong to play on Monday or any other night." I felt distressed. Thinks I to myself, "What shall I do?" At that moment the Duke appealed to Lady Durham, who gave a faint assent to what he had said. I, of course, was silent, when his Royal Highness, suddenly leaning forward from the immense armchair in which he was half-buried, addressed me: "I think, my dear Madam, it is considered a sin to play any game on Sunday in your country." I replied instantly in a calm, earnest, and emphatic manner, so that, although a little deaf, he did not lose a word: "Your Royal Highness is right. We think it a violation of that Commandment which bids us to keep holy the Sabbath Day, and we also think it is setting a bad example to our dependents, who cannot so well discern between right and wrong." The old gentleman drew himself back in his chair and remained silent for several minutes. A solemn pause ensued, and I felt almost frightened at what I had done. Still, I did not regret it. In the meantime the servants had set out the tables, but no one approached them, nor was the slightest allusion made to the subject again. The Duke did not retire until his usual hour, and continued in pleasant conversation all the evening, every now and then speaking with his usual kindness to me; and when he rose to retire he called out for me, saying, "Where is Mrs. Stevenson?" and when I advanced from a table where I had been looking at some drawings of Lady Mary's, he shook my hand with even more than usual cordiality, as he uttered his "Good night." I was glad not to have offended him, for he has been very kind to us; still, I felt very grateful that I had moral courage given me at the moment to do and say what I ought, despite the fear of man.

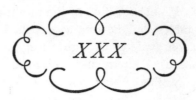

XXX

On Christmas Day, 1839, Mrs. Stevenson attended services at London's Trinity Church. That afternoon she wrote home a Christmas letter in which she sent a special message to her brother, Isaac, on the servant problem in England. She had no way of knowing, incidentally, that Enniscorthy, her old home in Virginia where this brother lived, had gone up in flames this same week.

The closing part of this letter deals with a matter keenly distressing to the Stevensons: the defection of her niece, Angelica Singleton Van Buren. This young lady and her husband, Major Abram Van Buren, returning home from their London visit, had poured into President Van Buren's ears fantastic tales of the "highfalutin" life the Stevensons were leading in the British capital. There was criticism, too, of Stevenson's ministry. And this, after the Stevensons had showered favors and courtesies on them and inducted them into the splendors of the British court and of social life there. It appears to have been a deliberate attempt to discredit the American Minister and his wife. It was to backfire disastrously on Angelica's father-in-law, the President.

Apparently Van Buren took little stock in what Angelica and her husband told him, but he made the mistake of permitting her to introduce British court customs at the White House. Installed as hostess of the Executive Mansion she began mimicking what she had seen in London, holding "Drawing Rooms" just as

(238)

did Queen Victoria. Guests were announced by uniformed flunkeys. Wearing a long purple velvet train with a headdress of long white feathers in the court fashion, Angelica seated herself on a raised platform and gave formal bows to curtsying guests. It was flagrantly at odds with American democratic tradition, and the Whigs seized on it as a major political issue in the 1840 campaign. Congress echoed with repercussions of Angelica's pretentious ways. In the House a skilled Whig spokesman fumed all day on the subject. This diatribe went down in history as the famous Gold Spoon Speech in which Van Buren was charged with aping the ways of royalty. He got the blame for his daughter-in-law's regal importations. It had much to do with ousting him from the White House.

London Decr 25th 1839

My beloved Sisters—

Mr. S. and myself laughed last night when you my dear brother talk of our not getting on in old Virginia with the servants. When we meet I will give you a chapter on this subject—to make you open your eyes. At this very time we are without a regular cook. The one we employed having received an offer of higher wages, acted in such a manner as to force me to turn her off, and whilst we are put to the greatest inconvenience as well as expense to get someone to come occasionally during the Christmas holidays to cook us something to eat, she actually refused to quit the house untill she was paid not only her wages for the month, but board wages—& is now frolicking about the town untill New Years Day when she takes her new place. I frankly confess we have deserved this by not taking the precautions English people do, who tie them up in a way to prevent impositions of this sort, but if you omit the least thing in the way of a bargain they take advantage of it, and summon you before a magistrate—& you who know Mr. S. will readily believe the advantage the wretches will have over him. He made the bargain with this cook—and in the multiplicity of things he has had to do he failed to tie her up suffi-

ciently tight—& in consequence we have come near having—
no Christmas dinner—and by way of a little seasoning to myself
—I have been without a ladies maid for the last month indeed,
ever since my return to town. The house maid dresses me, or
rather fastens my dress, & yesterday I did even that. She said
to me a few days since, "That she had never seen any lady who
required so little waiting upon". This is something in favour of
my not being spoiled, is it not dear Bett?

I have read your letter three times as if by reading I could
find out something more. I thank you for all the family news.
You perceive how prudent I am. I never allude to any thing
you tell me . . . .

As to what you tell me of Angelica it does not surprise
altho' I must confess it pains me that she should not have
written you as soon as she returned. Let us endeavor to remember always she is our Sister's daughter. I assure you I had
to keep it in mind when she was here & often has it restrained
me when I was about to offer a retort. As to what I have
written you dear Betsy it has fallen so far short of the reality,
& I softened down so much that I thought I had made her
quite presentable to the whole family, her Mother & all, knowing
as I did in what an exaggerated form it would be all given to
the "President" as well as to her own Parents.

I endeavored to give you some light upon the subject
altho' there is so much I shall never communicate except
verbally. I must, however, in justice to myself, say, I suffered
with Job-like patience, injury for benefits—insults for kindness
—annoyances of every kind & sort which could have been in-
flicted by one's greatest enemy, and when I look back upon her
past life, remember her as a dear little scary black eyed child
whom it was my delight to caress and fondle. Then as a young
woman just on the threshold of life, when with much pride &
pleasure we presented her to the world with feelings almost of
parental fondness, and when afterwards she formed the connec-
tion which decides the fate of woman for happiness or misery,
how fervently did I pray for her happiness, here & here after,
and how little did I think that the being on whom I had

lavished so many cares & so much tenderness would endeavor to sting the bosom that had thus fondly cherished her—But so it is—and I endeavor to console myself by remembering that in no one thought, word or deed have I ever injured her & the course she pursued here would not have been betrayed by me, but for her own conduct. She has forced me in self-defence— the first law of Nature, to speak, but I have spoken as little as possible of her follies to say the least of them. I find in this world if one is patient & conscientious, returning good for evil & will be content to pursue the even tenor of their way—all things then right themselves after a while. Witness my old enemy & caluminator Mrs. S—— Others it seems have now found out her want of truthfulness, that first of virtues, the foundation stone on which all the other rest. A woman who will utter deliberate falsehoods, knowing them to be so, why, such romance lovers should write novels, and publish them as such, not as veritable true stories!

XXXI

ON HER WEDDING MORNING—February 10, 1840—happy Queen
Victoria scribbled a hasty *billet doux* to her soon-to-be bridegroom, Prince Albert of Saxe-Coburg Gotha, who was lodged in
a far-off apartment in St. James's Palace. "What weather!" she
said. "I believe, however, the rain will cease."

At the American Legation, Sallie Stevenson "opened my
eyes upon a pouring rain." Like everybody else in London she
was "dying with curiosity to see a queen married."

The rain didn't cease as Victoria thought—and Sallie Stevenson hoped—it would, but it made no difference, nor did it dampen
the breathless excitement that held London in its grip. Not only
did Mrs. Stevenson watch Victoria plight her troth to Albert,
but she extracted a bit of humor from the scene and carried off
a sizable piece of the mountainous wedding cake from the reception after the ceremony. Romantic Sallie Stevenson carved her
slice into several pieces. One she despatched to her niece, Sally
Rutherford, in Richmond, Virginia; another to her friend, Margaret Hone, daughter of Philip Hone, New York's diarist extraordinary. A young Englishman just leaving for America volunteered to carry the packages of the Queen's wedding cake as
far as New York. Both pieces arrived safely. On March 11, 1840,
Philip Hone duly entered in his diary, "My daughter received as
a present from London a piece of the Queen's wedding cake, enclosed in a letter from Mrs. Stevenson, Lady of the American

Minister, and brought in by the Great Western by Mr. Cracroft. . . ."

London Feby 19th 1840
32 Upper Grosvenor St.

My dear Sally,

I find there is no other way of getting a letter from either you or your good mother but by addressing mine especially to you, putting your names both inside and out. I must say it is very hard work for me to write such volumes as I do to your Aunt Betsy and then be obliged to write individually to each person; but as you follow your mother's example, I must not scold you, but reserve the outpourings of my wrath for her. I have written so often & so much lately that I am afraid I must have tired you all, especially since the burning of our good old home, the Enniscorthy mansion, has made my letters perfect jeremiads. But now I will not blight thy young spirit by touching on anything disagreeable. "Sufficient unto the day is the evil thereof." I remember, dear Sally, when I was at your time of life everything was couleur de rose. Hope spread her gay illusions round me, and played the dear deceiver's part. I will not say that my hopes are less bright now than they were then, but they have changed their object, & soared beyond this little scene of things. But I find myself relapsing again, & will amuse you with some account of the Queen's marriage.

The ceremony took place on the 10th in St. James Chapel Royal, which was fitted up especially for the occasion; but as it is very small, it could hold only a few of her Majesty's subjects, who were dying with curiosity to see a queen married. We ladies of the diplomatic corps began to despair of an invitation, but at the eleventh hour it came, all, however, in good time. It was expected that she would be married at half-past eleven, which rendered it necessary for us to be up before eight, at work upon our heads, &c., which were to be full-dressed. I opened my eyes upon a pouring rain, which continued with very little intermission all day; but rain or shine, we must be at our posts. Uncle Stevy figgeted and fretted, but notwithstanding it rained on, & the new liveries were well soaked, but, then, everybody else was in the same plight, and you know there is some consolation in that. We of the diplomacy had what is called the Queen's royal closet. It afforded us an excellent view, but we were miserably cold, with our bare arms, necks, & heads, with nothing to cover the latter but the graceful white plumes. As for me, I christened my beautiful India satin cloak, which I exhibited for the first time on that day.

After two mortal hours of shivering, the trumpets proclaimed the approach of royalty, and Prince Albert arrived, as you will see in the "Court Journal," which I send you. Soon after the Queen entered, attended by a numerous cortege. Her dress you will see described in the "Court Journal." It was rich, beautiful, & in perfect taste. The train was held by twelve fair girls, daughters of the highest nobility, all in white, with orange flowers in their hair. The deportment of the royal bride was really beautiful. It blended the sensibility of the woman with the dignity of the queen and that calm & quiet self-possession for which she has been so remarkable ever since her accession to the throne on all public occasions. Her agitation was only discoverable in the marble paleness of her brow and the shaking of the orange flowers. The prince is very handsome and graceful, and looks older than he is by several years. Both made the responses very audibly, but her tones, tho' soft and low, were yet so perfectly distinct that every one in the chapel heard her vow to love, honor, & obey; and when he promised to love and cherish her, she turned her sweet & innocent looks upon him with an expression that brought tears into every eye that saw it. There was another part of the ceremony that touched me deeply, when she threw herself on her knees at the foot of the altar as if her whole soul was in the petition she was offering up for a blessing. The Archbishop of Canterbury performed the ceremony, with the assistance of the Lord Bishop of London (He asked, "Who gives this woman," &c. &c. and "I, Victoria, take thee, Albert &c".) The Duke of Sussex gave her away, and the only comic part of the whole affair was when the poor German prince "endowed her with all his worldly goods." They left the chapel together hand in hand, and I must say that, take it all together, it was a beautiful & impressive scene. The whole palace was filled with spectators, through which they passed, and it is said by some of the curious and prying that they were observed to squeeze each other's hands most affy. I sincerely wish they may pass through the thorny paths they probably will have to tread hand in hand till they reach that bourne to which even kings and queens must come at last. At night the whole city was splendidly illuminated. We dined with the whole diplomatic corps at Lord Palmerston's, a party of forty, & ordered our carriages to return at half-past ten, thinking we would see something of the illuminations before we went to the Duchess of Sutherland's grand party, given in honor of her Majesty's nuptials. But at half-past 12 o'clock we heard from our footman that the carriage was in Piccadilly, where it had been from half-past 7 when we dismissed it, blocked up with hundreds of others, not a very comfortable predicament. Fortunately we got a hack, and returned home after One, and this occurred, as we heard the next day, to one half of the Duchess's invited guests. So much for the 10th of Feb'y, the happiest day in all the year to Britain's youthful Queen. Notwithstanding she is unpopular with the Tories, there is much loyalty & good feeling evinced toward her on this, I hope, auspicious day. On her way to Windsor in the evening there were 30 triumphal arches erected to do her honor, and her sight-loving subjects took the rain as quietly as if it had been a passing April shower. And now, dear Sally, I must bid you adieu. I have already sent you some cake by a Mr. Cracroft, a nice young Englishman who is going over, he says, to lose his heart to some pretty American; but you had better keep yours for some one of your own countrymen. When Mr. Heth goes, I will send you a larger piece, & I wish you to give the Ritches, Watsons, Maj. Heth, & the Misses Skipwiths some in my name, and be sure to give Mr. Palmer a piece to dream on, if he is not married. . .

This is obviously the logical niche for Mrs. Stevenson's facts-of-life sequel to her account of the wedding of Victoria and Albert. On May 29, 1840, three months after the royal nuptials, she wrote a short, revealing letter to her sister in law, Mrs. Julia Coles, wife of her brother, Isaac. This paragraph tells the story.

London is now in the meridian of the Season, balls, dinners, concerts & without end. The Queen has given several Drawing Rooms and one ball, at which she was permitted to dance *very little,* & to take her steps with great circumspection. To the great joy of her leiges she is, as "Ladies wish to be, who love their Lords" & I suppose I may add in her case, who love their subjects. The Prince is very popular and seems universally liked, for tho' humble minded & modest and most devoted to the Queen, he yet has the spirit to assert his authority as a husband.

XXXII

TRYING TO KEEP an aged Duke awake, with the novelist, Bulwer Lytton, looking on amusedly, was a novel experience for Mrs. Stevenson yet that is what happened the night she and her husband dined with the Duke and Duchess of Somerset. She failed in her endeavor. Morpheus beat her to it.

The Duke of Somerset was Lord Robert Edward Henry Somerset. Incidentally, his brother, Baron Raglan, was one day to give the fatal order for the Charge of the Light Brigade at Balaclava in the Crimean War.

32 Upper Grosvenor St.
Feby 30th [sic] 1840

You see beloved sister how impossible it is for me to send off one sheet to you. I wrote yesterday to be ready for today and last night I received a beautiful pair of slippers from Sophy Hope Vere, the daughter of Lady Elisabeth of whom I have spoken in a former letter, and as Mr. Rush tells me I have half an hour to spare I shall copy her note & her sister's, the charming Hannah's. First however I must explain to you what her allusions mean.

Yesterday we dined with the Duke and Duchess of Somerset, and it was my fortune to sit by the Duke, and not far from the Duchess. His Grace was exceedingly talkative & agreeable until he had finished his dinner, when the most invincible fit of drowsiness seized him, a usual thing, no doubt, for his wife seemed to be watching him, & discovered before I did the first symptoms. She immediately leant over to me, & said: "Pray talk to the Duke & don't let him go to sleep." So on I floundered, every now & then getting an unmeaning smile, with closed eyes; but the moment I ceased, the Duchess would urge me to "talk on, ask questions, talk mathematics!" Think of that? "Ask him," she said, "what was the problem he was solving this morning." Imagine me talking mathematics to a stupid, dosing old duke, who, if he had been wide-awake, had not a dozen ideas. I stood it as long as possible, but finding myself unequal to the task imposed on me, I spoke to Madam Rothschild (the great banker's widow), behind the Duke's chair, & said: "For Heaven's sake help me to keep the Duke awake!" She kindly lent her aid and we talked at him with all our might; but it would not do. He gave audible signs that he had quit us and mathematics for the land of dreams, & involuntarily we both laughed outright. Bulwer Lytton, who sat opposite to me, seemed to enjoy the sport most unromantically.

By the way, his Lady is dashing away in Paris and I hear is patronized by the Casses. It is a pleasant thing to be able to quit a bad tempered tyrant, with a heart capable of enjoyments but it seems she is as merry as if she had never been galled by the shackles of an ill assorted marriage. And now for the note.

"A thousand thanks dear Mrs. Stevenson for your most affec & charming note which I assure you I truly value as I know how fond you are of your dear happy land & home. How very kind of you to write me when your heart & head (for with you they act together) were so busy. I am much better today. We dined this evening en famille with the Cleveland's. We go to Lady Hamlyns on Saturday. I know you are to be there. Do not disappoint us. I heard from Mamma of your gallant beau, the Duke of Somerset. Sophy & I were malicious enough, dear Mrs. Stevenson, to laugh at the thoughts of your dear face in this delicate dilemma."

XXXIII

THE SOCIAL STATISTICS of the Legation in London were astounding and the Stevenson Letter Books in the Library of Congress amply corroborate Mrs. Stevenson's figures. Receiving visits, paying them back, acknowledging invitations involved untold labor.

Hardly had the spring "Season" of 1840 begun before the Stevensons were invited to dine with the royal bride and bridegroom, Victoria and Albert. They were the first of the Diplomatic set to be so honored. This close-up at-home picture of the royal newlyweds has much charm. It was quite evident to Sallie Stevenson that the little Queen had not as yet surrendered to the gallant Prince Consort any of her prerogatives though all England was wondering whether she would "manage" him or otherwise.

Incidentally, in this letter, Mrs. Stevenson refers to the second portrait of her painted by G. P. A. Healy.

London April 8th 1840

My beloved Sister,

It is almost incredible the amount of labour I perform—and you would probably think I had learnt the art of romancing if I were to tell you all I do—only imagine for one item upwards of 2000 visits not hundreds—thousands—the cards are all entered in a book, & the footman counted them the other day & told me there were then two thousand two hundred & forty six, since this time last year—every one of which I have returned—besides the necessity of receiving morning as well as evening visitors—writing notes. In the season I have taken in my basket fifteen, the product of one morning—all cards of invitation here are addressed to the ladies. Besides all this I am obliged to write letters all over the world even to the Celestial Empire. Dear Mrs. Coolidge! has Sally heard from her? I have had her splendid satin cloak made up, & it is the admiration of every one, and nothing ever was more acceptable than it has been to me. I have no doubt it has kept the "Rhumatics" out of my old bones this most inclement & disagreeable winter, besides giving me a very ambassadress look. My own maid made it, and did it very well, dress-making being the only thing she is really good for. I have often blessed the kind donor when I have wrapped its ample folds around me. When I get back, if I ever do, I will astonish you with my economy. I assure you I am astonished myself. I got only one dress last season, and shall get none this. I have had my satins dyed so well that I would defy any eye to detect the economical trick —my hats turned and cut into the fashion—my blond washed, & feathers cleaned—I have often wished for the gold turban I sent you, since I find you cant wear it this winter—however, I do very well, & look as smart as the best of them. I have been particular always in getting good things, thus they look well as long as they last & as I am very careful of them this last has been beyond all calculations—your munificent present my darling sister I thought it best to vest in my likeness, which is really a beautiful picture and the artist is so proud of it that he has painted me another to let him keep the large one for the exhibition. He thinks it his chef d'oeuvre.

In consequence of the Queen's marriage, the "season" has commenced at least a month earlier than usual by bringing the nobility so much sooner to town, who have endeavored to pass away this cold and inclement spring by giving dinners, balls, soirees, &c. We have sometimes received four invitations to dinner in one day, and last week 8 for the week, besides two or three parties every night. I have endeavored to follow Lady Grace's example in the play, by taking it "soberly." You remember when we used to play Lady Grace and Trunly. "Oh, my dear Lady Grace, how could you leave me so unmercifully alone all this time?" It is, as Lady Trunly says, a very different thing to live "soberly" in London, especially in our situation, for we receive invitations from all parties, and it is so ungracious always to refuse. We dined a short time since with the Queen, and are the only members of the diplomatic corps who have yet been invited. It was a very agreeable dinner, more so than any other state dinner we have been at before. The Queen looked so happy that it was refreshing to see her with her handsome, manly-looking young husband sitting by her. The etiquette was the same I have before described to you. She entered the grand drawing-room preceded by her gentlemen of the household, accompanied by Prince Albert, and followed by her ladies-in-waiting, and the mistress of the robes, and the tall graceful, and beautiful Duchess of Sutherland, "Who moves like a goddess, and who looks like a queen." We received her standing, and after shaking hands with us, she took her husband's arm and led the way to the salle a manger. The Duke of Argyll led me, and I found myself seated opposite the royal pair, between the dukes of Argyll and Norfolk. "His Royal Highness' Prince Albert sat on the left of his royal bride. Frequently during the evening they conversed, and several times laughed with merry glee at the communications they made to each other. But still there is something dignified and queenly in whatever this extraordinary young creature says or does. She appears much attached to her young husband, and her manner is certainly much more joyous and happy than I ever saw it before. He is said to be entirely worthy of her affections, and has already gained "golden opinions" from every one. The Baroness Lehzun told me, after dinner, in her broken English, that it was fortunate for "de nation that the Queen had married such a good and humble-minded person." He is very handsome, fine figure, and a very sweet and amiable expression of the face, something like his cousin the Queen, particularly about the mouth, when he smiles, and their complexions are very much alike. Both the Baroness and Lady Littleton told me that the hopes of the nation were not yet to be realized & &.

After dinner the Queen conversed with me for some time and I took the occasion of offering her my congratulations, which she accepted very graciously, and then presented me to her husband, who also conversed about the opera, &c, and told me he had seen me at the play some nights before, when we had gone with Col. Heth. He spoke also of commerce with interest, and when I complimented him on his very good English, he said: "Oh, no; it is just tolerable. I hope to improve." But he really does speak admirably well for a foreigner. They went out together to visit the Duchess of Kent, who was indisposed, and confined to her room. On their return, she led the way to a d.-room, where tables were set out, and Mr. S. was invited to play whist. The prince played 4-handed chess, and the Queen invited me to sit near her, with Lady Lansdowne, Lady Littleton, and the Premier, &c. The evening passed rather pleasantly, perhaps I ought to say very pleasantly for a royal circle, over which the spirit of dullness always broods. Prince Albert sat not far from his Queen, and when it was time to retire and he was still intent on his game, she leaned over to him and said in the softest, sweetest tones, "Albert!" But as His Royal Highness was too much employed to hear these soft and silvery accents, she repeated his name again and again, each time modulating her voice to greater earnestness, without losing any of its sweetness or tenderness. They do say, however, that, Queen though she be, he will not allow himself to be, in matrimonial phrase, "managed,"—that whenever it is necessary, he resists her firmly, though kindly, and I think it is the best security for their future happiness. And I think it is always bad when a woman inverts the laws of Providence by taking the reins in her own hands. You know I never, even in my palmy days, asserted the equality of the sexes. Man is the head of the woman, or rather, in Scripture phrase, "The husband is the head of the wife, even as Christ is the head of the church." Therefore "wives, submit yourselves unto your own husbands," &c. You will laugh at all this, and say it does not concern you. True; but it is good for me to remember it, and write it down occasionally for my own benefit; and it will be well for this dear, little, innocent-looking Queen to do the same.

The Marchioness of Lansdowne has given the most splendid fete of the season to her Majesty and Prince Albert. There was a platform erected for illuminating the exterior of the mansion and carriage-way with lights, which threw a brilliancy over every object exceeding the light of day. The interior presented even a more inspiring aspect. The grand vestibule, with its Corinthian columns, its beautiful and fragrant flowers, statues, liveried servants, and lights, presented altogether a dazzling coup d'oeil. The statue-gallery, one of the most magnificent in London, was used as the dancing-room, and besides the supper-room for the Queen and her court, there were three other rooms with supper-tables for the guests, covered with every kind of delicacy. The diplomatic corps had seats assigned them, which was very fortunate for me, I having scalded my foot only a few days ago, and it would have been severe duty to have stood on it all night. The Queen danced with the young noblemen of her court, and the prince with the daughters of the high nobility. We came away early. These things have but little attraction for us now that the novelty is over, and the happiest in the twenty-four is that in which sleep unites me to you. There has also been a d.-room, on the 9th, which was very splendid and crowded. I wore my green velvet train and embroidered satin dress which I got from France the first season I was here, and was the best dressed of the corps, for the others were dressed in gold and tinsel, which I never wear, and looked more like opera-dancers than representatives of nations. However, everybody to their taste. We left the presence-chamber before the court was over, and got home just at 4, tired to death. Fell asleep in my chair, and refused to go out in the evening. You see I shall never become a fine lady, or a lady of fashion. I refused so many invitations this year that I am thought almost unapproachable; but I find it quite as much as I can do to go to those places at which my situation here compels me to be present. I make my appearance, if only for five minutes.

XXXIV

In America's progress towards greatness and the things she believed in, her destinies often impinged on Britain's. It meant a constant succession of little crises that necessitated patience and skillful handling by the American Minister.

There was, for instance, the problem of the slave trade and the right of search that was irksome to both nations. Britain was zealous in her crusade against this nefarious traffic. Her men-of-war, off the African coast and around the West Indies, were constantly overhauling American merchantmen suspected of slave-running.

America had sought to suppress the importation of slaves, but she refused to grant any foreign power the right to search her vessels on the high seas. This ill-fated business—trading in black ivory—created many disagreeable incidents between the two nations. One by one Stevenson resolved them peacefully.

To add to the ministerial burdens in 1840, Legation Secretary Benjamin Rush resigned. This efficient young man—son of their old friend, Richard Rush—had been a godsend to the Legation. His departure was a blow, and his place really never was filled before the Stevensons went home.

Not long after the Stevensons reached London in 1836 a fine young American artist, G. P. A. Healy, had come to see them. This aspiring genius had arrived in the British capital looking for worlds to conquer, though not new ones, for he had not yet reached his zenith. Titled patrons, then as now, meant much to a rising artist. To Healy the Stevensons held out a helping hand. Many were the "introductions" they gave him to Very Important People. Indeed, through his friend the American Minister at Paris, Stevenson arranged for Healy to paint the celebrated portrait of King Louis Philippe of France.

Both the Stevensons sat for Healy. Of her he made two likenesses. The larger, depicting the brilliant lady dressed for the Queen's Drawing Room, was exhibited in England. It excited much admiration and won great praise for the artist. Brought to Virginia it survived until a few years ago when it was destroyed by fire. Healy's second portrait of Mrs. Stevenson belongs to one of her descendants in Charlottesville, Virginia.

In this letter, packed with social items, Mrs. Stevenson relates how she came to sit for Healy.

London June 12th 1840
32 Upper Grosvenor St.

My beloved Sisters, and
Edward, & Sally

You must really my beloved friends allow me to take you all together for since Mr. Rush's departure I have not had a moment I could devote to you my best beloved, and ever faithful correspondents—much as I dreaded his leaving my husband with the whole weight of the Legation upon his shoulders, I must confess the reality has surpassed my very worst imaginings. The morning after his departure Mr. Stevenson called me into the office & gave me six or eight pages of dispatch paper to copy, & the next morning another not so long. I began to think I should have a hard time of it, if I were to have the Secy's and my own business to do in the midst of a London Season, but I would not complain as long as I could hold a pen, as it is always my duty as well as my happiness to help my husband in his hour of need. The truth is nothing could have been more mal-appropos than Mr. R. leaving us at this time besides all the toil & labour of a London Season the town is overflowing with Americans, I assure you I am not romancing when I tell you, there are 20 at one boarding house, and every one who comes here, letters or no letters, expects some civility at our hands. Mr. Stevenson says some-times he shall go crazy, but as he has threatened this so often I begin to get used to it. Altho' I must say I pity him and myself too, for we have rather more than we can do. I sent you all long letters by Mr. Rush. We got back from Epsom Races just in time for Mr. S. to close his dispatch, he did not enjoy the race, however, from his anxiety to get back before Mr. Rush's departure, and I should not have gone but as Mr. S. intended taking the carriage & servants I thought I might as well go too, and enjoy the country air for one night—besides I did not quite like being left behind. The murder of Ld William Russel, has made cowards of every one, and they say there never was such a locking of doors as since this horrible event, for an amiable old nobleman to have his throat cut in the very focus of fashion in the polished capital of the world, is something to make people look about them—suspicion has fastened upon his Swiss valet, Couvoisier—but it is feared he will escape, notwithstanding, as he has been so cunning in destroying all the evidences of his guilt, that it is feared an English jury will not hang him. I shall continue to write just when I can snatch a half hour; since the above entry we have spent two days in the country at Whitsuntide with Mr. & Mrs. Charles Marryat about 20 miles from town, we took our own horses within five miles of the place, & then posted. They were very kind and we enjoyed the country & quiet, Mr. S. went out one day fishing & caught a large fish, and the other day of our absence we went to see the pictures at Pansanger, Earl Cooper's, lunched in the road, & upon the whole had a pleasant day. We met Capn Marryat, & Miss Mynaham, the latter is the lady who had such a terrible passage over. I asked her to come & make my house an hotel for a few days untill she could make arrangements to join some friends who expected her and accordingly on our return to town she came to us and stayed three or four days. I believe she was heartily tired of it, for we dined out every day, & two & three parties every evening, and during the time I was at home I was always writing notes, or resting, she said the day she left me raising her hands, "Well, I could not at all understand this untill I came to stay with you, and how you do so much business, & undergo so much fatigue is to me quite marvellous". She said she should die in a week, but I told her there was nothing like use. She compliments my system & industry as beyond any thing she ever saw. What will Helen say to this?—Without system I should not be able to get on at all—for all the notes of invitation, &c, go through my hands, and in the last month we had 20 odd invitations out to dinner & about double that number to evening parties. What would become of us if we trusted to memory. & since I have been in England I have never made a mistake, whereas old stagers of a life time, make some very odd ones—for instance a lady intended giving two dinners & wrote all her invitations for one day in consequence of which she had 40 guests instead of 20—& pretended to be taken violently ill—so as to send them all off —as to us, we do not give many dinners, but Miss Bessy says she believes we eat more than 365 in the year. We returned from the country to dine with Baron & Lady Alderman, charming persons, where we met, Amelia Opie and Sigismendi &c—the latter sat by me, at dinner, & the former not far off, so that I had the benefit of their conversation. Mrs. Opie is a large stout looking old lady dressed as a Quaker, high white caps—quakerish satin dress with long sleeves. The moment I entered the room I was struck with her appearance, and Lady Alderman said she would bring her up & present her to me but I said, "No, if you please, I will go to her". I cannot say she came up exactly to my idea of Mrs. Opie, I expected from her writings to have seen a thin spiritual looking being, a Joanne Bailie sort of person but whether it is that her dress gave her an outre appearance, I was disappointed—her manners are easy & polite, and her smile sweet & intelligent and gives to her countenance an expression of benevolence, & sensibility, but when her features are in repose they express nothing but what I have seen in the face of thousands of good kind hearted old ladies, nor is her conversation either sparkling or brilliant but quiet &

subdued—sensible of course, for Amelia Opie could neither speak or write any thing that was not. We talked about her writings which I told her was much read & admired in my country, she spoke particularly of her illustrations on dying—&c. Sigismendi is on the contrary a very intellectual looking person, & in his broken English said some things to be remembered.

Just as we were going to dinner, one of the guests came in and said that he had been detained by an attack made upon the life of the Queen; that in passing down Constitution Hill she had been shot at twice by a ruffian within a few feet of her carriage, but escaped unhurt; that the excitement had been excessive; that instead of turning back in alarm, she ordered the carriage to be driven immediately to her mother's the Duchess of Kent's, to prevent her being alarmed by the report of the attempt on her life. What thoughtful tenderness and presence of mind! And yet this is the daughter who, the Tories say, is neglectful of her mother. On her return through the park, she was followed and cheered by crowds on horseback, in carriages, and on foot, and the enthusiasm was beyond anything. The gentleman who had come in just in time for his dinner said he had been led on by his feelings of loyalty to the palace gates.

Since writing the above, we have been to the palace to a ball, at which I had much conversation with the Baroness Lehzun. She says the Queen told her that when the first pistol was fired, she said to Prince Albert: "How imprudent that persons should be allowed to shoot at birds in the park!" and the report of the pistol having frightened the horse of one of the gentlemen in attendance, the prince ordered the postilions to stop. At that moment, she says, she saw the pistol directed at herself, and the assassin deliberately take aim, when she stooped her head towards her husband's bosom, and thought to herself, "If it please Providence, I shall escape." And it did please that kind Providence to which she trusted to deliver her. The baroness told me she said she did not feel at all agitated, and how thankful she felt that her equeries had been sent round to meet her at the park gate, otherwise one of them would probably have been shot, which she added, "would have afflicted me." This account of the matter I received from the baroness, although there are various others. Some say she stood up after the report of the first pistol and that the prince pulled her down; but I think that the probability is that Baroness L., who was with her immediately after the event, and to whom she speaks most freely, is better informed than any one else. The old lady is decidedly in favor of hanging the wretch, as she calls him. I suggested he might be insane, but she said, "Dere was too much of de method in his madness," for that she knew he might have been practising for six weeks before he attempted the life of the Queen. I asked if she thought the Queen would sign the death-warrant, when she gave me a piece of information as to English jurisprudence of which I was previously ignorant, that the Queen was not called upon to sign death-warrants, only pardons. The deportment of the young man, who is not more than 18 or 19, was very insolent & indifferent as to consequences when first taken into custody, though more serious and thoughtful, it is said, now. I suppose the condemnation of Couvoisier has had some effect upon his nerves. The conviction of this hardened murderer was the most extraordinary thing ever known, he would have been acquitted the next day, for the want of evidence, when a paper published in France was the cause of his detection. After an article written upon the murder, the Editor inscribed a remark of his own, that it was surprising that no enquiries had been made at the hotels kept by foreigners in London, to ascertain whether any parcels had been left there, as the probability was that the stolen property would have been left there by the Swiss. On their being read by some one in the hearing of the mistress of the hotel, it reminded her that a parcel had been left with her, and on examination proved to be Ld W. Russels plate with his arms & initials upon it, &c and on being carried to the prison she recognised the Swiss as the person who had left it; upon which he confessed his guilt &c—strange and mysterious are the workings of Providence!!! I must now tell you of some charming new acquaintances we have made a pleasant change from the worse to the best of God's creatures. About six weeks ago we dined at Lord & Lady Stanleys of Anderly, (of whom I wrote you last autumn as having been very civil to us, &c,) there we met with a charming person, a Miss Tunno, with whom I became accidentally acquainted. She sat by Mr. Stevenson & I thought he neglected her, and after dinner, I endeavoured to atone for his want of attention, & somewhat struck too with her mild thoughtful countenance, I made up to her, & we entered into conversation, finding her intelligent & agreeable, I remained at her side almost the whole evening, and before we parted, she had given me a general invitation to visit her at her Villa near Windsor, she told me her Mother was an American, & she had been born in her mother's land, which had given her a kind feeling towards all of that country & therefore she was particularly pleased to have made my acquaintance, &c. Among other things by way of proving her birth-right, she said she was very fond of hominy—& thanks to Matt I had some, & told her I would send her a little parcel. When she called upon me I happened to be at home & received her & ordered the hominy to be put into her carriage—and by a singular coincidence when I called some days after to take leave of her, the wife of her only brother chanced to come in, & she asked leave to present her. This brought an invitation to dinner where we found all that wealth, taste & luxury could supply, and the most amiable persons in the world. Soon after this Miss Tunno left town for her country villa, but before doing so, she made me promise to go to her for a week at the time of the Ascot races. Then wrote, & fixed the 15th to the 20th and said she should send her carriage to meet us at the maiden-head-station about three miles from her house &c, &c. June 23d Well, dear Lucy we have had the most delightful visit to the Tunno's and now I can tell you all about them. Mr. Stevenson and myself were to have set off on Monday the 15th but Alas! for Mr. Rush! my good husband found it impossible to get away that night, so he took me, with Mrs. Jeffs & James the footman, for both of whom I have a special liking, to the rail road, & put me in, I must confess I felt rather forlorn, as the servants were in a back car, and I sat waiting for the steam to put us in motion, & thinking, well, Mr. S. is snug at home by this time, when I looked up, & saw him standing with folded arms and a most lover like look gazing on me as if he was taking a last look. Will you believe, I was silly enough to shed a tear or two as the thought past through my mind of that last parting which come's to all of woman born, but the steam soon put all my sentiment to flight and away we went at a speed that soon brought the turrets of Windsor castle in view but owing to the many stopages we did not arrive untill an hour after our time, that is instead of one hour we were just two, and I found dear Miss Tunno in great trouble looking for me in every car. She was in a handsome Barouche with liveried servants, &c, and a pony chaise for the luggage. From the wealth and splendour I had seen in her brothers house, I was prepared to see a comfortable respectable place, but I must confess I was astonished to find myself welcomed to one of the most beautiful villa's I have seen in England, the grounds highly ornamented & exhibiting the taste, as well as the opulence of the owner's. I found there were three sisters (all single,) living together— and this place had been left to them by their mother with the means of keeping it up—and certainly there cannot be a better appointed establishment—my friend is the eldest of the family to whom all the others look up, as their head & superior. She is from her appearance between 50 & 60, tall in person with a touching expression of softness & pensiveness in her counte- nance which is occasionally kindled into a smile the sweeter & more winning from the previously grave aspect which it softens and subdues. There is a something in her manner that impressed me with an idea that some great grief had cast its shadow over her, but that submissive to the chastening of Heaven, it had only purified her from the dross of Earthly passions, and upon a more intimate acquaintance I find this is the case. I found Mr. & Mrs. Tunno had arrived before us, and three or four other guests. Miss Tunno asked me if I felt disposed for a little walk before dinner which proposal I gladly acceded to after being confined for two hours in a rail road car. The grounds were so beautiful and inviting that I felt unwilling to leave them, shaded walks affording a hundred intricacies delicious to the eye and imagination which led us at last to a beautiful conservatory situated amidst flowers, & shrubs of rare beauty & fragrance. She pointed out several from her mother-land, my old friends and acquaintances, which I recognized with a thrill of delight. The evening passed most agreeably, music, chess, & conversation. They said they only wanted Mr. S. to complete their satisfaction but not so with me dear Lucy, for strange to tell, I thought incessantly of you and imagined how you would be delighted with these admirable and excellent persons, I could not resist the impulse I felt to speak of you to them, & told them how much they would like you. They are all highly cultivated, very literary in their taste & pursuits, Miss Tunno is an artist of the first order, her two drawing rooms are filled with her own painting, a likeness half or 3 quarters length of her Father & Mother, equal to Sir Martin Shee's who has painted a full length of herself, when in the meridian of her youth & beauty—besides many other paintings all beautifully executed. She speaks & writes, German, French, & Italian, & writes the most beautiful letter I ever read—her two sisters Marie, & Harriet, a little younger than herself, are also very accomplished & well read, but not equal to their sister. The next morning we looked out anxiously for Mr. S. but were obliged to set off without him, but about two miles from the house, we saw him coming under full sail, he & his man Cates in a little 4 wheeled vehicle he had got at the station, with much squeezing &c, we took him into the barouche, but having four horses to the carriage his weight did not make much difference. The day was beautiful the party all in good humour, & good spirits, and we soon got over the 14 miles and found ourselves on the Ascot race course, crowd like a D Room. Fortunately, the Miss Tunno's had had the precaution to have another barouche fixed upon the course, in a good situation indeed the best, for which they paid some two or three pounds and a man to take care of it into this we got, & saw every thing which was to be seen. The Queen with all her attendants in

5 or 6 carriages and 4 passed close by us, so that we had the benefit of her smiles, & some of the young gentlemen of our party joined in the cheering, which on the second day was really deafening—in the intervals between the races we walked about, & saw the roulette tables, thimble-rig, &c, &c, and I threw the dice once for Mr. Tunno, & lost him 2/6—upon the whole we enjoyed ourselves very much, and had a very pleasant time. At 2 the servants produced baskets filled with every delicacy to eat & drink with little baskets of strawberries for dessert. We got back at 5 o'clock and had time to rest a little before dinner, to which some guests from the neighbourhood had been added. I however stole off by ½ past 10 oclock. The next day, Miss Tunno took us all in two carriages to visit Tress-mere, the celebrated seat of Ld & Lady Granville, a most beautiful place a wilderness of sweets through which we wandered for two hours, finding something new & beautiful to attract us at every step. On the third day we went again to the races—the two days that the Queen was present, and enjoyed ourselves quite as much as on the first, with the additional pleasure of the days beginning with rain & wind & clearing off to a calm & beautiful sunshine just enough obscured to make it pleasant. On the fourth day we stayed at home, and as it rained the Miss Tunno's took us all over the house, each lady has her own bed room and sitting parlour to herself up stairs, through which they took us, and showed us all their comforts & conveniences —and my friend invited me to remain with her in her sanctum. Then it was she spoke to me of her past trials the loss of dear friends by death, a neice whom she had adopted as a child— a mother on whom she doated—(again I thought of you,) and to whom she had dedicated all the best days of her life—&c- &c. We left that little room, more bound to each other than ever.

You will be surprised to hear I have been sitting again tho' not for myself. The one that Mr. Rand exhibited in the Royal Academy has brought him so much into notice that Mr. Healy a young American artist of great worth & talent, (who has lately received the gold medal from the King of France, having taken by special favour a likeness of him,) made it a matter of particular favour that I would sit to him, at first I refused & told him it was impossible—that nothing but my love for a dear sister who wished to have my likeness and sent the means of paying for it, could have induced me to take the trouble & fatigue of sitting—but again, & again, he came, and said it might be the means of doing him much good &c, &c, what could I say? My means of doing good, are too limitted to refuse when I have the power, therefore I consented & have given him four sittings, with which he has finished a beautiful picture 3 quarters length—he has painted me in crimson velvet, with one arm over the arm of the chair, with Mr. Rogers richly embroidered hankerchief in that hand, and a beautiful bouquet of flowers in the other a gold turban very like the one I sent you &c, &c. He took it yesterday to the Duke of Sussex, who thought it a good likeness and a beautiful picture. He says, the Duke told him he had an affc. regard for me. But of course it is not mine, & I have nothing to do with it altho' I have no doubt at some future day he will present it to me.

This beloved sisters and you my precious Ned is only a slight sketch of the inmates of Taplan. I could write a volume, but time presses, and I must now hasten to thank you for your dear & welcome letters my dear Bett, & Emm, & you too my dear little name sake. Your kindness in writing me twice made my heart smite me for reproaching you, but still dear Sall, I will not take back what I have said. It is a duty to cultivate your talents, and if by doing so, you can also give pleasure & happiness to one who loves you tenderly & devotedly, how much more encumbent on you, and then there is another reason, your dear devoted mother is not fond of writing besides I know she has not much time for it & you save her trouble. These are potent reasons for writing—and can you give me one for not writing? As for want of time that would be no excuse to me—for I write without time. I have no idle moment—seize every one, as Uncle Stevy would say, "by the tail"—and you have no notion at all what may be done by a determined will. Not a word by the steamer from your dear brother—nor Sally—but

I have no reason to complain—you wrote so recently—still I pine to see even a scrip from your dear pen—and of all things I wish to know how you like your seal & key & what you thought of my likeness. I see dear Bett neither you nor Emily think it like, you are too good to mortify me by saying so, but I see plainly you think it "loves labour lost". I am glad nothing else has been thrown away upon it, as Mr. Rand took it for nothing, but the permission to keep the other which I had paid for.

So much for the pictures!—and now my beloved sister to reply to your kind & affec letter which brought tears into my eyes, and touched me deeply. I fancied I could see you with the picture—could hear you say, This is not Sally, and Emily responding—no—"It is not Sally." Well, I am sure I do not know whether it is like or not. I know I am flattered and that is all I do know about it. I certainly am improved in appearance greatly since you saw me, and you know how much I am improved in appearance by dress—and you must not suppose my dear sister when I boast to you of my little economical contrivances that I ever go into such a society as this, ill-dressed—no indeed, that, here is too much the test of gentility—besides, when I speak of dying satins, &c I ought to tell you how perfectly it is done here, also cleaning feathers, &c, quite like new. No indeed, altho' I am strictly economical, from principle as well as necessity, & have dressed on less than any one who has made so good an appearance, yet I have never forgotten, what is due to my station here and always dressed like a lady. But I have no time to dwell upon this subject now—more anon. I cannot tell you dear sister how eagerly I waited for your letter by Mrs. Moncure who did not get to town immediately, & when she did come, not understanding the etiquette she waited for me to call, not remembering it would be as easy to find a needle in a hay-stack. As soon as I heard of her being in town & ascertained her location I went, but found her out. We asked them all, Mr. Ambler and the little girl, to breakfast. When she brought your box, I could not open it whilst she staid. I wished no eye to see my emotion. I kissed each article as I took it out, with the reverence a Catholic would have pressed his lips to a holy relick. The reticule is very pretty & ingenious, & the pin cushion will never be used in this country, I could not bear that my maid should take out the pins your dear fingers have stuck in. The cape, or [illegible] as they call them here, is beautiful and just the thing I wanted. I wore it last evening at a small dinner party over black, (the Court is in mourning for the King of Prussia,) because it had been on your neck, I would not let it be done up untill I had worn it. I am glad you sent it so. Mr. S. must speak for himself. He has just been up with both hands full of papers for me to copy, & told me to cut short my dispatches, for there was work enough to last me untill the Queen went off. Luckily or unluckily his eagle eye spied my scrawled sheets. He snatched them up, and has fretted & fumed over every line. I could not help telling him I thought him as tyrannical as he of Syracuse, to restrict me in the pleasure of writing to my family. He says he shall write you & Edward a letter & give it to me—and that if Mr. Rush hears of my complaining it will be a mortal offence &c &c—gathered up his papers and disappeared growling all the way down stairs. So now as I think he has cooled down a little I must after him, and look very humble and penitent just as if I knew what offence I had been guilty of, and ask permission to have the honour to copy those odious papers—and if it is granted you will hear no more from me by the Queen. But before I go, I must thank you my precious sister for your presents. Had it come direct from the hand that gave it, I should have been touched & gratified, as she might make so delicate & just a reason for bestowing out of her superfluity but somehow or other, the more I feel your generous kindness the more I am unwilling to appropriate this gift to my own use. I shall write her when I have a little time and tell her I shall be happy to lay it out for her in something that may be useful or ornamental. But do not dearest & best beloved sister, give yourself the least concern about sending me any more money, I had rather you would not, dearest. I know how hard the times are in America —so pray do not think any more of it. I do very well, I assure you—and it is the business of my gude-man to supply the need-ful. I have a thousand things to say but must defer to another time. I cannot tell you how my heart is lightened & gladdened by hearing of your recovery. God grant it may be permanent.

XXXV

Mrs. Stevenson was duly impressed by the celebrated English actress, Fanny Kemble, but not by her American husband, Pierce Butler, whom Fanny married on her first American tour in the early 1830's. Mrs. Stevenson does not indicate it, but she must have known that Fanny Kemble was not sparing in her criticism of Southern institutions.

Maria Edgeworth, the novelist, was in her sunset years when she came within range of Mrs. Stevenson's eye and pen as this note indicates.

Nov. 18 1840

I dined yesterday at Mr. Kenyons with Fanny Kemble, Mrs. Butler. Mr. Kenyon called to enquire before he issued his tickets if I objected to meeting the *Ci-devant* actress, on the contrary I rather liked it. She is certainly a woman of genius —but has not lost either the air or manner of her profession. We were politely civil. Butler seems to be a good natured nobody. We had a large party in the evening from which we soon made our escape, bearing off the 'poet of memory' with us. He is truly a dear old man, & says so many kind things to us. He told me the other night of his bon-mot upon Prince

Albert, which he said, delighted the Queen so much, when he was introduced to the Prince, some one enquired what he thought of him, to which he replied—"He is very good looking —and looks good".

Maria Edgeworth is in town and has made us a visit, and written me a note. She is a nice old lady of 72—very small in stature, comes up to about my shoulders—her countenance does not indicate much talent except when she is excited in conversation. She has a good deal of action, and the Irish vivacity of manner. She says, "Paddy God bless him, I love him, tho' he cheats me every hour in the day". Her language is particularly felicitous, and her illustrations apt & beautiful. She talked of Dr. Johnson's "tripod sentences". I first called upon her. (The etiquette here—for the person of highest rank either to go first, or grant permission &c) and invited her to come to me, as I wished my husband to see her, (being too good a wife to have any enjoyment in which he does not share). She appointed the hour, and it so happened the Duchess of Cleaveland called at the same time, & was highly gratified to meet this gifted authoress. When Mr. Stevenson came up, I saw at once, that she talked to sustain her high reputation—and really she was not only brilliant, but most happy both in her subject, & her manner. She left us all delighted—and passed out of the room under Mr. Stevenson's arm saying to him the most flattering things, and professing herself to be the most honoured, & obliged, &c, &c.

Not a word of Mr. Heth yet. I hope dearest you did not get the money. I shall bring you a pair of clogs and India rubbers that are invaluable. I would if I could, take a pair also to Emily & Sally, but they cost a good deal of money, altho' they last a life time. I have got my maid making me up some summer dresses for America—and was kept awake last night thinking whether I could make her fit you in a pretty cheap silk dress. Oh for Midas' touch—how many very useful things I could take you free of duty. I am constantly thinking what I shall carry this one, & that one, untill I am half crazy. Heigho! If

my purse was as large as my heart—there would be no difficulty and my dear husband too is always thinking what he
shall do. God bless you beloved sister, I must leave you to
write to Edward & Mat. Your devoted sister

S. C. Stevenson

XXXVI

Mrs. Stevenson drew this chatty comparison between manners in America and manners in England in the late Eighteen-thirties for her niece, Sally Rutherfoord.

I cannot, however, dismiss this subject without saying a few words on the difference of manners in our country & this. With us, as soon as a woman marries, no matter how young, she retires from the great theatre of the world, and buries herself in obscurity & retirement. Her talents, & her accomplishments, if she has any, are neglected, or only exercised in the nursery. Here it is very different, young ladies are not permitted to appear in publick without accompanied by their mothers, or a chaperon, who is required to watch her with Spanish vigilance. The presence of sensible and dignified matrons give a higher tone to society, and has also the effect of making married women more solicitous both in adorning their minds & persons and of cultivating all those graces which embellish life, and gives to them charms, which even old Time, the fell Destroyer, cannot impair. When I first came to England I was, I confess, shocked to hear, how old women were whom I met in society, dressed out with all the care, & sometimes, with too much of the juvenility of blooming 18, but after being here long enough to look beyond the surface of things, I found that these very persons whom I met so often in the gay circles of fashionable society, were the benefactresses of the poor, giving not only their money, but their time to benevolent purposes; that time, which others would spend in sloth, or indolence, was actively & zealously employed for the good of their suffering fellow creatures, and that to those good works, they united an humble faith, and fervent piety, which exhibited itself not in empty words, but in the performance of every duty, which adorns and elevates the female character, and this too, to extreme old age. When a woman thinks herself too old to go into general society she does not shut herself up as with us, but she assembles around her own fire side, a little retinue of sensible and agreeable people and enjoys to the last the pleasures of intellect. Thus it is, with the Miss Barries, the loves of Horace Walpole!—Since I have been here, I have lost two friends, whose bitter end, showed that altho' they were in the world, they lived above it. The first, was a Mrs. Bowles, the sister of Lord Palmerston, who was obliged to be much in society, and yet who always found time and opportunity to do good, & I know from the best authority she, & her husband never omitted family prayers night & morning, they stayed at home always on the Sabbath evenings to read to their servants. She died like a Saint, and again, our dear & amiable friend, the Duchess Countess of Sutherland, who was ill only one short week, when a friend flattered her with getting well, she looked earnestly at him, and said, "Why should I wish it, I am now old and well stricken in years, my life has been not only long, but prosperous and happy. I have raised my children to be virtuous & good, & leave them possessed of every earthly blessing. Why then should I wish to remain here? My work is done, & I am ready & willing to depart". She died as peaceful & as tranquil as an infant. If this is not Christianity, what is?—No my dear child, I think it is our duty to make ourselves as innocently happy as we can in the situation in which God has placed us, to cultivate the faculties & the talents He has given us, and when we have devoted them in every way we can to His service, the next most pleasing and acceptable thing we can do, is to endeavour to make ourselves agreeable to each other.

You will think this a very dull long letter my dear child and really I do not know how I have fallen into so grave a strain to you, to whom I should have put on my most smiling & cheerful aspect, I believe it was all owing to Lady Cash, who has really haunted me like a dream, ever since I saw & heard her. Yesterday we had a very pleasant dinner at Sir Frances Chauntry's the great sculptor, and afterward went to Lady Minto's; London is becoming very gay—as Walpole says, "all the town has come to town" to night we are to go to Lord Denmans, another of Englands great men—&c, &c, &c, &c, &c

But positively I will write—no more—your letters are so short & unsatisfactory, they might all be published in the Enquirer, by the way give my kindest remembrances to them all, notwithstanding Mr. R's neglect of my long letter—and now dear Sally, let me ask it of you to do as I have done, put a large sheet of paper on your table & whenever you have a moments leisure scribble whatever comes first into your mind —tell me how Mamma & Papa look—what they are doing— saying—, &c,—the children—how much they have grown, who they look like—if they remember me &c &c—of Aunt Betsy's looks—doings—sayings—&c &c—Uncle Tucker—Aunt Helen —of all the Richmond people, especially of your dear Grand Father, & of all the family—but your dear old Grand Papa, is, I confess, the delight of my heart. I remember the pleasant jokes & frolicks we have had together—we can neither of us jump as well as in the days of yore, but we are both I believe something of evergreens, in spirits at least, and will laugh, & play chess as long as we live, I hope—Kiss him for me dear S, for many a kiss he has stolen from me, when I was better worth kissing than I am now—but you will be a good substitute for me in my best days.

Ever your affectionate aunt—S C S

XXXVII

ON THE AFTERNOON of November 21, 1840, Mrs. Stevenson was writing away with her portfolio on her knees when church bells began chiming. Presently cannon boomed and there was excitement in the street outside the Legation. She knew what it meant. Queen Victoria's first-born had arrived safely at Buckingham Palace; this was the Princess Royal, Victoria Adelaide Mary Louisa.

In due time American Minister Stevenson would transmit to the Queen, through Lord Palmerston, a letter of congratulations from President Van Buren, but the Minister's Lady did not wait for the tedious processes of official protocol. She proceeded to write at once her own few words to welcome the newcomer and wish the royal mother well.

Excitedly, she dashed off a note to her homefolks in Virginia. They would be interested, too.

And now I must hasten, while I have a little time, to tell you of the birth of a princess royal, which took place last Saturday, the 21st, to the surprise of all her Majesty's lieges, who did not expect the happy event for a week or ten days. She was taken at 2, called up the household at 4 in the morning, and by 2 in the day gave birth to the little chubby princess, who gave audible demonstration to the attendant ministers &c., in waiting of her discontent in being brought into this working-day world in so public a manner. The old etiquette of the court has been strictly kept up on this occasion. All the ministers of state, officers of state, were summoned, and waited in the adjoining room with the door of the Queen's apartment partly open, so that those who deemed it necessary might look in. I dined yesterday with the Lord Bishop of London, whose duty it was to be present, and he told me in one minute after the birth of the child it was wrapped in flannel & brought into the room, the nurse laying it on the table for inspection. He says he saw in the Queen's dressing-room (which was fitted up as a temporary nursery until her little royal highness's apartments were got ready) a marble and a silver bath for the young stranger, & her gorgeous cradle made in the form of a nautilus &c. But I dare say you have no interest in these things, and, to confess the truth, since my husband has turned his face so resolutely homeward, I am losing my interest in all these matters, & I sometimes reproach myself for want of gratitude to those who are so very kind to be glad to leave them. Mr. Stevenson only waits to hear the result of the elections, & either way he sends in his resignation. The fogs have been intense for the last week, darkness at midday, and I congratulate myself in thinking I shall not be another winter in London—indeed but for the necessity of Mr. S's being in town we might be in the country now, as we have invitations from various places, Mrs. Davenport to Caperthorn—Lady Stanly to Anderley—and yesterday I got quite a long letter from Lady Westminster telling me of an accident that had befallen the Marquis and inviting us to Eaton Hall—these are all in the way to Ireland, to which the Lord Lieutenant of Ireland, have invited us to make him a visit this winter—but I don't know whether Mr. S. will go. I should like him to give up his house at New Year—pack every thing & hire a room to put the horses in.

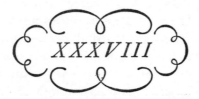

XXXVIII

It is strange that her own people apparently continued to resent the popularity Mrs. Stevenson and her husband had won in England. Even her talented brother Edward had written that it appeared to him as if they had nothing to do but be entertained. Consistently the good lady defended their way of life in Britain. She was proud of her husband's diplomatic achievements. Not the least of them she pointed out, was persuading Lord Palmerston to consent to arbitration of the touchy, critical Northeastern Boundary problem which had brought the two nations to the verge of war.

The tragic burning of her home, Enniscorthy, the winter before had saddened her considerably. She yearned all the more for her own people and America. Her brother, Isaac, who had inherited Enniscorthy in 1808 when John Coles II died, had beautified and enlarged the house. It was still the home of Mrs. Stevenson's heart though she had not lived there since her marriage. Its destruction left a void. Incidentally, not until 1850 would Enniscorthy rise from its ruins.

Christmas Day, 1840, brought back many happy memories though they were tinged with nostalgia. The best she could do was to reach out across three thousand miles of water with her pen for a long chat with her sister Emily, Mrs. John Rutherfoord of Richmond, Virginia.

Christmas Day

My beloved sister,

A merry Christmas and a happy New Year to you all! and may the next find us united in persons, as we are in hearts, and infinitely more merry & more happy under our own bright, clear, cold skies. The very thought makes my heart flutter, and seems to brighten this murky atmosphere—which now at mid-day is so dense that it looks tangible—and is scarcely respirable. It affects me in the most extraordinary manner, you know I was always atmospherial, & I now cough as if I were in the last stage of consumption, the cold has been so intense this winter, that it has aggravated all the miseries of fog & smoke. The Serpentine and the water in all the parks have been frozen over for more than ten days and last week 40 persons fell in skating, and were all rescued, such is the vigilance of the Humane Society and the value which is here put upon human life. It has been fine fun for the skaters who seldom have so long an interval of frosty weather. The fog's have been unusually severe—dense dark & yellow, it is impossible for one who has never seen a London fog to form any idea of it. It sometimes falls so suddenly upon the city that one feels as if an extinguisher had been put upon the sun, and very serious and fatal accidents occur, besides some that are truly ludicrous. Some few evenings since Lady Elizabeth Hope Vere, & Sophy spent a sociable evening with me & when I saw Sophy the next day she told me that it had been with the greatest difficulty they had found their way home a distance of only a few hundred yards, that the coachman after much driving found himself a mile in the contrary direction, & it was only by the aid of a boy they got home at all—and that the whole house had been kept in a state of anxiety untill one or two oclock in the morning in conse-quence of the absence of the different members of the family. A French maid of Lady Elizabeth's had been permitted to go to the theatre with the house keeper, and after much wandering they were brought home, the poor French girl in hysterics declaring that she believed the world was coming to an end. When these fogs occur it is in vain to light lamps. The gas which generally makes the town so bright & brilliant, cannot be seen, the atmosphere is too thick for the rays of light to penetrate, & often it puts them out. Imagine such an air to be breathed for months together, & you will not be surprised that I do nothing but cough. To be sure I must confess, it is not always so bad as this, but there is always at this season more or less fog in London, when the country is beautifully clear. When they do occur they are frightful. I heard from a gentleman a few days since that he had attempted to make his way home from the club in St. James St., and that he thought he had got hold of an iron railing which would lead him directly home—but that to his surprise he continued to walk & walk, untill he was sure he had gone five times the distance when lo! he found he had been walking round & round the railing which surrounds King Charles Statue & was too happy to get back to the club, & pass his night there with many other disconsolate husbands & bachelors in their arm chairs. This is really a long yarn upon fog, &c—but in truth I have but little else to write about since my last long letter to you on the 4th of Decr which was sent by a Boston Steamer. My cough has been so bad that I have de- clined all invitations out either in the evening or to dinner. At this season there is not much going on, but always something —in the last ten days I have declined dinners to Ld Cheif Justice Tindal's, a dear old man, so good, & so wise, & so very fond of us—Mr. Rogers—whose dinners can only be exceeded in agreeableness by his breakfasts—Sir Robert Harry Inglis —one of the most pure & zealous Christians that any country has to boast of—& the Countess Devon of Essex, besides several evening soiree's all of which I have declined & stayed quietly at home. I must confess but for my love of books, which thank Heaven has rather encreased than diminished I should often have found it very lonely without any companion—but my husband who is always too busy to have much time to spare altho' that little is so precious to me that without it I should be utterly forlorn—he is so kind & so affectionate that his presence always brings joy, & the expectation of seeing him makes his absence endurable. You may laugh at this, in two old people that have lived together 24 years—but for 5 years we have been all the world to each other—& without children to love, our hearts naturally cling more closely together. He has given me a Respirator which enables me to go out in this foggy atmosphere, & in short he watches over me like a child. I believe he has been a little frightened by the hollow sound of my cough —in consequence of it he has not allowed me to go to church today, indeed, I should not like to have disturbed the congregation with such discordant sounds—altho' I feel much disappointed. But we are told the humble & fervent prayer will be accepted no matter where offered. Mr. Rush has just been in to make me the compliments of the season—and we have had a long talk on religion. I have been persuading him ever since his illness to become a communicant & I think he is half, nay, almost quite resolved. It would be a high gratification to me to see him commune. It is so dark today that one can scarcely see to do any thing—and really the denseness of the fog seems to cloud my intellect. I have written you a most scrawling rambling sort of a letter—but I have lately got a little out of practice. As I hope to see you so soon, I shall reserve what I have to say in the way of narrative 'till we meet. Since my return from the country, I have been reading—History—Sophy Hope Vere sent me "Cromwell" and after going through that, I felt an irresistible desire to refer to Hume and have gone on from volume to volume with still encreasing interest—and when to this you add the newspapers, reviews, &c, to say nothing of more serious reading, I have found full enough occupation to keep away ennui—besides—the never ceasing occupation of note writing—& when I say notes—I mean two & three sheets of note paper. The 'Hopes' as Charlotte Mansfield calls them, I see often—and the dear girls cannot speak of my going away that the big tears do not roll down their cheeks & dim their beautiful eyes—indeed from every part of England & Scotland we have received letters filled with regrets at the prospect of losing us, as they are pleased to say. When I return, if please God I do, I will show you letters from persons whose names the trump of Fame have sounded through our own dear land of the far far west. Invitations pour in upon us from various quarters to beg for a visit before we go. I believe I wrote you that Lord Elsington, the Lord Leiutenant of Ireland, had invited us to make him a visit at the castle of Dublin this winter—& that Lady Westminster had also written to 'remind' us of our promise to go to Eaton Hall. The Stanley's, Davenports, P &c, &c all in the way to Ireland. But I fear we shall not be able to go. It takes too much money, & we want all we have got now to prepare for house-keeping in America. Indeed, our thoughts are now all bent on our return and making arrangements for it. I cannot sleep for thinking, as soon as my head is laid upon my pillow, "imagination bodies forth" the forms & faces of those I love so well. I endeavour to fancy you all looking as when we parted—but this I cannot realize. You are right when you say we have stayed too long away. We are consigned to the oblivion of the tomb, before we become tenants of it. I have not received a line from Emily or Sally since my separate letters to them early last summer, & have never heard whether they have received the things I sent them by Col Heth. In short I know nothing but what you write me, even my dear & faithful Edward has failed me of late, ever since he joined you last summer at the Springs. I would not, & ought not beloved sister, to pain you by the expression of these feelings— but really the o'er-fraught heart must speak, or break—and what makes me feel this so much now, is the high state of excitement I have been in since I knew I was certainly to go home in the Spring and the hope of getting letters from my friends rejoicing at the prospect of seeing us, when the steamer's arrived, but both have come & brought me not one line from any one. The Queen & Great Western—both in—and no letters— really it is enough to overcome the patience of Job!

Decr 29th
On looking back to what I have written conscience forces me to acknowledge this letter is but a poor offering for Christ-

mas & New Year. I will hope the next will find us happier & more contented. Since the above I have received a long letter from Edward, & dear Sally by Drs Randolph & Page. Sally's was one of the most affec letters I have received for a long time & was accompanied by a pair of beautiful slippers worked by her own dear hand. These little offering of friendship & affection came to me at a fortunate moment when like the thirsty traveller in the wilderness the last drop of patience was exhausted. It has been balm to my wounded spirit, & cheered me under disappointment & mortification. I see from the papers that there was an immense fall of snow which blocked up all the roads, &c, and I flatter myself this must be the cause why your letters did not reach Washington in time for the steamers —or—if they did Mr. Forsythe was too long looking over the election returns—or in preparing to meet Congress, &c, &c, to attend to forwarding your letters. I can, & will believe any thing rather than that you ever neglect me beloved sisters. I am rejoiced to hear from Edward & Sally that your health continues to improve & sincerely hope & pray that this cold weather may not have an injurious effect upon you. You ought to play Battledore "The Graces" or walk in the house, when you cant get out. I find I cannot do without walking exercise, but such a cough as I have got, you never heard in our dear sunny clime. Yes, I remember one winter my dear Emm had just such a one and we all got frightened about it. Tell Sally in my imaginings—I see her a tall, graceful, gentle creature—full of health & spirits—but one who seldom stains her fair fingers with the ink of friendship. I have no news to write you. My health or rather, my cough has been too bad to go out except for exercise—and at this season of fog & discomfort in London every one who can, flies to the country.

The Queen has recovered sufficiently to go to Windsor for the Christmas. I heard the other day an anecdote of her and the prince most honorable to them both. A day or two after her confinement she asked Dr. South if Prince Albert might read to her. He objected, saying he was afraid the prince would read a novel, which would be too exciting. To which she replied, "No, he would read to me the lessons for the day, and as he has done so ever since we were married, it would be particularly gratifying to me now." This anecdote came directly from Dr. South himself, and cannot therefore be doubted. The little princess royal is said to be very pretty, & very thriving.

Dr. Randolph & Page have brought us letters from Edward and in consequence we have invited them to dine with us to-day, with three or four English gentlemen & Mr. Rush. Our dinners are few & far between now and it always puts me out of sorts to have to give one, since I have heard of some of our country peoples saying our salary must be quite sufficient if we could live in such stile, &c & Mr. Tucker's report has had considerable effect in curing us of our hospitable habits—however, it is very silly to regard the malice of a world which has always been uncharitable & will be untill Time is, no more. These reflections have also been called forth by Edwards letter—in which he tells us much that the world have been saying about my dear husband which has pained me very much—not so much that the world—or some disconted person has said it—as that he my ever kind (& except in this instance) my ever considerate brother, should have repeated it to us, because it answers no good purpose but to embitter Mr. Stevenson's mind against his country & his own people—and take from us that feeling of intense happiness we should otherwise have in returning to our country & friends. But enough—& perhaps more than enough—I cannot, however, help feeling the deepest mortification, when I hear from all sides, & all parties in this country such unqualified praises bestowed upon my husband & not the least justice accorded him in his own. My good brother says, "The impression which is very generally if not universally entertained, that he has had but very little to do"—no minister ever had so easy and agreeable a time in England—nothing to do but to enjoy the luxury & high life of the nobility, & the many good things of old England"—I rather think if he had had one half or one third of the labour to perform which Mr. S. has had—Sally & the children would not have been so well taken care of. The truth is Mr. Stevenson's friends in America seem not to know what he has done. Look at the Boundary question and the labour & trouble he has had with that. I dont know what you all think but here I assure you the people believe, & know that he has kept the peace between the two countries, but for Mr. S. the government here would never have consented to arbitrate the matter again, they refused to do so, and Mr. Stevenson succeeded in getting them to yield. Then as to the Slave question which Mr. Van Buren commenced & did nothing with, why that itself cost more labour than the whole of the French claims which Mr. Rives got so much credit for —besides the 30 thousand pounds, Mr. S. got to the astonishment of every one, he discussed all the great questions involved in Slavery—indeed, Mr. Calhoun's famous resolutions & speach which they give him so much credit for, had been discussed by my husband. Bye the by, I have seen a very curious correspondence between Mr. Calhoun & Mr. Stevenson on the subject in which Mr. C. compliments Mr. Stevenson very highly in his letter but takes care to say nothing in his speach. When to all this is added the Canada troubles—African Slave trade— questions in relation to our affairs in the Pacific—which I have heard untill I could almost discuss them myself, and there are, I know, innumerable questions of minor importance which take all my husbands time as I know to my sorrow. As to our annual tour, that has been necessary for my health, and indeed, as a relaxation to himself—besides, the pleasure of being received with such marked kindness & hospitality, every where, a distinction which we have reason to know is payed more to the individuals than to the office. Edward says this very popularity will make against him on his return—strange that he should be condemned for endeavouring to fill in a proper manner the office to which he has been appointed, & for obtaining an influence which may enable him to benefit his country. I cannot believe this will be the case with those whose good opinion is worth having. He says also that Mr. Stevenson gives offence by not writing to his political friends. I believe I can venture to assert that he has never failed to answer every letter that has been addressed to him, knowing as many persons as he does can it be expected that he would volunteer letters—where would he begin or where end? He would offend every one that he did not write to by selecting, &c. But really I have no time nor heart to go over all the ground my dear brother took. If, he so good, so loving, & so charitable speaks to us thus, how will it be with those who have evinced so little affection or interest in us. For myself as I said before I am very proud of the reputation my husband has acquired here among men who stand foremost in the world. At Cambridge he spoke before 3000 persons, & stood side by side with the greatest men of the age, and it is admitted here that he did not lose by a comparison with Peel in all the blaze & splendour of his eloquence, & with all the advantages of laborious preparation. Now, my dear Bett, it will be quite time enough to condemn him if these things make him vain or presumptious—but wait—and do you not pass sentence, & say—Why this sister of mine must be crazy to be always boring me with her husbands perfections. The truth is I think my dear husband has had very severe measure meted out to him both by friends & foes—and whilst I care not what is said of me, I am alive to unjust censure upon him—besides, other strange & unaccountable things Edward has heard, that some one told him that a friend of his had heard Mr. Stevenson say, "That in consequence of his wifes neice marrying Mr. V. B.'s son he should remain here 6 years longer"—did you ever hear any thing so ridiculous? In the first place we thought every friend we had, knew that we were only detained at this Court, by the natural desire Mr. S. had to finish the Boundary question as he had had so much trouble with it, he felt it was but fair that she should reap the honor of concluding it if he could. Now altho' I touched as lightly as possible upon our neice's course whilst here & since her departure always remembering she was the daughter of a dear loved sister—still I thought it needed no 'ghost come from the grave', to tell that she had been any thing—but a bond of union—a medium of good will & friendship—but of all these things we will talk when we meet. Now I must hasten to say a few last words about what I shall bring you & Emily & Sally. Let me know in time.

Sally has sent for some more stockings shall I get you any more? or any thing else—say so to Mr. John Rutherford or any of our friends or all you may think we should like to oblige —would you like a cloth riding habit? linen—chintz? &c. We have been all day buying things for house-keeping—& for our negros. Who has Dr. B's old house? & where does Julia & brother Isaac stay this winter? Is it a good boarding house? &c. When I think of being with you my beloved sister I feel as if I could soon get a house ready for your home. Emily must not complain that we shall take possession of you altogether. I think I never saw such bargains as we met with today. I wish Emily would let us do something for her. This is her last chance. Mr. S. desires me to say to Mr. H. that he shall be much gratified to do any thing for him & that he must write for what he wants & pray say so to Emily. You must all send your memorandum's but no money—we can pay for what you want & settle when we meet. I shall write again to inform you when we shall sail and in what vessel. I think we shall take a steamer. We shall have an immense quantity of luggage which we shall send direct to Richmond to the care of Mr. Palmer our very good friend. Now the time is coming so near—I think of nothing else & take but little pleasure in any thing here— which is very ungrateful in me—but nature is too powerful to be restrained even by the coldness of those we love. Dear Sally Coles I see I shall love her profoundly you dont know how I am touched by kindness from any member of my family I have lived so long upon crumbs from them.

A packet in to day, & Mr. Rush got a letter, or rather letters as usual, he is a happy man in that respect. I believe he gets 10 to my one—and I am sure he does not love his family better than I do. I beg you will enquire of Jack Heth about the bonnets, as I want to ascertain if the milliner here has cheated me. Adieu—A few more letters & I think I will give up my pen—like others. Love to Emily Mr R. Sally & all & believe me beloved sister your devotedly attached S. C. Stevenson. How does John R. Junr come on? Love to him. This letter is for yourself alone.

XXXIX

DESPITE MRS. STEVENSON's eagerness to return home—even though Enniscorthy lay in ashes—England still had its bright spots. One seems to have been a dinner at Sir Francis Chantrey's, England's foremost sculptor. Here she met Sir Benjamin Brodie, Surgeon-to-the-Queen, probably the most skilled surgeon of his day. Another guest was Samuel Rogers, poet and conversationalist *extraordinaire*. She was quite fascinated by the brilliant Rogers—and he by her.

It should be noted that the Stevensons extended hospitality to their countrymen without stint, or regard to party or section. She mentions how delighted two of her countrymen were with their reception at the Legation. The President of Brown University, Francis Wayland, celebrated cleric and educator, apparently found an evening with the Stevensons most exhilarating, as did Anthony King, of South Carolina, who came armed with a letter of introduction.

London Feby 2d 1841
32 Upper Grosvr St.

My beloved Brothers & Sisters,

Your most welcome letter of the 30th of Decr was received by the last Boston Steamer and I avail myself of the first steamer that returns to thank you for it—and to tell you how happy it made me. It was so like yourself, so kind and so affc that it melted me into tears and I reproached myself for having thought your last cold, & not so kind as usual—no my own dear and excellent brother, I know your kind heart, too well to doubt it—to me—you have ever been all that was affc & good—but I thought your remarks were rather hardly upon my husband—and you on whom a kind Providence has bestowed a 'jewel of a wife', ought to know how to appreciate this wifely feeling which is much more alive to all that touches her husband than herself. But soon, very soon, now, I shall be folded to thy noble, generous, and loving heart—my brother! And we shall read in each others eyes the happiness we feel in our re-union—and my sweet sister too whose gentle virtues I have learnt to love even the better for our separation but above all—I love her for having been to you—Heavens choicest gift—and tho' last not least in the joys that await me under my brothers roof, will be the sight of our dear children—whom I fancy gazing upon me with that look of enquiring confidence which seems to ask, "Is this my dear Aunt Stevy, whom you have been teaching me to love?" How touching to me will be that look, for it will tell me of the parents love for their dear and childless sister. What you tell me of my dear brothers and sisters comforts me—for they themselves have been so silent that I know nothing of their feelings, notwithstanding the many efforts directly and indirectly to call them forth. But a little while will end all doubts—we shall soon meet face to face and read there whose hearts have been most constant. There will be one great draw back to my ever feeling happy again on our dear old mountain. Enniscorthy—dear Enniscorthy in ruins! I cannot tell you how much I was touched by your discription of its present state. I imagined myself standing at your side with our back's to the pitiless ruin and gazing upon the bright & glorious sunset on which we have so often looked in childhoods happy hour, when the summer air felt as balmy as our dreams of Heaven, and the deep blue skies shone so serenely over our heads lifting the grateful happy heart "Through Nature, up to

Natures God". Truly I can say, some of the purest devotional feelings I have ever known have been called forth by a summer evenings sunset, at Enniscorthy. & to this cause, I believe, I can trace my passionate love of Nature. I learnt in early life to see the Creator in His works, and to worship Him in His own glorious Temple. Ah, my dear brother how many sweet memories will this loved spot have power always to awaken, for it

> Is to our heart of hearts endeared,
> The House, where we were born & reared!

and where too we have heard dear voices we shall hear no more, rejoiced in the care and tender love of dear parents we shall see no more on Earth, and whose memory ought to be to us as a sacred bond of union—rendering even the ruins of their domestic sanctuary—a holy spot, where we ought to bury every unchristian feeling, which would grieve their spirits if on Earth.

Since my last long letters to you and Sally, we have been very much at home, excepting dinner parties, which have no end here, and which I must say are very pleasant, such pains is taken by dinner givers, to group their company and to bring together persons of congenial taste & pursuits, and it is the ambition of every one to have as many stars as can be obtained. We dined a day or two ago at Sir Francis Chantrey's and I had him on my left. Sir Benjamin Brodie on my right, and Mrs. Rogers, in her best mood, just opposite, & I assure you, we had so much wit, and mirth, & pleasant anecdote, among us, that the other end of the table were filled with envy & uncharitableness. Lord Denman, & Mr. Stevenson sat on each side of Lady Chantrey, and are really so much alike that Mr. Stevenson might be taken for Ld Denman's younger brother. Rogers is always a lion wherever he goes for his fine coloquial talents, and for his peculiarly bland & amiable manners, I dont know whether I ever described him to you, but now that I have seen so much of him I think I could do him more justice. In stature he is rather below the middle size, & stoops a little in the shoulders, his countenance is un-naturally pale, with a look as refined and intellectual as if his "body thought" —his manner is indescribably soft and gentle and his voice as low and persuasive in its tones as a womans—his conversation is delightful and one wonders in listening to him how so much wit—wisdom and eloquence can be packed in so small a compass, almost every epithet has an individual aim, and serves to point, amplify, or modify the thought. But to me, his greatest charm is his sensibility & feeling, he cannot speak of any action which has in it, the least touch of the moral sublime that his eyes are not suffused with tears—and when to all this, he professes to be my devoted admirer & friend, can you be surprised at my admiration. A few days since we dined together and at dinner he had a seat nearer to the fire than mine which he insisted on my taking. I refused—when he raised his finger, and shaking it at me, said to a friend next him, in his emphatic manner, "Behold, there is a woman, who is truth itself, & yet she says what she does not think for politeness sake". I have been much flattered at hearing many kind things of his saying of me, among the number that "he would not give my heart, for the best head in Europe". The parties are just commencing but I do not go to any from which I can stay away. The only parties I like is when I can get my dear young friends the Miss Hope Vere's (daughters of Lady Elizabeth, who is the daughter of the Marquis of Tweedale) to come and spend the evening with me sociably. I sometimes invite a few of my compatriots to meet them, and they never fail to go away delighted, last night we had with them Professor Wayland and Mr. Anthony King of South Carolina, a very clever person, and they were so perfectly enchanted I could not get them away before 20 minutes to one. It was "Still another song, Miss Hope Vere, just one more", &c—and to confess the truth such is the charm of her voice that I had no idea we had even reached the witching hour of 12, when I found it so near one, her voice is thought to excel Grisi's in sweetness, and always brings to my mind those beautiful lines in Milton's Comus of "linked sweetness long drawn out," which "lap'd" the spirit in "Elysium". Hannah the syren, is about 18 or 20—beautiful as a dream, with large dark eyes, whose expression is as sweet & soft, as the liquid tones of her voice—a delicate & fair, yet beautiful, & sunny complexion, with just enough of embonpoint to give roundness and symetry to her person and to all those charms there in, that air distingue which pleases and impresses the mind, without our knowing why, and which frequently bears the palm of admiration away from beauty itself, her sister Sophy is not so handsome, but quite as intelligent, and as amiable but with all their beauty, talents, rank and accomplishments their crowning grace is goodness. When I receive from them such proof's of devoted attachment, and see the tears streaming down their cheeks at the thought of parting with me, a mysterious feeling of deep gratitude steals over me, & I believe it is the goodness of Him who rules the hearts of all his creatures that has inspired the hearts of these innocent and charming girls to love me, who have no offspring to "rise up and call me blessed". I cannot tell you what comfort they have been to me. They come at all hours, and all times, they set at my feet and leaning on my knees, they disclose to me all their little troubles, as well as the most sacred secrets of their young hearts. I assure you their affection for me has fallen upon me like the dew of Heaven, softening, refreshing, refining, & keeping me unselfish and loving in the thorny wilderness of the world—where self—under the most polished exterior is still the governing principle with all. They have just returned from the country where they went to spend their Christmas. We had promised to make several visits, but when the time came it was really so cold & inclement we determined to stay in town and enjoy this "festival of the fire-side" at home. In this country they enjoy this season of festivity with a strong and sacred affection, it is with them a thorough holiday. Christmas day all the shops are shut, labour in a great measure ceases, and the poor join with the rich in repose and worship. Parliment adjourns and all who can, fly to their country seats, eager for enjoyment, & storms, frost & darkness is no interruption to the fireside enjoyments & merry spirits within doors. We resemble the land of our forefathers in so many of our customs &

habits that all this is very familiar to us. The more I see of this glorious land from whence we sprung the more pride I feel in our common ancestry, and rejoice to think their laws, their literature, their language is ours, and that they upheld the same principles of liberty with ourselves.

My dear brother what a long, long letter I am writing you, but it will probably be the last except the one to say—we are coming—coming—coming—I wish you could see the number of letters I have written and count the pages, you would say "my good sister deserves—a clerkship—let me see, 12 to Betsy —4 to Emily—7½ to Sally—8 to Mat Singleton, & his Mother, 4 to Lewis Nigen, in reply to his—4 to Mrs. Platt—reply—4 to Sarah Moore and tho' last not least this token as a *Bonne bouche* to you—7 or 8 as it may be, & now we will add up, if my multiplication will hold out. I make it between 51 & 2— besides—letters to Paris & notes without number. It is really well for me that my time is drawing to a close, the labour of writing so much is becoming intolerable, but not one of my family will write unless I address them a separate letter & not always then—besides, the labour of writing so much, one has to repeat themselves in every letter. Of course I must be guilty more or less of tautology but I hope it will not be deemed plagerism to quote from oneself—and now, dear brother, I must bid you and dear Sally, Adieu! I have no more news to write you. Yes, I forgot to tell you, I have seen Maria Edgeworth, she is now in town, & we have interchanged visits. Her sister told me her age was 72—and she quite looks it, notwithstanding the vivacity of her manner, which has all the frank hilarity of the Irish—in stature she is very low, & would not, I think, more than come up to my shoulders her countenance does not indicate much talent except, when animated in conversation, which is brilliant and sparkling. The Court is now at Claremont but the Queen returns next week for the christening of the little Princess Royal, which is to take place on the anniversary of her marriage in the Royal Chapel with all the pride, pomp, & splendour of Royalty. It is reported in the Court circles that her little Majesty will have another festival of the same sort this time next year. Positively I will close this long letter. God bless you all my beloved friends and grant us a happy re-union—in peace—& love & joy—is the prayer of your attached and devoted sister

S. C. Stevenson

THE STEVENSONS were going home. All day carriages were stopping at the Legation to bring visitors and *bon voyage* presents or to leave cards from the great and not-so-great. The Duke of Wellington came to say England would miss them, always remember them, a parting accolade they never forgot

On October 18, 1841, Mrs. Stevenson brought her letter-writing to a close with a farewell note to her "Own & Precious Sisters." The "negotiations" she mentions were the high-level talks, started by her husband, on the touchy Northeastern boundary dispute, now nearing a treaty that would end the long tension between the two nations.

The new Minister, Edward Everett, had not yet arrived. President Harrison had died after a month in office. His successor, President Tyler, and the Whig hierarchy in the Senate wrangled for months before appointing a Minister to take Stevenson's place at the Court of St. James.

On October twenty-first, Andrew Stevenson had a farewell audience with Queen Victoria, who wished him and his lady godspeed and expressed her pleasure at having known them. They must come again to England. Two days later these two Americans, representative of diplomacy at its best, embarked at Bristol on the *Great Western*. After a voyage of seventeen days Sallie Coles Stevenson reached New York and set foot again on the land she had longed to see for five years—America.

32 Upper Grosvr St.
Octr 18th 1841

My own & precious Sister's,

Another letter—yes—another—but the last I trust untill we meet. Soon very soon dearest I shall be in your arms, if it is the will of Providence. Our passage is taken, & paid for in the Great Western on the 23 of this month and we are packing up every thing to send to Richmond except our wearing clothes which we take with us; Mr. S. has written to Edward to procure a man servant for him in New York, & I shall depend on myself alone—but a man will be necessary to take charge of the luggage. I cannot tell you how nervous and anxious I feel about hearing from you all once more before our departure. God grant we may be (all that remain) spared to meet in peace & love. I write in great haste & confusion—packing—person's calling, letters, notes, &c &c. I feel very ungrateful to be so glad to leave those who are loading us with kindness attentions—presents &c &c and who weep floods of tears when they say Adieu! Well, nature is stronger than any thing else—and my Heavenly Father has been very good to me to inspire so many good & kind hearts with affection for me in this distant land. I shall not write you any news sufficient for one & the last letter to say when you may expect to see us. My husband has not been very well, & is terribly afraid the publick interest may require him to stay—but I will not hear of this, and he only fears it. 20 days now & we shall leave London in all human probability forever. We are very anxious for the next steamer. And now dearest sisters—brother—& you my dear Sally I bid you Adieu for a little while. Kiss the children dear Emm for me & tell them who is coming. We shall not loiter long by the way—altho' we must stay a little with my beloved Edward & his family. God bless you all my darlings—

Your dearest Sister
S C Stevenson

I had scarcely finished the last word when Mr. S. came up with a newspaper in his hand a packet in. Tyler vetoed two bills, Cabinet cut, &c appointments & Everett confirmed glad of it—a good thing for us as well as the two countries if it had been sooner done. Everett will now probably not get here untill just as we are starting & be ignorant of many things he might have learnt from Mr. S. relative to the negotiations &c, &c. Well so be it—his loss not ours. No letters. Your own devoted

Sister
SCS

Index

Coles, Mary Eliza, [Mrs. Robert Carter], 9
Coles, Rebecca, 3
Coles, Rebecca [Mrs. Richard Singleton], 10, 34, 146, 211
Coles, Selina Skipwith, [Mrs. John III], 107, 164, 231
Coles, Stricker, 31
Coles, Tucker, 10, 97, 98, 99, 144, 231, 274
Coles, Walter, 9, 31, 189, 190, 231
Cook, Mr. & Mrs., 219
Coolidge, Ellen Wales Randolph, 199, 200, 201, 250
Coolidge, Joseph, Jr., 199, 201
Cooper, Earl, 257
Cornwallis, [Lord], 4
"Coronation Letter," 10, 142 ff.
Court Journal, 135, 136, 141, 156, 244
Couvoisier, 257, 260
Covent Garden, 106
Cowley, Lord and Lady, 79, 84
Coxe, Mr., 224
Cracroft, Mr., 243, 245
Creevey, [Thomas], viii, 211
Crimean War, 247
Crinman Canal, 183
Cromwell, Oliver, 196
Culloden battlefield, 174, 183
Cumberland, 182

Dalmacordock, 183
Dalmatia, Duke of. *See* Soult, Marshall
Dalwhinnie, 183
Darnley, [Lord], 173
Davenport
  Mr., 236, 281
  Mrs., 236, 276, 281
Davy
  Lady, 201
  Sir Humphry, 201

Decatur, Stephen, 5
Dedel, Madame, 53, 54, 82, 111
Delafield, Lady, 70
Denbigh Hall, 182
Denman, Lord, 274, 289
Deputies, Chamber of, 129
Devon, Countess, of Essex, 279
Devonshire, Duke of, 39, 154, 161
Devonshire House, 154
Dieu, Hotel, 127
Diggeswell, 113
Dingwall, 183
Dolce, Carlo, 28
Douglas, ——, 169, 175
Dryburgh, 167, 168, 169, 182
Drummond, [poet], 174
Dudleys, the, 49
Dunken
  Lady Anna Maria, 39, 41, 42, 67
  Sir Rufane, 39, 67
Duer, John, 53, 229, 230
Dunkirk, 183
Dunn, 53, 87, 88, 104, 127
Dunrobin Castle, 164, 174 ff., 191
Duprez, [Gilbert], 124
Durham, 181, 183
Durham
  Bishop of, 183, 236
  Lady, 123, 236
  Lord, 123, 233, 236
Dutton, Miss, 94, 95

Eaton, Peggy, 203
Eaton Hall, 146, 276, 281
Edgeworth, Maria, 269, 270, 292
Edinburgh, 169, 172, 174, 182
Egerton, Lord Francis, 177
Eildon Hills, 168
Eliza of Abelard, 127
Elizabeth, Queen, 24, 76, 98, 107

Ellice, Edward, 44, 50, 68, 71, 124, 208
Elsington, Lord, 276, 281
Enniscorthy, 3, 4, 5, 9, 12, 105, 119, 238, 243, 277, 287, 288, 289
Enquirer, Richmond, 45, 57, 130
Epsom Races, 257
Erskine, Mr. Justice, 208
Esk, the, 168
Esterhazy, Prince Paul, 64, 70, 71, 145, 148, 160
Estouteville, Va., 9, 164
Everett, Edward, 12, 294, 295

Fashee bridge, 182
Fay, Theodore, 13, 15, 16, 21, 34, 65, 123
Fendal, Lord Chief Justice, 207
Firth Cray, 232
Fisher, Miss, 126
Fisher, Mr. and Mrs., 197
Fonthill, 17, 20, 24 ff.
Forsyth(e), John, 36, 97, 214, 226, 282
Fox, Charles, widow of, 79, 81, 82
France, 124 ff.
Freetown, 183
Fulham Palace, 198

Gagarini, Princess, 103
Galantha, Prince of. *See* Esterhazy
Gallashields, 182
Galspie, 183
Gardiner, Gen. Sir John, 197
George III, King, 3, 7, 24, 45, 56, 72, 100, 134, 199
George IV, King, 63, 117, 170, 179
George, Prince, of Cambridge, 134, 141
Gibbs, Mr., 156

Glasgow, 178
Globe, Washington, 44, 52, 57
Gloucester, Duchess of, 58, 155, 215
Godey's Lady's Book, 6
Grace, Lady, 66
Graham, Sir S., and Lady, 197
Grandvilles, the, 125
Granville, Lord and Lady, 264
Great Western, 9, 10, 12, 243, 281, 294, 295
Green
   Mr., 165, 236
   Mrs., 182, 236
Grenville, Lord, 49
Gretna Green, 183
Greville, Charles, 34, 73, 113, 217
Grey
   Lady Georgianne, 50
   Lord, 44, 50, 112
Grisi, Giulia, 63, 66, 124, 158, 230, 290
Grosvenor
   Eleanor. *See* Westminster, Lady
   Robert. *See* Westminster, Lord
Grote, Mr. and Mrs., 205
Guensloff, Baron, 109
Guido, 28, 82
Gunnersburg Park, 158

Hacknall Torchard, 197
Hallam, [Henry], 201, 232
Harrison, Mrs., 61, 66
Harrison, William Henry, 294
Hastings, Lady Flora, 113, 217–18, 221–22
Hawthorn-Den, 174
Headfort, Marquis of, 109
Healy, G. P. A., 8, 249, 255–56, 265
Henry IV, King, 129

Rush-Bagot Treaty, 73
Russel, Lord William, 257, 260
Russell, Miss, 188, 189
Rutherford
  Emma, 31
  John, 9, 23, 51, 56, 286
  Sarah [Sally], 199, 242, 243,
    272
Rutherfords, the, 231
Rydal Mount, 164
  Rydal, falls of, 166

St. Boswell Green, 182
St. Cloud, 125
St. George's Church, 47
St. George's Society of Philadel-
  phia, 153
St. Giles' Church, 173
St. James's, Court of, 6, 8, 11,
  294
St. James, Palace of, 21, 63, 243
St. James Chapel Royal, 243
St. James' Park, 136
St. Paul's, 17, 25, 68, 134, 136
Sali, Countess de. *See* Williams,
  Lady Hamlyn
"Sally," [niece], 23, 60, 180, 225,
  226, 250, 256, 265, 266, 270,
  274, 281, 282, 283, 285,
  286, 289, 292, 295
"Sall," [niece], 128, 131, 265
Salisbury, 24, 25
Salisbury
  Marchioness of, 84
  Marquis of, 44, 48
Sallie Coles Stevenson Collection,
  10
"Sandbach," 193, 194
Scarborough, Earl of, 193, 232,
  233, 234
Scotland, 164 ff.
Scott, [servant], 15, 19, 23
Scott
  Anne, 170

Scott (*continued*)
  Michael, 169
  Sir Walter, 28, 30, 82, 168,
    169, 170, 175, 179, 182, 192
Sedgewick, Miss, 20
Senate (U.S.) Chamber, 129
Seymour
  Lady, 162
  Mr. and Mrs., 28
Shee, Sir Martin, 263
Sheffield, 194
Sherbourne, 95
Sherbourne
  Lady, 89, 95, 96, 123
  Lord, 94, 95, 123
Sherman, William Tecumseh, 6
Sherwood forest, 194
Sigismendi, 258, 259
Singleton, Angelica, 34, 70, 97,
  98, 156, 181, 198, 207
  See also Van Buren, Mrs.
  Abram
  Mat, 209, 213, 223, 226, 229,
    261, 271, 292
  Richard, 10, 70
Singletons, the, 231
Skipwiths, the, 231, 245
Sligo
  Marchioness of, 209
  Marquess of, 133, 136
Smith, Sydney, 134, 138, 139,
  206
  Mrs., 206
Somerset, Duke of, 106, 220, 232,
  247–48
  Duchess of, 160, 209, 220, 232,
    247–48
Somerville, Mrs., 34, 35
Soult, Marshall, 142, 145, 147,
  148, 151, 154, 161
South, Dr., 282
Southey, [Robert], 143
Soutri, Prince, 161
Speare, Miss, 195